S0-CBD-325

3 0700 10673 1430

CHARISMATIC AUTHORITY IN
EARLY MODERN ENGLISH TRAGEDY

CHARISMATIC AUTHORITY
—*in*—
EARLY MODERN ENGLISH TRAGEDY

Raphael Falco

The Johns Hopkins University Press

Baltimore & London

© 2000 The Johns Hopkins University Press
All rights reserved. Published 2000
Printed in the United States of America on acid-free paper
1 3 5 7 9 8 6 4 2

THE JOHNS HOPKINS UNIVERSITY PRESS
2715 North Charles Street
Baltimore, Maryland 21218-4363
www.press.jhu.edu

Library of Congress Cataloging-in-Publication Data
will be found at the end of this book.
A catalog record for this book is available from the British Library.

ISBN 0-8018-6280-9

FOR ANI

CONTENTS

PREFACE

As I was completing this book I happened across a passage in Malcolm Bradbury's *The History Man*: "'What did you do over the summer? Did you go away?' 'No, we didn't,' says Barbara, 'we stayed right here, and Howard finished a book.' 'A book,' says Myra, 'Henry tried to write a book. A very profoundly solemn book. On charisma.'" Needless to say, the last phrases had a sobering, not to say alarming, effect when I read them. They made me wonder whether writing a "solemn" book on charisma was as ridiculous as Bradbury makes it sound. On reflection I concluded that it probably was, although it was consoling to recall how many solemn books on the subject have been written and continue to appear. Of course, this fact in itself is no excuse to add another to the list and should perhaps have been a deterrant. But I have added one to the list nonetheless, reasoning that my book is different from the others because it assuages the solemnity of charisma with the leaven of tragedy.

This is, then, a book about charisma and tragedy. It combines analyses of different kinds of charismatic authority with criticism of early modern tragedies by Christopher Marlowe, William Shakespeare, and John Milton, as well as a few of their contemporaries. Chapters take up such topics as the routinization of charisma, lineage charisma, and erotic charisma, focusing particularly on the effects of group formation and group breakdown on tragic dénouement. My methodological approach is interdisciplinary, although, inasmuch as saying something about tragedy is my aim, literary analysis drives the discussions. In setting a critical tone for the book I have resisted the temptation to aestheticize sociology while applying sociological or sociopolitical

arguments to tragic drama. Concomitantly, I have avoided politiciz-
ing my literary arguments, few of which in any case could be deemed
strictly aesthetic.

References appear in parentheses in the text and are keyed to the
bibliography. Notes are reserved for discursive remarks or occasionally for extended citations. All translations, except where otherwise
noted, are mine.

Many people and organizations who have contributed significantly
to this book do not appear in the notes and bibliography. I first began
talking about Max Weber with David J. Rothman, and our early discussions helped me to connect charisma and tragedy. Stanley Rothman, David's father, made helpful suggestions early on and supplied
several crucial sources. Other colleagues and friends have read chapters, discussed ideas, and offered useful advice, much of which I have
incorporated into the book (usually without acknowledgment). I am
most grateful to Anthony Low, Leeds Barroll, William Sherman, Blan-
ford Parker, Catherine Labio, Shawn Shieh, Lyell Asher, Steven
Shankman, Deniz Şengel, Arthur F. Kinney, Thomas Vargish, Wolfgang Mommsen, Donald R. Kelley, James Siemon, Rosanna Camer-
lingo, Matthew Proser, Casey Charles, and J. W. Binns. Kenneth Daley
has been a steadfast, intelligent listener since I began this project. Elizabeth Mazzola read the entire manuscript twice, in consecutive summers, and did a great deal of invaluable editing swiftly and with her
customary grace. Without her efforts this book would have been
much less than it is. My wife, Ani, to whom I dedicate the book, has
attended its completion with curiosity, humor, and a bit of well-timed
exasperation.

I am grateful to the Folger Institute for two grants-in-aid allowing
me to participate in seminars during a critical period of my research,
and to the University of Maryland Graduate School for awarding me
a Summer Faculty Fellowship in 1994. I would like to express my
gratitude to the Humanities Forum at the University of Maryland,
Baltimore County, for the invitation to give a lecture on "Charisma
and Mass Dissent" in 1995. And I thank the editors of *Theory, Culture,
and Society* and of *Exemplaria: A Journal of Theory in Medieval and
Renaissance Studies* for permission to reprint earlier versions of the
Introduction and Chapter 2, which first appeared in those journals.

CHARISMATIC AUTHORITY IN
EARLY MODERN ENGLISH TRAGEDY

INTRODUCTION

From Charisma to Tragedy

Tragedy is the preeminent discourse of the failure of charisma. This may not seem surprising in that tragedy tends to record the failure of many kinds of human enterprise. But because tragedy has a particular affinity for representing both leadership and social chaos, both equilibrium and entropy among groups of followers, it is an ideal showcase for the transformations and the dilutions of charismatic authority. Since Aeschylus, tragedy has provided sobering reflections of the central paradox of charisma and group function: emphasis on a group ideal tends to destroy the individuality of the human being at the group's core; and, conversely, emphasis on the autonomy of an individual charismatic leader destroys the group ideal.

This paradox, which frustrates and destroys so many tragic protagonists, forms the conceptual core of this book. It is not difficult to see how such a paradoxical (and ubiquitous) conflict could eventuate in tragedy. In fact, the preservation or gradual breakdown of charismatic bonds often contributes to the tension of tragic drama leading to the catastrophe. But little critical attention has been paid to group dissolution as a significant component of tragedy. While the isolation of tragic figures dominates our analyses, we have neglected the ramifications of tragic isolation, in particular the devastating effect on group function of isolating a charismatic leader. In the present book I hope to redress this neglect, or at least to make a beginning. My analysis concentrates on the dissolution of charismatic groups in early modern tragedies. So far as I can determine, this approach to tragedy has not yet been explored—which is remarkable, I think, given the prevalence of charismatic figures on the early modern stage

1

and the clear dependence of these figures on their royal courts, their armies, or their marauding bands.

The concept of charisma with which I began my research—indeed, with which twentieth-century sociology on the subject begins— derives from Max Weber's *Economy and Society* (*Wirtschaft und Gesellschaft*). As will be immediately apparent, however, to inveterate Weberians as well as to others, I have at times wandered far from Weber's basic thesis regarding charismatic authority. Charisma is something of a cottage industry in contemporary sociology, and in many of my wanderings I am merely following Weber's superb critics, such as Edward Shils and Thomas Spence Smith; in other wanderings I have adduced recent literary and cultural theory, especially views of human subjectivity. And where appropriate I have ransacked the treasures of social psychology stemming—and branching away—from Freud's *Group Psychology and the Analysis of the Ego*. The final map is my own, although I must emphasize my ongoing debt to Weberian thought and to the lively, fertile reactions Weber continues to inspire.[1]

Group and Agency

Although sociologists use the term *charisma* in a value-free sense, in common usage charisma tends to receive a positive valuation. We speak of charisma as a kind of heightened personal attractiveness, a desirable attribute. Moreover—again, if usage is any measure—we regard charisma as a zenith of individuality, a subjectivity so exceptional it stands utterly alone. But this notion of charisma occludes the actual workings of social authority and also gives too optimistic an impression of the relation between individuality and charismatic domination. Whether we consider charisma a revolutionary social force or merely a disruptive and disorderly state of affairs—as, for instance, in a pirate band (like Menas's) or a street gang (like Poins's)— we should nonetheless recognize that charismatic social authority sustains itself as a relation between an individual and a group. As Donald McIntosh puts it, "charisma is not so much a quality as an experience. The charismatic object or person is *experienced* as possessed by and transmitting an uncanny and compelling force" (1970, 902).

Charisma is therefore a *shared* experience. This is perhaps the most important, and most misunderstood, fact of charismatic group formation. The ideal of pure individuality which we typically associate with charisma does not really fit charismatic group psychology.

The key to charismatic authority is its shared quality, what S. N. Eisenstadt calls "the intense personal nature of the response to charisma" (1968, xix; Camic 1980, 7). Charismatic leaders either triumph or fail on the basis of an ongoing emotional interchange with their followers, a dynamic of interdependence. This dynamic provides the basis for the legitimacy of charismatic authority. As Weber describes it, "this basis lies . . . in the conception that it is the duty of those subject to charismatic authority to recognize its genuineness and to act accordingly" (1978, 1:242). Although Weber concludes that the recognition of charismatic genuineness is, psychologically, "a matter of complete personal devotion to the possessor of the quality" (1978, 1:242), it is clear that no charismatic authority can be sustained in the absence of an interdependent relation between it and a group. As we will see in subsequent chapters, tragedies often turn on the breakdown of that interdependent relationship and on the loss of the shared experience of charisma.

Because both the validity and the legitimacy of charismatic authority depend on the active, dutiful participation of those subject to the authority, the inner workings of charismatic groups are distinct from those of other kinds of groups. The reliance on extrasocial authority, while it can sometimes coexist with charisma, remains secondary to the personal bonds of charisma. For example, military rank would not suffice to produce a charismatic group, because the legitimacy of, say, a captaincy does not depend upon its recognition by a group of sailors. To get a sense of charismatic leadership we need only contrast such Shakespearean soldiers as Othello, Hotspur, or Antony to the time-serving officers of a standing army. The authority of rank bears an external imprimatur. Those subject to that kind of authority are by and large irrelevant to its legitimacy. Military authority is impersonal, and, while it may be slandered or impugned or even disobeyed, it retains an abstract existence apart from and outliving both those holding a particular rank and those subject to the authority. Actual leadership in battle may at times be charismatic, but military hierarchy itself, as well as military discipline, are both antithetical to the personal and impermament conditions that produce a charismatic group (see Weber 1978, 2:1148–50; Smith 1992, 168).

The binding relationship between the recognition of charisma and its validity fosters what might be called a systemic mutuality in charismatic groups, a uniquely fragile form of membership. Significantly, this systemic mutuality has its roots in the first explicit text on charisma, Saint Paul's 1 Corinthians 12. Explaining the function of the charisms (Greek *charismata*, gifts of grace) in the congregation of

Christ, Paul's letter provides a remarkably durable myth of charismatic authority. Here is the Geneva Bible version:

> Now there are diuersities of gifts, but the same Spirit.
> And there are diuersities of administrations, but the same Lord.
> And there are diuersities of operations, but God is the same, which worketh all in all.
> But the manifestation of the Spirit is giuen to euery man, to profit withall.
> For to one is giuen by the Spirit the word of wisedome: and to an other the word of knowledge, by the same Spirit:
> And to another *is giuen* faith by the same Spirit: and to another the gifts of healing, by the same Spirit:
> And to another the operations of great works: and to another, prophecie: and to another, the discerning of spirits: and to another diuersities of tongues: and to another, the interpretation of tongues:
> And all these things worketh one and the selfe same Spirit, distributing to euery man seuerally as he will.
>
> (1 Cor. 12:7–11)[2]

The nine official charisms are wisdom, knowledge, faith, healing, great works, prophecy, discerning of spirits, speaking in tongues, and interpreting different tongues. Although they are distributed by the same spirit "seuerally as he will," the individual charisms do not carry equivalent force or importance. As Paul soon makes clear, his list represents a hierarchy of descending charismatic value (cf. 1 Cor. 12:28–30). But his hortatory rhetoric of cooperation and collectivity tends to obscure the overall effect of the hierarchy on the equality of congregation members.

By uniting the physical body, the spiritual body, and political authority, Paul permanently establishes the social dynamics of charismatic authority. Revolutionary religion provides an incomparable pretext for this union: the physical body, always a convenient metaphor for the political body, is transformed through politics to a spiritual body, simultaneously leader and follower in the Christian congregation. This is a chief message of the apostolic mission. Paul's theological program unites the three bodies (physical, spiritual, political), linking magical properties to the pragmatic politics of his ecclesiology. Paul binds the metaphors together with a new version of charisma, appropriating (for the Revolution) the ideal of the charismatic leader from the texts of the Hebrew prophets, and even as it might have been conceived from the example of Jesus. He deliberately divides the culture of charisma from its progenitors, from Moses, Eli-jah, and David, as well as from Jesus' charismatic contemporaries like Honi and Hanina ben Dosa, all of whom are exemplary recipients of the divine gifts of grace (see Vermes 1973, 79 and passim).

Paul's new congregational charisma has an egalitarian flavor, blending a curious mixture of hierarchy, equality, and divine inspira-tion in the lives of a privileged group. Suppressing the exceptional nature of charismatic power, he transforms every Christian into a charismatic; every congregant's access to the Christian god is compa-rable to the relation of a prophet of Israel to Yahweh. Of course, not every member of the congregation is granted prophetic gifts per se. But every member has unobstructed access to the same source of power, men and women together. Given this, we might say that Paul democratizes charisma through a rationalization of it. His classifica-tory analysis of charismatic attributes, which theretofore had been massed together mostly in Hebrew men-of-deed, institutionalizes the Christian claim to charisma. Indeed, the very idea of the chosen group changes insofar as the Corinthians (and Romans, Ephesians, and others) seem to be self-selecting, a community composed of extra-ordinary needs rather than a genetically determined tribe or race. This self-selecting quality of the new charismatic ideal has significant ramifications for tragic representation: most charismatic figures in tragedies are leaders of self-selected groups. Not lineage kings or queens but outsiders and near-outsiders demonstrate charismatic authority: we need only think of Tamburlaine, Hamlet, or Boling-broke to recognize the vitality and suggestiveness of the Pauline model of charisma on the early modern stage.

The background of Paul's revision of Hebrew men-of-deed is worth recalling. Paul was writing for polemical reasons. His letter to the Corinthians was delivered in response to a political crisis in which his own authority had been threatened. He invents his charismatic theory to censure the "spiritual aristocracy" of the church at Corinth, a group "inclined to pride themselves on the possession of pro-founder wisdom and deeper mystical experiences than their brethren or even than the apostle himself" (Chadwick 1967, 33). The Argument to 1 Corinthians in the Geneva Bible explains that, during Paul's absence in Syria,

> false Apostles entred into the Church, who being puffed vp with vaine glorie, and affect at eloquence, soght to bring into contempt the simplicitie which Paul vsed in preaching the Gospel. By whose ambition suche factions & schismes sprang up in the Church, that from opinions in pollicies & ceremonies they fel into false doctrine

and heresies, calling into doute the resurrection from the dead, one of the chiefest points of Christian religion.

The crisis was severe, and the translators clearly recognize it as political. The language of Reformation polemic proves as much, particularly reference to "factions & schismes."

Paul roundly rebukes the Corinthians for their arrogance and for neglect of his teachings; and he makes certain to assert his predominance: "Am I not an Apostle? am I not fre? haue I not sene Jesus Christ our Lord?" (1 Cor. 9:1). His apostleship—indeed, his divine authority—he sets in hierarchical relation to the Corinthians' particular fascination with ecstatic utterance, the gift of speaking in tongues. As Henry Chadwick concludes, "Paul could not afford to deny that the gift of ecstasy was a genuine manifestation of the Spirit, but was alarmed by its divisive possibilities and told the Corinthians that the enthusiastic utterance they especially prized was the last in the graded hierarchy of supernatural gifts" (1967, 45–46).[3]

From inception (or invention), then, the charisms were components in a hierarchical order designed to promulgate a centralized and personal authority. Paul clearly uses the charisms to dismantle the threat of aristocratic hierarchy presented by the Corinthians. The distribution of the gifts of grace pretends to anatomize the very concept of the leader in whom all extraordinary powers are concentrated. Although a particular gift might distinguish one recipient from another in the congregation, the implication is that everyone will receive grace in some form and that everyone bears a responsibility at some time to lead the others.[4] Each charism remains a part of the whole, and the charismatic presence of each gift of grace preserves the stability of the group, even if individually such charisms would appear to disrupt the normal order of social action and behavior. The disequilibrium of charismatic individualism becomes, in Paul's ecclesiology, a *definition* of functional stability—very nearly a complete reversal of meaning. Pauline charismatic theory might be defined as a continual deconstruction of charismatic monarchy, resulting not in pure egalitarianism but in a dialectic between graceful leadership and leaderless grace.

Predictably, the strongest Pauline injunction is leveled against the autonomy of any one charismatically endowed Christian in the congregation. He compares autonomy to a mutiny of human bodily parts. The new church of Christ, he says, is one body. But "the bodie also is not one member, but many. If the fote would say, Because I am not the hand, I am not of the bodie, is it therefore not of the bodie? And if the eare would say, Because I am not the eye, I am not of the

bodie, is it therefore not of the bodie?" (1 Cor. 12:14–16). The attempt
of any one member to act as an individual agent would destroy the
"one body." The figurative harm done to the body of Christ, or to
Paul's ideal of a living Church, would be realized in the literal dismemberment of the body politic (see Ziesler 1990, 58). This systemic
mutuality guarantees both the equality of individual members and
the integrity of the congregation as a whole. Yet, diversity notwithstanding, the individual agency of any one member systematically
undermines the structure of the group as a whole.

This is the paradox that I mentioned earlier. It effectively defines
the charismatic group as at once governing and governed by a symbol of its own grace and power. The ambiguity is systemic; when
extended beyond the sacred confines of the early church, it is manifest in an interdependence of leader and follower, subject and objec-
tified other, following the pattern of the relation between the Christian and his or her god. While the charisms may not be "exceptional
things" in Pauline theology, the notion of charisma in secular terms
is synonomous with exceptionality, uniqueness, extraordinary status
in society. In Weberian terms, a charismatic leader is by definition
"outside the common run." But we would do well to recall that the
discourse originates in an economy of mutual dependence, with a
double-edged system of governing.

The paradox of group agency—or group *and* agency—suggests the
dialectical nature of charismatic power. Like most charismatic move-
ments in their first stages, Christianity was forged and advanced in
dissidence. But, ironically, the emblematic signs of that revolutionary
church, the charisms themselves, came into being as a suppression of
the dissident voices at Corinth. This irony is the result of Paul's rationalization of charisma. He uses a rhetoric of equality to quash the
spiritual rebellion of the Corinthians, emphasizing the revolutionary
egalitarianism of Christianity. His suppression of the dissidence, like
all such suppressions, purports to serve both the congregation and
the incipient Church at large. As John Colet explained in his commentary on 1 Corinithians (1513), "God has established harmony in the
body, giving more abundant honor to that which was deficient, so
that there may be no schism in the body. In this way all in the Church
are balanced by a kind of equality, so that in it there may be only oneness arising from charity and charity arising from oneness. For likeness and equality are the mother of love."[5]

But likeness and equality are also the mother of the peculiar class
consciousness of the early church. The Pauline congregation is both
egalitarian and hierarchical, led from below and governed from above.
The "one body" of different members cannot survive in a leaderless

vacuum: Paul's hierarchy of the charisms supplies the conditions of authority by which the group rules itself. His totalizing discourse is unmistakable: it is all for one, he says, or else neither the all nor the one can exist. The ongoing dialectic between equal membership in the body of Christ and subordination to higher endowments categorically defines the basis of power in Paul's charismatic organization.

The conflict between the "one body" of Pauline theology, consisting of diverse and equal bodily members, and the unique, self-contained charismatic body of a leader has never been resolved in the West. A permanent dialectic accompanies charisma in the post-Pauline world, set in motion by Paul's democratizing romance of the congregation. Even in the early church charismatic authority met with stringent checks reflecting an uneasy alternation between individual authority and group membership. For example, as Peter Brown points out regarding the first centuries of Christianity, the difficulty of balancing leadership and egalitarian membership inspired arbitrary regulatory practices: "Christian communities soon had to lay down rules as to how to treat prestigious wanderers endowed with prophetic gifts. A visiting preacher of the kingdom must be welcomed 'as if he were the Lord himself'; but he could be fed and lodged by the local householders for only three days. If he so much as ordered a special meal for himself, he was to be shown the road: he was a false prophet!" (1988, 43). This instability in the charismatic preacher's status is different not so much in kind as in degree from the status of political leaders, monks, or pirates. Undoubtedly the early Christians recognized the claim of their "prestigious wanderers." But the standards of proof were so strict that the formation of the "one body" of the congregation was continually threatened by individual authority—by the displacement of the congregational body by the human body at the group's center.

The Charismatic Subject

The conflict between the human and the congregational body originates in the ambiguities of Pauline anthropology, but I do not have the space here to explore such a large subject in detail. Briefly, the ambiguities stem from the difference between *sōma* and *sarx*, both words for *body* in Greek, as well as from the variable meanings of *sōma* in Paul's letters.[6] *Sarx* has tended to be interpreted as the body in the world, the fleshly body, whereas *sōma* has been seen as a description of the body as both external mortal shell and spiritual or psychological depth. Thus *sōma* at times can mean 'flesh' and at times can mean "supramundane body," in the latter meaning containing *sarx* but extending far beyond it. In J. A. T. Robinson's view, "*sōma* is the nearest equivalent to our word 'personality'" (1952, 28). But it is also the word Paul uses to describe the congregation as the "one body." The confusion of meanings, besides its theological significance, inevitably affects our conception of the charismatic body, whether we think of that body as an individual human leader or as a collective political entity. According to Robert Gundry, this confusion can be found at the very heart of Paul's message:

> where Paul uses the phrase, "the Body of Christ," he discusses the *inner* structure and workings of the body in the interrelationship of its various organs and limbs. Paul nowhere relates the Body of Christ to outward activities in relationship to others. Thus the cohesiveness and harmonious function of a single physical body, considered by itself, provides Paul with a model for the Church in the interrelationships of its own members. (1976, 226)

The physical body provides a model for the "one body" of the congregation.[7] But that same physical body also becomes the site of irresolvable oppositions like those between *sōma* and *sarx*, sacred and profane, or individual and member, all stemming from "the intoxicating boundary-blurring ambiguity of Christ's body" (Beckwith 1993, 25). Unfortunately, the social—in contrast to the spiritual—function of either the body of Christ or of the single physical body gets little attention in the theological debate. The focus instead tends to be on the distinction between Christ's human body and the collectivity or solidarity of the body of Christ whose members are believers.

Nevertheless, we can extrapolate from this debate to form a clearer picture of the social structure of all charismatic groups. The relation between the physical body and the collective or organic whole determines group function to a greater extent in charismatic groups than in others, chiefly because charisma (in its pure, early stages) relies on the human leader at its center. A balance, or a dialectic, develops between that leader's body as flesh and the leader's body as a symbol of charismatic unity. Mirroring the relation of Christ to his church, the economy of power in the Pauline organization (the hierarchy of endowments) schematizes the delicate relatedness of personal power to political leadership and, consequently, to spiritual survival. The natural body is the center not only of the disposition of individual power but also of the mythification of group power. Thus subjectivity itself must be redefined to accommodate the charismatic experience.

In recent years there has been a good deal of critical interest among literary critics in defining and tracing the development of early modern subjectivity. This critical interest rarely extends to group subjectivity, however, and in most cases is confined to literary examples with only a dusting of anthropological or sociopolitical theorizing. The line of argument usually taken poses a strict opposition between the notion of a continuous interiority and that of a discontinuous subject. But to my mind—and certainly where charismatic groups are concerned—it is inaccurate to characterize subjectivity in the sharply polarized terms suggested by such critics as Catherine Belsey (1985, esp. 33–34, 39–40), Jonathan Dollimore (1984), and numerous others who have adopted similar terminology. In reviling "essentialism" and "liberal humanism," these critics posit both an evolutionary model of the "unified subject" (Belsey's term) and an either/or pattern characterizing a protagonist as *either* a continuous interiority *or* a discontinuous collocation of exterior impressions. But the either/or pattern fails to account for the ambiguous status of group identity and intrasubjective dependence which we find in all charismatic groups, and which the Pauline congregation idealizes. Further, as Alan Macfarlane showed years ago, the evolutionary historical model of judging the emergence of individualism does not have much credence in England (1979; cf. Huizinga 1959, esp. 29–39). By extension, we should be skeptical about the sudden emergence of subjectivity, let alone about the putative dark ages of its nonexistence.

It is not my intent to defend the concepts of "essentialism" or "liberal humanism," but merely to express a bit of exasperation that such crude nomenclature should govern an important debate in the field. Notably, Stephen Greenblatt, who is often cited among the pioneers of revisionist Renaissance subjectivity, takes a balanced view in his early work, although he too eventually comes to extrapolate an overpolarized thesis. In a discussion of More's *Utopia* in *Renaissance Self-Fashioning*, he observes that the author connects self-conscious individualism to private property, while implying that communal ownership dissolves such individualism: "Private ownership of property is causally linked in *Utopia* to private ownership of self, what C. B. Macpherson calls 'possessive individualism'; to abolish private property is to render such self-conscious individualism obsolete" (1980, 38–39). Greenblatt frames his discussion in psychological terms—"the scope of the ego" (1980, 39)—but his observation of More's distinction between communal and private individuality might be profitably translated to the charismatic relationship between group members and each other, and particularly between leader and members. The communal "ownership" of the charismatic mission completely alters the status of individualism, or subjective autonomy, conflating in a dependent relationship the interiority of a subject and the external forces by which that subject comes into being in the context of charismatic group action.

In a later study Greenblatt concludes in regard to early modern identity that "the concrete individual exists only in relation to forces that pull against spontaneous singularity and that draw any given life, however peculiarly formed, toward communal norms" (1988, 75). He bases his conclusion on very thin evidence, specifically his own overdetermined interpretation of a "cheerfully grotesque story" (his terms) about sexual hermaphroditism in a sixteenth-century text. He says of Marin le Marcis, the accused hermaphrodite, "the drive to be reabsorbed into the communal is sufficiently strong in his case to make us doubt that individualism, in the sense of freestanding and irreducible particularity, had any meaning or value to [him]" (1988, 75). In my view there is not enough to go on in the story to support this conclusion, and certainly not enough to stand as a foundation for Greenblatt's final generalization: "It has been traditional, since Jakob Burckhardt, to trace the origins of autonomous individuality to the Renaissance, but the material under consideration here suggests that individual identity in the early modern period served less as a final goal than as a way station on the road to a firm and decisive identification with normative structures" (1988, 75–76). This is doubtful, not so much because it cannot be so for the early modern period as that it cannot help but be so for all periods in which "normative structures" exist. But this is not an observation best understood in terms of individual psychology. Rather, it would be more prudent to reduce the scope of Greenblatt's generalization and to see it as a plausible observation on group psychology. Moreover, we should once again avoid the polarizing either/or implications of seeing identification with normative structures as a supersession of individual identity. The relation between these two emotional or psychological states is dialectical and unresolvable, as will be repeatedly demonstrated in our analyses of charismatic groups. Highlighting the discontinuity and porousness of individual subjectivity in the realm of group experience, charisma brings into sharp relief a fragile balance between individual identity and normative structures, and between autonomy and collective identity.

This fragile balance as a systemic structure of mutuality can be traced back to 1 Corinthians, a text at pains to redefine subjectivity *in tandem with* new normative structures. For the present study we will be concerned more with the effects of this redefinition on charisma than on those structures through which normative Christianity emerged. Yet it must be acknowledged that, despite secularization, Pauline discourse continues to influence our understanding of charismatic authority. Of course, Paul's ideas should not be seen as purely original in regard to the charismatic ideal, but as important revised descriptions of how charisma works. While neither Paul nor the Hebrews had invented charisma, Paul recasts and rationalizes the ideals of subjectivity and authority as they were manifest in Hebrew prophecy, chrism, and personal obedience to the Law.[8] We will see a more explicit recasting of the Hebrew charismatic ideal in Chapter Four, with Milton's adaptation of the Book of Judges for *Samson Agonistes*. But, inevitably, the Pauline model stands behind Milton's representation of charisma, just as its influence is felt in so many literary renderings of charismatic authority during the sixteenth and seventeenth centuries. Paul's letter to the Corinthians incised rationalized charismatic organization on the cornerstone of the Christian church, establishing a new myth of the mutuality peculiar to all functioning charismatic groups. Reformation discourse fetishized Pauline ecclesiology and with it the myth of a new mutuality (inseparable from the myth of a new individualism, pace Greenblatt). This powerful subtext of mutuality and individualism undergirds the relation between charismatic group function and early modern tragedy.

Weber and Weberians

Given Paul's ongoing influence, it seems fitting that Weber should have taken the term *charisma* from Rudolf Sohm's *Kirchenrecht* (1892), in which Sohm describes what he calls the "charismatic organization" of the itinerant teachers of the gospel (*didaskaloi*) during the first centuries of the Christian church.[9] When first invoking the term (in *The Sociology of Religion*), Weber uses it to mean "extraordinary powers that have been designated by such special terms as 'mana,' 'orenda,' and the Iranian 'maga' (the term from which our word 'magic' is derived)" (1978, 1:400). He later expands his use of the term and concludes that charismatic authority is one of only three legitimate types, the other two being traditional and legal-bureaucratic authority. Charisma, he notes, refers to "a certain quality of an individual personality by virtue of which he is considered extraordinary and treated as endowed with supernatural, superhuman, or at least specifically exceptional qualities or powers" (1978, 1:241).[10]

"The power of charisma," Weber states, "rests upon the belief in revelation and heroes, upon the conviction that certain manifestations—whether they be religious, ethical, artistic, scientific, political or other kind—are important and valuable; it rests upon 'heroism' of an ascetic, military, judicial, magical or whichever kind" (1978, 2:1116). The charismatically endowed person is thought to have powers or qualities that are inaccessible to ordinary people, even divine in origin (see Weber 1978, 1:241). As Robert Tucker suggests, "charismatic leadership is specifically salvationist or messianic in nature" (1968, 743; cf. McIntosh 1970, 909). A charismatic leader—in Weber's sense of pure charisma—must have a mission, and that mission must be recognized by the charismatically enthralled group of followers. But the charismatic leader's presence will be alien to normal social organization because charisma comes into being in response to extreme or extraordinary circumstances, generally crises:

> All *extra*ordinary needs, i.e., those which *transcend* the sphere of everyday economic routines, have always been satisfied in an entirely heterogeneous manner: on a *charismatic* basis. The further we go back into history, the more strongly does this statement hold. It means the following: that the "natural" leaders in moments of distress—whether psychic, physical, economic, ethical, religious, or political—were neither appointed officeholders nor "professionals" in the present-day sense . . . but rather bearers of specific gifts of body and mind that were considered "supernatural" (in the sense that not everybody could have access to them). (Weber 1978, 2:1111–12)

This is a crucial passage in Weber's definition of charisma. But it should be noted that in his emphasis on the supernatural gifts of the charismatic figure he does not develop the notion of heterogeneity. His point seems to be that because the followers' needs are by no means the same in all "moments of distress," the preconditions of charisma must be seen as heterogeneous (cf. Tucker 1968, 742, 744; Camic 1980, 7, 12). The implication would be that charisma cannot be reduced to a single essence.

Nevertheless, certain features of charismatic authority always remain constant—according to Weber, in any case. Chief among these constant features are the notion of the charismatic's mission and Weber's conviction (in his later work) that pure charisma is a revolutionary, disruptive force. The actions of the "'natural' leaders in moments of distress" necessarily break the constraints of everyday routine (*Alltag*). In this sense, pure charisma can be subversive of either traditional authority or bureaucratic organization:

> Genuine charismatic domination knows no abstract laws and regulations and no formal adjudication. Its "objective" law flows from the highly personal experience of divine grace and god-like heroic strength and rejects all external order solely for the sake of glorifying genuine prophetic and heroic ethos. Hence, in a revolutionary and sovereign manner, charismatic domination transforms all values and breaks all traditional and rational norms. (Weber 1978: 2:1115)

Weber quotes Jesus as an example of this transformation of values: "It has been written . . . but *I* say unto you." The followers of a charismatic who claims such power must respond to the revolutionary challenge with the courage to abandon themselves, "to overcome the external and internal limits of daily existence" (Dow 1978, 83). Jesus required his disciples to reject their families, their livelihoods, and their possessions before joining him. Such sacrifices of subjective identity depend on submerging individual subjectivity in an identification with the charismatic leader, "in that the leader, on the basis of his apparent gifts of body and mind, his heroism, is perceived as a model of both release itself and the apparent power that makes release possible" (83–84).

The crucial question is this: to what extent does charisma disrupt the social order? Camic notes that in *The Sociology of Religion* Weber demonstrated that "the potential consequences of satisfying extraordinary dependency needs . . . are sometimes disruptive and sometimes conserving of the existing social order" (1980, 20). But Weber's later work, culminating in *Economy and Society*, repeatedly emphasizes the disruptive nature of charisma and places charismatic rule in an antithetical relation to both traditional and rational rule:

> Charisma, in its most potent forms, disrupts rational rule as well as tradition altogether and overturns all notions of sanctity. Instead of reverence for customs that are ancient and hence sacred, it enforces the inner subjection to the unprecedented and absolutely unique and therefore Divine. In this purely empirical and value-free sense charisma is indeed the specifically creative revolutionary force of history. (1978, 2:1117)

This disruptive element makes charisma particularly relevant to tragedy, a genre in which varieties of social disruption often collide.

Weber's description of an "inner subjection" in conflict with reverence for sacred customs might be applied to all the tragic figures in this book, from Tamburlaine to Hamlet to Samson to Cleopatra. Indeed, the suffocation of their "creative revolutionary force" both defines and palpably augments our experience of their separate catastrophes.

The "inner subjection" to which Weber refers also calls to mind Paul's requirements for the Corinthian congregation. The mutuality of membership in the Pauline church implied a choice not to dissent from the dissenters, absorbing the deviants at Corinth into the larger, unchoosable pretext of dissent on which the Christian apostolic mission was founded. The pivotal function of the charisms for Paul seems to have been their ability to bind members to the congregation as individuals while simultaneously neutralizing the threat of individual domination. Only through what Weber calls inner subjection would this kind of binding succeed. And this internal element separates charismatic change from other kinds of change: "rationalization and rational organization," according to Weber, "revolutionize 'from the outside,' whereas charisma, if it has any specific effects at all, manifests its revolutionary power from within, from a central *metanoia* [change] of the followers' attitudes" (1978, 2:1117).

But a change of attitudes does not necessarily mean social disruption, as Weber's critics have pointed out. It must also be acknowledged that the concept of pure charisma is something of a hothouse concept, clearly suitable for fiction that is full of pure charismatics but perhaps nonexistent in such pure form in society.[11] As Edward Shils argues, "The extraordinary charisma of which Max Weber spoke was the intense and concentrated form. Its normal form, however—attenuated and dispersed charisma—exists in all societies. In this form it is attributed in a context of routine actions to the rules, norms, offices, institutions, and strata of any society" (1982, 118). This radical revision of Weber's "concentrated" charisma demotes the importance of the mission. Shils maintains that "normal" charisma contributes to the function of routine actions in society, bringing together the Weberian poles of charismatic and traditional domination, of charisma and bureaucracy. Weber too saw the inevitable collapse of these poles, and his discussion of the routinization of charisma is the precursor to Shils's "normal" charisma. The difference is in degree. Weber believed that a pure form of charisma was the originating or legitimating force behind all attenuations, while he also suspected that pure charisma, insofar as it demanded a belief in transcendent values, was increasingly impossible in the modern world.

In contrast, Shils is inclined to see more balance between the types of authority, so that, due to a "mediated, institutionalized . . .

propensity . . . charisma not only disrupts social order; it also maintains or conserves it (1982, 120; cf. Camic 1980, 20). Liah Greenfeld puts
it slightly differently. She maintains that "genuine charisma is revolutionary" because "acceptance of charismatic authority is based on the
destruction or complete neglect of all previous norms and values."
"But," she adds, "genuinely charismatic authority necessarily and
very soon leads to the establishment of new values or re-establishment
of the earlier ones" (1985, 128). This latter point echoes Camic's notion
that "figures deemed sacred generally do not revolt against the moral
standards of a social order; they are special because they uphold these
standards" (1980, 20). Again the example of Jesus is apt: he came, he
said, to fulfill the Torah, not to overthrow it.[12]

Shils's flexible notion of charisma has valuable applications. But it
should be borne in mind, I think, that to operate *charismatically* even
within the boundaries of a particular order is usually accomplished
in the name of dissent: just as Paul silences the dissenters from the
already socialized dissent of the early church, any charismatic conservation of a social order is manifest in a group identification with
change or, in heightened political circumstances, even with subversion. Eisenstadt notes that "a crucial aspect of the charismatic personality or group is not only the possession of some extraordinary,
exhilarating qualities, but also the ability, through these qualities,
to reorder and reorganize both the symbolic and cognitive order"
(1968, xl). Echoing Shils and others, Eisenstadt implies that Weber
fails to acknowledge the administrative talents of charismatic leaders. The irony of this view is that an ideal of revolutionary change,
with its promise of particularized individual freedom, becomes the
instrument by which subversive impulses are controlled and turned
toward conservative, protobureaucratic—or, in any case, antiindivid-
ual—ends. Such an irony has considerable force when applied to
early modern England and especially to the charismatic Elizabeth I.
For all her revolutionary conduct (like refusing to marry), Elizabeth
obviously demonstrated conservative impulses in regard to societal
change.[13] As critics have noted, her government often used apparently subversive or revolutionary phenomena in the service of the
containment of potentially more subversive or more revolutionary
impulses.[14]

But charisma should not be seen merely as the furtherance of a
repressive psuedoindividualism. It is also a barometer of the balance
between subjectivity and domination, and, more broadly, between
order and chaos. The decline to conformity and regulatory organization—to "routinization" in Weberian terms—simultaneously undermines charismatic power and protects the centralized authority of a

new organization derived from that charisma. Yet a conflict arises between the charismatic leader as a pragmatic force and as a hypostatized symbol of the group, because, when the existing social order is shattered, people become dependent on leaders who "are able to present to them new symbols which could give meaning to their experiences in terms of some fundamental cosmic, social, or political order" (Eisenstadt 1968, xxviii). But the danger to the charismatic leader is that he or she will be absorbed by the symbols, a situation that often amplifies the isolation of charismatic figures in tragedy. As the Willners point out, "the charismatic leader can be seen as a double-visaged Janus, projecting himself on the one hand as the omniscient repository of ancient wisdom and on the other as the new man of the people" (1965, 87). This double visage inexorably leads to the double bind in which all charismatic authority is caught: "While charismatic leadership may contribute in many ways to the consolidation of the state, its exercise may also delay the kind of institutionalization and continuity of authority needed for concrete tasks of development. The charismatic leader may become trapped by his own symbols and substitute symbolic action as ends instead of means" (87).

The last point is particularly important for tragedy. The substitution of charismatic symbols as the ends of group function rather than as a means of achieving certain goals undermines most tragic protagonists. For instance, Marlowe's Tamburlaine becomes obsessed by the symbol of his charisma, by the notion of his marauding army as an end in itself. Similarly, Othello substitutes the ideal of charismatic generalship for actual charismatic behavior, as is evident in his disciplining of Cassio. In both plays the idealized version of the charismatic group has become hypostatized along with an ideal of the leader. But the once-disruptive symbolic order has been mistaken for the action of disruption, separating the human being who leads the group from his own symbolization.

This is an irony of charismatic agency. The corpus agens of the leader is displaced from the center of charismatic movements by the very transcendental ideals which its exceptional powers inculcate. In the case of Jesus the displacement is itself an ideal, an allegory of the shuffling off of the body in pursuit of spiritual apotheosis. For ordinary humans, whose authority remains earthbound, the displacement of individual relevance by a hypostatized symbol of that relevance results in either the overshadowing of individual charisma or a destructive series of compromises with putatively permanent, rather than palpably revolutionary, authority. In other words, the idealization of the charismatic mission reifies it, occluding the individual at its center.

Freedom from choice accompanies membership in a charismatic group (see Newman 1983, 204; cf. Fromm 1941). But that freedom binds the members to conformity in the satisfaction of their special needs, while at the same time locking the leader to the members' needs. The group makes the charismatic leader "the prisoner of his or her own gifts" (Newman 1983, 203). This tight interdependence is what I earlier called systemic mutuality. The breakdown of such a mutuality destroys the group system and all the social, political, legal, or other functions that depend on the group. But, conversely, the survival of that binding mutual relationship threatens the individuality of the charismatic leader.

Moreover, this conflict between individuality and an ideal form of mutuality is exacerbated by the inherent instability of charismatic groups. In the Weberian model, pure charisma really only exists *in statu nascendi*:

> The pure type of charismatic rulership is in a very specific sense unstable, and all its modifications have basically one and the same cause: The desire to transform charisma and charismatic blessing from a unique, transitory gift of grace of extraordinary times and persons to a permanent possession of everyday life. This is desired usually by the master, always by his disciples, and most of all by his charismatic subjects. Inevitably, however, this changes the nature of the charismatic structure. (1978: 2:1121)

The transformation of pure charisma to a "permanent possession of everyday life" is accomplished through a process of routinization. This process compromises the original disruptive action, ultimately destroying the uniqueness of the gift of grace and its bearer. Routinization takes many forms and has many justifications, most commonly the need of the charismatic followers to preserve their livelihoods (see Bendix 1977, 296, 326). In a striking metaphor Weber observes that "every charisma is on the road from a turbulently emotional life that knows no economic rationality to a slow death by suffocation under the weight of material interests: every hour of its existence brings it nearer to this end" (1978, 2:1120).[15] This is not merely a sociological abstraction. Human beings struggle to survive the end of every ruined charismatic movement, or they attempt to restructure it to their benefit. Between the straits of a "turbulently emotional life" and the "weight of material interests" there is a fertile human dimension comprising all manner of ambitions, frustrations, manipulations, destroyed hopes, and furious losers. The failure of charisma may be inevitable, but its death throes have an infinite variety.

Most recently, Thomas Spence Smith has analyzed this variety, making the provocative suggestion that charismatic groups might very well be unable to function *without* some degree of decay. He suggests that certain types of groups thrive in dissipative structures, in the entropy and mild chaos that allow leaders to emerge (1992, 110–11).[16] In this respect Smith is close to Weber, although he expands on the moment of emergence whereas Weber passes quickly to later stages. Smith notes, for example, that one of the constants of charismatic interaction is that it seeks to preserve itself. Therefore, if mild chaos were to provide a criterion for control, then a charismatic leader might extend or encourage a dissipative structure rather than gravitate toward stability, inasmuch as entropy guarantees a sharp dependency among followers. And here again we encounter a paradox: the notion of a *structure* that defines itself in dissipation. Such a structure is evident in the Pauline congregation, which allows a charismatic group to be led from above and simultaneously govern itself from below, thus systematically destabilizing itself as a group while requiring that same systematic destabilization to continue to function. Smith speaks of this kind of social phenomenon as "non-equilibrium functionalism," suggesting that social organization may well depend on the generation of disorder rather than order: "Disorder in this perspective is a sort of fuel for social life, and it is eaten up by engines that produce order" (1992, 14).

In drama, if not always in life, disorder-eating engines affect charismatic authority by bringing about the simultaneous defeat of both individual centrality and group function. The shared dissent that links the charismatic leader to the group also severely limits the individuality of that leader. In Smith's terms, "all dynamics leading in a far-from-equilibrium direction are either toward disorganization and chaos or toward dependency and centralization, undermining autonomy" (1992, 198). Management of the "far-from-equilibrium" dynamics—some form of dissipative structure—becomes a necessary component of preserving the charismatic relationship. But one of the typical means of managing a dissipative structure is the idealizing of the charismatic movement itself, turning it into a symbol. Once idealized, a charismatic mission alienates itself from its own origins, and the self-alienation precipitates a breakdown between group and leader.

For this reason, Oedipus the culprit clashes with the ideal of Oedipal charisma, a stable symbol of the original riddle-solving mission of the hero, who, in a time of distress, had fulfilled the extraordinary needs of the Theban polis. In the new emergency (the plague) Oedipus is trapped by the idealization of his charismatic rulership, a routinization of the original charisma with which he and the populace

have stabilized the political situation. The crushing irony that Oedipus is himself the cause of the new miasma only reinforces his
abstraction from the original needs and the original charismatic
bond. There is a lesson for all charismatic leaders in Sophocles' play,
and an indication of how the routinization of charisma can frame a
tragic situation. Limited by the group dynamic on one hand and by
transcendental idealization on the other, charismatic agency, if successful, defeats its own centrality. The inevitable erosion of power can
be stemmed only by generating further disorder, only by integrating
entropy as a permanent feature of authority. But individual autonomy is an unavoidable casualty of this kind of group function. And
tragedy may be our most eloquent lamentation of that casualty.

Tragedy

In *Democracy in America*, Tocqueville observed that "when the revolution that subverts the social and political state of an aristocratic people begins to penetrate into literature, it generally first manifests itself
in the drama, and it always remains conspicuous there" (1967, 95).
The Reformation was a revolution that subverted the aristocratic
state, even if the subversion was primarily conceived to have been
religious. Moreover, the centuries of the Reformation were prolific
times for the reassessment of the individual's relation to society,
destiny, and divinity. Tragedy was reborn in the kiln of these transforming relations—reborn and restructured to engage social and psychological realities significantly different from those of the primary
tragic models, Seneca and (for those who read them) the Greek trage-
dians. That the middle ages produced no tragedy identifiable as such
remains an unsolved sociological mystery. But that the Renaissance,
and particularly the Reformation, developed a poetics focused on a
newly defined relation of human beings to their world is not surprising in light of such profound disturbances as Luther's revolutionary
stance, the Copernican upheaval, or the sudden growth of the mer-
cantile classes in tandem with European expansionism. One might
have predicted something like the tragedies of Shakespeare and
Racine, exemplars of the defeat of individual centrality, just as one
might have expected something like the English Civil War.
    In the tragic setting, the failure of charisma captures the struggle
between the individual and the collective. The rise and decline of
charismatic authority exemplify the paradoxical constraints of group
identity, anticipating what the Frankfurt School writers spoke of as the
"gradual liquidation of the autonomous subject in modern society"

(Jay 1973, 178). This liquidation is most pronounced as an absorption of the individual (whether leader or follower) into the symbols of a group, an acquiescence to stability under the auspices of (a now neutralized) dissent or disruption. It is ironic that the word *individual* should come into English usage at this time, precisely when self-consciously Protestant society began to circumscribe the autonomy of the individual subject. The repressive grip of Calvinism probably had the strongest influence on delimiting the individual. The doctrine of election, emphasis on obedience, and the acceptance of the uncharismatic magistrate as unchallenged authority all pit the notion of individual autonomy against the reality and necessity of repression which Calvin advocated. In fact, Calvin himself, as Michael Walzer points out, "was acutely aware of the vast increase in social control that would result if human beings could be made to will that control themselves and consent to it in their hearts" (1968, 47). With such authoritarianism in the air, the developing use of the word *individual* might almost be seen as a protest. And the isolation of the tragic protagonist could be cast as a kind of heroic, morally exempt subversion—a defiantly secularized version of what Weber calls the "unprecedented inner loneliness of the single individual" under the strictures of Calvinistic election (Weber 1958, 104; cf. Rozett 1984).[17]

But one would be mistaken to conclude from this general observation that any particular play is therefore subversive. To the contrary, early modern tragedy—particularly the tragedy of charismatic figures—reflects not only the subversion of the social and political state but also the defeat of the individual in the course of that subversion. In this respect charismatic tragedies call to mind Nietzsche's *Birth of Tragedy*. Nietzsche conceived a link between tragedy and individuation, suggesting that tragic emotion reflects "a world torn asunder and shattered into individuals" (1967, 74). He speculated that the origin of tragic emotion was in religious ritual, particularly ecstatic possession, and in this respect too there is a connection to charismatic authority. For Nietzsche the ritual *sparagmos* which accompanied Dionysiac religious frenzy was the trace of a seminal moment in the history of the imagination and therefore the wellspring of Greek tragic representation. Although this is finally an insupportable premise, the spirit of Dionysus is difficult to banish and Nietzsche's theory can be intriguing for a consideration of tragedies involving charismatic groups.[18]

Individuation, dismemberment, and irrationality, if not rigid elements of a universal formula, haunt the background of much tragic drama, severally and as a triad. A cursory look at postclassical tragedy from Marlowe and Shakespeare to Racine and Büchner repeatedly confirms their proximity to certain kinds of tragic circumstances. It may be an exaggeration to claim Dionysian dismemberment as the founding horror of all forms of tragedy, as Nietzsche attempted to do. On the other hand, symbolic dismemberment—what Nietzsche calls the "spell of individuation"—invariably precipitates the catastrophes in tragedies centering on charismatic authority and charismatic group function. This is not surprising. Dismemberment is after all Saint Paul's metaphor too, the most profound threat to the "one body" of the congregation. The tragedy of a "world torn asunder and shattered into individuals" is precisely the tragedy of charismatic group break-down, reminiscent simultaneously of Saint Paul's warning to the "members" of the church and of such destructive individuations as Othello's or Coriolanus's.

But this is not to suggest that the essence of charisma is Dionysian, as Dow has done (1978, 84). Not even in tragedy can the charismatic experience be reduced to a single essence. The "Dionysian" stamp does a disservice to the plurality of charismas, just as in Nietzsche's hands it failed to accommodate the variety of tragedies. Camic's notion of the heterogeneous causes of charismatic authority, as well as Shils's description of attenuated charisma, should be sufficient warning against too reductive or homogenized a characterization of charismatic needs and gratifications.

Nevertheless, individuation, the symbol of group dismember-ment, remains *the* constant threat to charismatic groups. The revolu-tionary and sometimes subversive character of charismatic move-ments is therefore kept in check by the repressive character of group regulation. Because charismatic authority is vested in the extraordi-nary leadership of one person while being manifest in the mutuality (or democracy) of group power, it arises in an aura of subversion, a revolutionary magnetism. But since it must maintain its ascendancy by stifling dissident voices, even if they are perfect imitations of the charismatic authority itself (like the ecstatics at Corinth), the force of subversion is at one and the same time a force of repression. Tragedies that reflect the charismatic relationship therefore problematize the notion of subversion or dissent, no matter how morally legitimate the rejection of the status quo may appear to be.

Tragedy alone among literary genres requires the rejection of the status quo, the breakdown of social order. One can hardly gen-eralize beyond that, except to note the prevalence of suffering, death, horror, misrecognition, and blinding pride. Yet in virtually all trag-edies there is a disruption of the sociopolitical status quo, an irrepara-ble rent in the fabric of social stability. The irreparablility of the dis-ruption distinguishes tragedy from comedy (also full of disruptions, but reparable ones) and romance (whose disruptions are resolved and whose fabric is reconstituted through magic). Epic is the inverse of tragedy (even if tragic emotion stems in literary history from the *Iliad*): epic narrative records the reconstruction of order after (usually) one shocking disruption. Romance is often compared to epic, since its narrative also records the reconstruction after disruption (Tasso refers to "dispersion"), except that in romance the disruptions multiply outlandishly along with the supernatural interventions by which the reconstruction is set on course and eventually accomplished.

The chief difference among these genres, however, is that only tragic protagonists strive to interpret their own actions. Only tragedy can be said to explore the consequences wrought not only by actions but also by the interpretations (or misinterpretations) of actions. Comedy and romance tend to be "oversocialized," ignoring the mechanisms by which people interpret their societies (cf. Kalberg 1994, 25). Dramatic comedy depends on the existence of (and blind acquiescence to) a belief system whose meaning is hypostatized and apparently permanent. Dramatic romance relies on the intervention of otherworldly action to restore thisworldly social order, imbuing the system rather than human action with meaning; and, similarly, while tragicomedy threatens both social order and belief system with individual deviance, it soon retreats from the threat, confirming the existence of and acquiescence to the extant order and belief while suppressing the chaotic dangers of individual choice. Only tragedy attempts faithfully to recapitulate the relation of the individual to society by examining the power of choice and interpretation in fostering action. As Stephen Kalberg has observed, Weber's fundamental premise of social action—manifest in his notion of *Verstehen*, or interpretive understanding—is that people are *"cultural beings* endowed with the capacity and will to take a deliberate stand toward the world and to lend it *meaning (Sinn)"* (1994, 24; see Weber 1949, 81). This idea has provocative implications for understanding tragedy. For in tragic representation, action consistently depends upon a deliberate stand or choice by which, in Weber's terms, palpably *cultural* beings lend meaning to their actions.

Moreover, Weber's categories facilitate our recognition of how thinking and self-reflection contribute to tragic paradigms. Weberian sociology advocates a multicausality in social action, refusing to raise any one factor, such as religion or economic need, to the privileged position of a constant. In contrast to Marx, for example, who considers historical forces and the class struggle to be permanent features of society, largely independent of the thoughts of individuals, Weber emphasizes the importance of ideas and their effect on individual and group conduct in the development of society. This emphasis leads to a proliferation of causes to match the variety of social situations, and it provides a flexibly comprehensive set of categories by which to analyze shifts in authority, belief, custom, and political economy. All such shifts, changes in authority most prominently, are reflected somewhere in early modern tragedy. The Weberian categories, though by no means necessary to understanding tragic representation, add, I think, a new degree of interpretation to the experience of tragedy by helping us to construe the tragic paradigms more closely with society.

The place of thinking in tragedy—the cultural place—is unique. It appears as both lion and arena, both local cause and what we might call universal cause. Thinking (including choice) integrates the horror of tragic emotion and the action of the catastrophe. Hegel observed that Shakespeare's tragic characters develop "by virtue of the image in which they contemplate themselves objectively, in theoretical reflection, like a work of art" (Kaufmann 1968, 329). No such contemplation or objectivity occurs in comedy or romance, not even in Shakespeare's. Characters of comedy and romance do not know themselves. They are actors in an unreflective medium, and their pain and suffering (generally to be mended) afflicts them externally. There is no metanoia in comedy or romance as there is in tragedy, no inward change that affects (or effects) social action. To be comprehensive, therefore, the analysis of tragedy must contend with tragic agonists as thinking sufferers who recognize themselves as cultural beings, and it must incorporate the social roots and social ramifications of catastrophic action insofar as they are the products of characters' reflection. Indeed, in this context one of the meanings of anagnorisis might well be the sudden recognition of oneself as a cultural being in a particularized social reality—in contrast to seeing oneself as an idealized figure of imagination or delusion (a divine prince, the Scourge of God, Isis). The tragic deflation of the recognition scene from Oedipus to Edmund (who learns "Yet Edmund was belov'd") forcibly demonstrates the *social* connectedness of the protagonist, wresting that protagonist's mind from an imagination of himself (or occasionally herself) as supernatural, extrasocial, or controlled by fate rather than subject to social forces. And for charismatic figures the deflation can be especially precipitous. Some form of self-delusion, what Smith calls "illusional conviction," is a necessary component of charismatic leadership (1992, 168). Recognizing the absence of a supernatural aura shatters both the individual at the center of the charismatic group as well as the idealized symbols of the original charisma.

Tragedy captivates the imagination as an irresistible example of what Smith calls "processes that generate disorder." That such disorder could be "fuel for social life," as Smith puts it, "eaten up by engines that produce order," reminds us how often the disorder of tragedy casts the tragic protagonist down into the rational, order-driven realities of society from the heights of such powerful abstractions as genealogical superiority or semidivine bodily status (Smith 1992, 14). Charismatic protagonists are particularly vulnerable to the engines that produce order. Indeed, for them, tragedy might be seen as a fall into ordinary social life.

1

REVOLUTION TO ROUTINIZATION

Tamburlaine's Pure Charisma

The two parts of *Tamburlaine the Great* chart the course of charismatic group function with exceptional clarity, from the rising up of a martial hero to the enthralling of followers to the inevitable problems of charismatic succession. The first cracks in the Scythian shepherd's astonishing charismatic hegemony are evident in Part 2 of the play, and I think it is fair to see that incipient breakdown as an early form of the shattering of charismatic groups in such tragedies as *Richard II* and *Antony and Cleopatra*. Marlowe's play provides a useful analytic tool for the present study because Tamburlaine embodies as clear an example of the ideal type of pure charisma as Elizabethan drama has to offer.[1] But the play is more than merely an analytic tool, just as Tamburlaine himself, viewed in Marlowe's "tragic glass" (Prologue), has more breadth and human substance than the limits of an ideal type allow.

Critics have held mixed views of *Tamburlaine*, particularly in regard to Part 2. Many have considered the second part of the play much inferior to the first, a more or less perfunctory and poorly structured attempt to capitalize on the popularity of Part 1 (cf. Kuriyama 1980, 4–5). In contrast, Harry Levin, in his still useful book, observed that there is no tragedy until Part 2. He suggested that because Part 1 had exhausted Marlowe's source material, the playwright was forced in the second part "by the very impact of his creation, to face the genuinely tragic conflict that was bound to destroy the monster he created" (1952, 35). This is a reasonable way of linking the two parts without asserting, as Roy Battenhouse had earlier done, that they constitute a single ten-act morality play (1941, 252–53). To my mind, the two parts of the play are, if not seamlessly linked, then interdependent, with the tragic force of the second part growing out of our recognition of changes in the group dynamics surrounding Tamburlaine's charismatic status. As Helen Gardner long ago observed in defense of Part 2, "the Tamburlaine spell is not working" at the beginning of the second part ([1942] 1974, 204).

. I would like to analyze that broken spell as the spell of charisma and to discuss the consequences of its malfunction as they are manifest in the changed relation of Tamburlaine to his followers. Tamburlainian heroism never exists in isolation, and, despite the suggestiveness of Eugene Waith's influential thesis (1962), I doubt that the classical figure of Hercules best characterizes the charismatic experience of Tamburlaine and his warrior band. Whereas Hercules performs alone—he is, to be sure, the consummate lone wolf—Tamburlaine's feats all occur in a group context. Consequently his tragedy develops in tandem with his increasing alienation from followers and from the symbols of his own charismatic rise to power. As the play progresses from Part 1 to Part 2, the function, cohesion, and even the fundamental dynamic of the charismatically bound group begin to alter. But Tamburlaine remains oblivious to the alterations, unaware of subtle and ominous threats to his charismatic claim. A perilous gap opens between the reality of group function and Tamburlaine's consciousness of his charismatic control. This gap has been somewhat neglected in criticism, and the importance of group function to Tamburlaine's success, as well as to his failure, has been glossed over. The present chapter is an attempt to remedy the neglect. I agree with Constance Kuriyama when she says that "it is fatal to approach this play with the conviction that the author is a totally conscious creator, or that his works are shaped exclusively by the philosophical systems or values of his age" (1980, 8). But even with these caveats in mind I would still argue that the dramatic implications of group breakdown are demonstrably present to Marlowe's mind. The transformations of charisma pattern and motivate his "two tragicall discourses," as the play is called on the 1590 title page."

Charisma is never a stable condition, and Tamburlaine's charisma is no exception. As little by little his authority becomes less revolutionary and more conventionally imperialistic, there occurs, in Weberian terms, "a central *metanoia* [change] of the followers' attitudes" (1978, 2:1117). With the passage of time the followers begin to adapt as rulers themselves, moving from the constant crises of conflict and rebellion to the relative stability of satrap government. They become vital members of the Tamburlainian body stretched across Asia. Their concerns or "extraordinary needs" naturally shift in concert with the material changes in their lives, and as soon as they begin to depend on rational economic conduct they become anxious about the preservation of their privileges. Needless to say, Tamburlaine must respond to this metanoia in his followers' attitudes if he hopes to maintain his charismatic ascendency. Marlowe positions his tragic glass deliberately to reflect the limits of Tamburlaine's success in this endeavor.

A Calling to Conquest

Tamburlaine begins his quest as a paradigm of pure charisma. On the surface his authority is revolutionary, defying sacred traditions, traditional authorities, rational economic organization, and conventional military discipline. As C. L. Barber puts it, "Tamburlaine moves *through* geography, cosmology, royalty, but there is nowhere for him to arrive; he is essentially a disruptive energy, to be defined only dynamically, that is, dramatically" (1988, 58). Barber's analogy between dynamic and dramatic definition underscores the link between group function and tragic representation. But, notwithstanding that Tamburlaine "Daily commits incivil outrages" (I.1.1.40), thinking of him as "essentially a disruptive energy" ignores his knack for imposing Tamburlainian stability along the way. He is a master at manipulating "processes that generate disorder" (Smith 1992, 14) and he fulfills Eisenstadt's requirement that the charismatic personality not only possess extraordinary qualities, "but also the ability, through these qualities, to reorder and reorganize both the symbolic and cognitive order" (1968, xl). Reordering the symbols of rulership and authority becomes Tamburlaine's mission. His violence, disruptiveness, and defiance of tradition dovetail with his power to stabilize the economic, political, and even emotional situation within his charismatic group.

Tamburlaine's charismatic claim depends on his ability to manipulate the symbols of destiny and power in a pragmatic manner. With supremely rational ends in mind, he exults in scenes of chaos and destruction, citing fate, oracular truth, pagan myth, and tutelary gods as suprarational proofs of his superiority. His band of followers functions successfully in spite of the contradiction between irrational auspices and rational ends, or indeed because of that contradiction. As A. D. Hope has noted, Tamburlaine "partakes of the divine" and "subsumes all values unto himself" (1986, 48). His physique is consonant with this extraordinary superiority, and even in the eyes of his opponents Tamburlaine "subsumes" the symbolic mythologies of origin, sovereignty, and ambition in his own natural body. Every one of his bodily parts, while recognizably human, is also emblematic of divinity:

> Of stature tall, and straightly fashioned
> Like his desire, lift upwards and divine.
> So large of limbs, his joints so strongly knit,
> Such breadth of shoulders as might mainly bear
> Old Atlas' burden. 'Twixt his manly pitch
> A pearl more worth than all the world is plac'd,
> Wherein by curious sovereignty of art
> Are fix'd his piercing instruments of sight,
> Whose fiery circles bear encompassed
> A heaven of heavenly bodies in their spheres,
> That guides his steps and actions to the throne
> Where honour sits invested royally.
>
>   (I.2.1.7–18)

Marlowe here combines *effictio* with *notatio*, the outward physical description with its moral implications. The continuum between physical stature and divine blessing extends to Tamburlaine's cognitive state, the "desire" that will propel him to rulership. A human giant with the strength of a god, a Scythian Achilles, Tamburlaine's burning ambition shines from eyes which are weapons in themselves, "his piercing instruments of sight." But the zenith on which Tamburlaine has set his sights, "heaven of heavenly bodies," is simultaneously a reflection of the divine auspices that guide his destiny, leading him toward a throne where the charismatic quality of honor, rather than hereditary kingship, "sits invested royally."

Tamburlaine's supernatural, or suprahistorical, appearance has an irresistible magnetism. He appears to be in the midst of a permanent *aristeia*, a charismatic state of excitement that repeatedly sweeps up converts to the conqueror's cause. Moreover, the presence of the warlike Tamburlaine provides an instant mythology to those around him. He is at the center of a shared experience of symbolism through which all followers can participate in what might be termed, with Saint Paul's charismatic model in mind, a congregation of conquest. Here are two members of the original band:

> *Techelles.* As princely lions, when they rouse themselves,
> Stretching their paws, and threatening herds of beasts,
> So in his armour looketh Tamburlaine.
> Methinks I see kings kneeling at his feet,

And he with frowning brows and fiery looks
Spurning their crowns from off their captive heads.

Usumcasanes. And making thee and me, Techelles, kings,
That even to death will follow Tamburlaine.

(I.1.2.52–59)

Likeness to the Achillean lion and the "frowning brows and fiery looks" of Mars combine to paint the image of a raging demigod. "To be a King," says Usumcasanes later on, "is half to be a god" (I.2.5.56), to which Theridamas replies, "A god is not so glorious as a king" because a king commands obedience and has the "power attractive" to breed love among opponents and subjects. This is the kind of kingship Tamburlaine seeks, achieved through meritorious conduct, what he calls 'honor,' and it is sustained by the systemic mutuality of charismatic relations. Tamburlaine's future crown depends on his personal responsibility for his followers and, concomitantly, on their unflagging willingness to follow him "even to death."

Tamburlaine's opponents (especially in Part 1) are uninitiated in the symbols of his agency, unable to decipher the signs and portents accruing to him. Baffled by the source of his superiority, they are inclined, like Meander, to puzzle whether "Some powers divine, or else infernal, mix'd /Their angry seeds at his conception" (I.2.6.9–10). But Tamburlaine leaves no room for ambivalence in his own interpretations of martial successes. Providing a running hermenuetic, he insists that the source of his power *is* divine. While his enemies portray him as a thief and a pirate parading his "vagrant ensign in the Persian fields" (I.1.1.45), Tamburlaine casts his exploits as heroic rebellions necessary to maintain his "life exempt from servitude" (I.1.2.31). A shepherd by birth, he claims the charisma of the anointed, a David rising against oppression. This is his salvationistic or messianic strain (cf. Tucker 1968, 743), proven by the special protection he claims to receive from the gods, as when he dares Theridamas to attack him:

Draw forth thy sword, thou mighty man-at-arms,
Intending but to raze my charmèd skin,
And Jove himself will stretch his hand from heaven
To ward the blow, and shield me safe from harm.

(I.1.2.177–80)

Similarly, he exults before the newly crowned Persian king Cosroe that

fates and oracles of heaven have sworn
To royalise the deeds of Tamburlaine
And make them blest that share in his attempts.

                                        (I.2.3.7–9)

He says this to persuade Cosroe to join him, but his exultation is merely a confirmation of the opinion Cosroe already holds. Before meeting Tamburlaine, Cosroe had marveled at his singular destiny, calling him "the man of fame, / The man that in the forehead of his fortune / Bears figures of renown and miracle" (I.2.1.2–4). Then, face to face with Tamburlaine, he emphasizes his trust in the latter's miraculous fortunes: "even as from assurèd oracle, / I take thy doom for satisfaction" (I.2.3.4–5).

Tamburlaine's mission, ordained by heaven, guarantees heavenly blessing to those who join the group and participate in the charismatic experience. This may be Tamburlaine's distinguishing attribute as a leader. According to Weber, the holder of pure charisma, in addition to working miracles and performing heroic deeds, must prove the validity of his or her mission "by *bringing well-being* to his followers" (1978, 2:1114). Tamburlaine fulfills this exacting requirement from his first military ventures, building his reputation on a shared experience of glory and aggrandizement, a group dependency on both the symbols of charismatic cohesion and the material rewards of that cohesion.

Marlowe's chief historical source for the play, George Whetstone's *The English Myrror* (1586), describes this aspect of Tamburlaine's method at the start of the shepherd's martial career (presumably the beginning of "life exempt from servitude"):

> *Tamberlaine* (having a ruling desire) after an othe of obedience, commanded every man to sell his cattaile: and to contemn their mean estate, and to follow him as their captaine: and in smal time, he assembled 500. heardmen, and laborers, whose first act was to rob the marchants that passed that way: he parted the spoyle continually among his companions, and intertayned them with such faithfulness and love, as the rumour therof dayly increased his strength. (Marlowe 1981, 321).

Somewhat like Jesus, who tells his disciples to abandon their livelihoods and families, Tamburlaine demands the condemnation of class confinement ("mean estate") and the liquidation of the material possessions that identify that class. By sheer force of rebellious innovation, Tamburlaine breaks the constraints of everyday life (Weber's

Alltag), promising to reward those who follow and obey. He divides the spoils among his companions, ensuring their continued loyalty and confirming the interdependence of group members. Because this means of economic conduct is irrational, it is bound to be routinized as time passes. But at this early stage before the "slow death by suffocation under the weight of material interests" (Weber 1978, 2:1120), before the entropy of rational organization sets in, Tamburlaine distributes spoils not as an exchange for services, nor as a form of salary, but as a spontaneous sharing of booty.[2]

Tamburlaine's irrational economic conduct satisfies a prime criterion for Weber's ideal type of pure charismatic group function:

> Charisma rejects as undignified all methodical rational acquisition, in fact, all rational economic conduct. . . . In its pure form charisma is never a source of private income; it is neither utilized for the exchange of services nor is it exercised for pay, and it does not know orderly taxation to meet the material demands of its mission. . . . In the case of charismatic warriors, the booty is both means and end of the mission. In contrast to all patriarchal forms of domination, pure charisma is opposed to all systematic economic activities; in fact, it is the strongest anti-economic force, even when it is after material possessions, as in the case of the charismatic warrior. (1978, 2:1113)

Weber could easily have had Tamburlaine in mind here. In Whetstone the robbing of the merchants comprises "both means and end of the mission." In Marlowe's version, which is more condensed and more ambitious in sketching a personality, Tamburlaine's thievery has a miraculous aura, proof of divine approbation in random material bounty. Thus, after claiming that the fates and oracles will "royalise" his deeds, Tamburlaine can assure Theridamas that Jove "rains down heaps of gold in showers /As if he meant to give my soldiers pay" (I.1.2.181–82). This statement marks the inculcation of a charismatic symbol, a good example of irrational conduct manipulated toward the rational end of group cohesion. In Part 1 of the play Tamburlaine's conquering army resists any bureaucratic or systematic structure in attaining its wealth, as if it were a point of dignity or machismo or *virtú* for them to reject methodical acquisition. The booty of Tamburlaine's raids, which runs the gamut from crowns to highborn slaves, reinforces the divine auspices of his mission, proving in yet another way his vocation to conquer.

Unlike some charismatic groups, such as mendicant friars, Tamburlaine's warrior band does not reject the notion of owning or making money. Their unique sanction takes an acquisitive form. Tamburlaine sees the plunder he accumulates, along with his enduring ability to plunder, as further evidence of the rectitude of his mission, a palpable gift of grace to complement his own personal gift.[3] This antisystematic form of economic organization, while absolutely necessary to the material support of the troops, raises the irrational, emotionally turbulent nature of Tamburlaine's charismatic style to a symbolic standard. At first this symbolism operates as an organizing principle, through what Thomas Spence Smith refers to as "disinhibiting practices" (1992, 169). But eventually Tamburlaine will become a prisoner of such symbols, reducing his action to the preservation not of the ends of his mission but of the means first used to achieve those ends. As his revolutionary mission loses urgency he becomes a purveyor of his own myth, wrapped in the petrified symbolism of his early reputation.

But booty does not tell the whole story. The inculcation of charismatic symbols could not occur without an affective component. Even in Whetstone's account we find that Tamburlaine's relation to his band of followers includes more than material rewards: he also "intertayned them with such faithfulness and love, as the rumour therof dayly increased his strength." In Marlowe's hands this Tamburlainian "entertainment," reflecting that "power attractive" of which Theridamas speaks, becomes a uniquely poetic synthesis of hyperbole and passion. The rhetoric of excess meets the dramatization of exceptional needs, and a rendering of charismatic mutuality results. Indeed, Marlowe's intuition of charisma most convincingly reveals itself in his extrapolation of Tamburlaine's affective genius from the welter of other superlative attributes.

The persuasion of Theridamas supplies the best example. It begins in high astounding terms, with Tamburlaine promising the Persian an equal share in unimaginable power and riches:

> Forsake thy king and do but join with me,
> And we will triumph over all the world.
> I hold the Fates bound fast in iron chains,
> And with my hand turn Fortune's wheel about,
> And sooner shall the sun fall from its sphere
> Than Tamburlaine be slain or overcome.
>
> (I.1.2.171–76)

As noted above, Tamburlaine offers Theridamas his bona fides, claiming a connectedness to Jove as well as a personal command of destiny. Jove will rain down showers of gold, Theridamas's troop of a thousand horse "shall sweat with martial spoil" (190), Christian merchants "Shall vail to us as lords" (195), and "mighty kings shall be our senators" (197). Praising the fruits of disruption and chaos, Tamburlaine's most powerful rhetoric promises that he and his followers shall thrive in the upheavals of traditional culture. This is the heart of his charismatic claim, and the repetitions of "our" and "we" confirm the ideal of a shared experience, a new form of subjectivity to match the new form of world authority Tamburlaine vows to provide. Class revolution and divine mission combine to form Tamburlaine's charismatic agency:

> Jove sometimes maskèd in a shepherd's weed,
> And by those steps that he hath scaled the heavens
> May we become immortal like the gods.
> Join with me now in this my mean estate
> (I call it mean, because, being yet obscure,
> The nations far removed admire me not),
> And when my name and honour shall be spread
> As far as Boreas claps his brazen wings
> Or fair Boötes send his cheerful light,
> Then shalt thou be competitor with me
> And sit with Tamburlaine in all his majesty.
>
> (I.1.2.198–208)

Tamburlaine uses the informal "thou" to address Theridamas, which suggests an egalitarian attitude as well as a hint of condescension. Yet Theridamas will be a "competitor," or partner, in Tamburlaine's majesty, an exceptional status to expect, even granting the hyperbole of the moment. Tamburlaine is inviting Theridamas to take a share in charisma, to turn away from his past loyalties (like a disciple), and to submerge his fortunes in those of the group.

Weber speaks of a share in charisma as *kleros*, the word from which *clergy* is derived. He compares the separation of the charismatic hierarchy with the division of laity from clergy (cf. 1978, 1:251). But the idea of sharing remains crucial even to the act of division. J.-P. Vernant defines the *kleroi* in ancient Greece as "inalienable family possessions, allotments, each belonging to one of the households making up the state, and not to a private individual" (1988, 15). Only if we attempt to combine these two concepts of *kleros*, appreciating the conflict between becoming separate from the group and sharing as a group member of the state, will we begin to understand the peculiar interdependence of Tamburlaine and his followers. Both the separation (in order to administer) and the sharing (in order to be governed) must be absolute. The conflict between these two conditions guarantees an inherent instability in the group, which paradoxically heightens the need for mutuality. As in 1 Corinthians 12, the threat of dismemberment demands a greater emphasis on the shared experience of the "one body" of the group. Therefore it might be said that the *kleros* that Tamburlaine offers, while acting as a "disinhibiting" practice and freeing Theridamas from conventional subjectivity, also locks both men into the systemic absolutism of mutual interdependence.

Referring to Theridamas's betrayal of Cosroe, Meander complains that "wicked Tamburlaine"

> could with gifts and promises
> Inveigle him that led a thousand horse,
> And make him false his faith unto his king.
>
> (I.2.2.24–27)

But Meander is one of the uninitiated and he misreads the encounter. Bribes alone do not persuade Theridamas. The inveigling, if we can call it that, reaches well beyond material considerations. An extraordinary charismatic bond develops between Tamburlaine and Theridamas, a suddenly personal and libidinized bond. The erotic emotion of the scene is palpable, accompanied throughout by Marlowe's heavyhanded impishness. As Theridamas remarks after listening to Tamburlaine's promises, "Not Hermes, prolocutor to the gods, / Could use persuasions more pathetical" (I.1.2.209–10). Cunningham glosses "pathetical" as "emotive," and it is indeed emotion that sways Theridamas rather than gifts or promises. He makes it clear that he is not won over merely by lucre, even if it is rained down in heaps from heaven. Rather, Tamburlaine's charismatic attributes induce him to switch loyalties. Amazed, he asks "What strong enchantments tice my yielding soul?" (I.1.2.223). And, following a sophistical exchange with Tamburlaine regarding the betrayal of Mycetes, Theridamas exclaims:

> Won with thy words and conquered with thy looks,
> I yield myself, my men and horse to thee:
> To be partaker of thy good or ill
> As long as life maintains Theridamas.
>
> (I.1.2.226–29)

The language of wooing is unmistakable. Theridamas may use military metaphors, but the conquest remains personal, even libidinal. We might compare Othello's amorous conquest of Desdemona; "strong enchantments tice" Desdemona as well, although Brabantio suspects outright sorcery. The sorcery of charisma pervades Tamburlaine's enchantment of Theridamas, the magic of a figure who can both identify and then satisfy rare human desires. Othello's relation to Desdemona is openly erotic, but Theridamas and Tamburlaine conceal the libidinal undercurrent of their union in martial language. They bandy about words like "won" and "conquest" and "yield," used not literally but as metaphors for exceptional persuasion, just as those same words have always been used to describe the results of amorous courtship. We must smile at Marlowe's ironies in this passage. While his two heroes stand in full regalia on the battlefield, he has them use military metaphors not to describe the campaign but rather to describe a kind of love. The soldiers imitate lovers imitating soldiers discussing a conquest. The scrambling of signifiers, in addition to shifting attention from the public sphere to the personal, allows Marlowe to weave in the homosexual subtext which, according to Kuriyama, pervades the allusive rhetoric of the play (1980, 19–33).

It is important to recognize, however, that in the context of charisma homoerotic impulses are not subversive. The formation of charismatic groups depends in varying degrees on the erotic undercurrent that binds members to a leader. As long as erotic needs remain activated but unrealized, regardless of whether they are homosexual or heterosexual in objective, they can act as the glue binding a group together. Thus Marlowe, who seems well aware of this fact, buttresses Theridamas's persuasion scene with the remarkable irony of a *necessary* homoeroticism, albeit unconsummated. No other scene in the two plays gives the playwright such latitude to interrogate the amoral mechanism of group cohesion. As he sketches an erotically charged, emotional magnetism between Tamburlaine and Theridamas, he also captures the essence of the aim-inhibited libidinal ties that contribute so much to the formulation of charismatic groups (cf. McIntosh 1970, 905, 911).

Here we can turn to one of Freud's later, more sociologically germane theories. In *Group Psychology and the Analysis of the Ego* he says that "the essence of a group lies in the libidinal ties existing in it" and that group members are to double duty bound: "each individual is bound by libidinal ties on the one hand to the leader . . . and on the other hand to the members of the group" (1960, 30).[4] The desire that binds group members is never satisfied erotically; libido, or simply love, is inhibited by a shared asceticism in which individual needs are sacrificed to group function. Freud speaks of this phenomenon as a limitation of narcissism which allows group members to "behave as though they were uniform, tolerate the peculiarities of . . . other

members, equate themselves with them, and have no feeling of aversion toward them" (1960, 43). And he concludes that "love for oneself
knows only one barrier—love for others, love for objects" (1960, 43).[5]

In charismatic groups this libidinal binding is enhanced by the
need among followers to experience—or to think they experience—a
personal relationship with the leader. Therefore, as Ralph Hummel
has pointed out, charisma might be called "a special type of love relationship" (1975, 759).[6] But the special love relationship must be
defined in terms of special needs. Eric Erikson spoke of a "charisma
hunger" which is fed by experiences of extraordinary behavior (1958;
cf. Smith 1992, 169), and his concept is a useful addition to the libidinal component of group formation. Charisma hunger is pervasive in
Tamburlaine, as the persuasion of Theridamas amply reveals. Theridamas seems positively starved for charisma when we first meet
him, and his gratitude to Tamburlaine for suborning him is effusive.
He gushes with grateful emotion when he is accepted into Tamburlaine's band: "Nor thee nor them, thrice-noble Tamburlaine, /
Shall want my heart to be with gladness pierced /To do you honor
and security" (I.1.2.248–50). His libidinal "gladness" of heart is sublimated in "honor and security." His charisma hunger is fed, indeed
overfed, because Tamburlaine's grandiose presence overstimulates
his followers, calling forth in their minds what Smith (following
Heinz Kohut) terms "idealizing selfobject transferences" (1992, 169,
185). Kohut argues that there is a regressive need in individuals for
awe-inspiring idealizations of the parental imago, and Smith relates
this to charisma by noting that "transfers of omnipotence to idealized
selfobjects are manifestations of the hunger for powerful figures, an
appetite that arises out of the inability of the child to stabilize its own
sense of self-worth or to give direction to its life" (1992, 174–75; cf.
Kohut 1971, 302).[7]

Paradoxically, warlords like Tamburlaine become ideals of stability through their "risk-taking exhibitionism supported by conviction
and grandiosity" (Smith 1992, 175). They mirror the imagined
strength of a never-existent yet now-idealized authority figure in the
childhood memories of group members. But there are consequences
for the leader in fulfilling this fantasy; the trap of the charismatic symbols begins here, at the level of transferences. Because charisma is a
mutually experienced phenomenon, the psychological transferences
are also mutual:

> The leader . . . demands and gets idealization, and we have a situa-
> tion that amplifies her grandiosity and conviction to extraordinary
> heights. In return, she produces in her followers an ever more

adventurous, stimulated, and exhilarated condition that substitutes for their deficits of mirrored strength. It fills them with excitation, which they continue to stabilize by repeated idealizing transferences. The circle of transference—the leader's exhibitionism and mirroring, the followers' voyeurism and idealization—is what constitutes the positive feedback in such extraordinary groups. (Smith 1992, 175–76)[8]

The Tamburlainian crew are in a constant state of exhilaration fostered by their leader's ever-surprising adventurism (particularly in Part 1). The "circle of transference" remains intact so long as Tamburlaine protects the mutuality of the libidinal ties binding group members, and so long as the idealization of his charisma produces symbols that advance his mission.

The extraordinary moment of charismatic acclamation at the end of act 2, when Tamburlaine takes Cosroe's crown and puts it on his own head, demonstrates the perfect balance Tamburlaine has attained between exhibitionism and voyeurism, between the mirroring of deficit strength and the idealization of that strength. The scene reflects these oppositions in its emotional extremes, beginning with the desperate outrage of the betrayed and mortally wounded Cosroe and ending with Tamburlaine's grandiose and gloating self-crowning. "Barbarous and bloody Tamburlaine," Cosroe cries,

> Thus to deprive me of my crown and life!
> Treacherous and false Theridamas,
> Even at the morning of my happy state,
> Scarce being seated in my royal throne,
> To work my downfall and untimely end!
> An uncouth pain torments my grievèd soul,
> And death arrests the organ of my voice.
>
> (I.2.7.1–8)

Cosroe feels an "uncouth pain" in proportion to the uncanny power of Tamburlainian charisma. But Tamburlaine does not really direct his power toward Cosroe. His triumphant exhibitionism is meant for his followers, and his response to Cosroe's suffering is almost perverse in its apparent self-regard:

> The thirst of reign and sweetness of a crown,
> That caused the eldest son of heavenly Ops
> To thrust his doting father from his chair
> And place himself in th' empyreal heaven,

Moved me to manage arms against thy state.
What better precedent than mighty Jove?
Nature, that framed us of four elements
Warring within our breasts for regiment,
Doth teach us all to have aspiring minds:
Our souls, whose faculties can comprehend
The wondrous architecture of the world
And measure every wand'ring planet's course,
Still climbing after knowledge infinite
And always moving as the restless spheres,
Wills us to wear ourselves and never rest
Until we reach the ripest fruit of all,
That perfect bliss and sole felicity,
The sweet fruition of an earthly crown.

(I.2.7.12–29)

A. D. Hope has called these celebrated sentiments the "humanism of war" (1986, 46–47). He rejects the view, expressed by various critics, that Tamburlaine's aspirations for both "knowledge infinite" and an "earthly crown" represent a contradiction in terms. I would agree that there is no absolute contradiction between the first and last parts of the speech, no decline from noble ideals to bathos as Una Ellis-Fermor claimed (1967, 29). But contradiction is irrelevant unless it threatens the management or the promulgation of the charismatic symbols.

Tamburlaine's sublime fantasy has a more heterogeneous etiology than either a sole passion (however dear to the Renaissance imagination) or the conflict between idealism and pragmatic advancement. His speech is not a political platform, nor, on the other hand, is it narcissism in the conventional sense. It would be more accurate to call the speech a form of mirroring, a portmanteau articulation of the "circle of transference." Emily Bartels has noted that Tamburlaine's rhetoric tends to reflect or even to copy statements he has already heard (1992, 11). This is an interesting point, if somewhat misleading in regard to Tamburlaine's innovative force. Tamburlaine transforms verbal cues with irresistible originality. But Bartels nonetheless astutely recognizes that the source of Tamburlaine's charismatic rhetoric is at least partly external, composed of the half-expressed desires and inchoate anxieties of those he intends to lead.

It is a fact of imaginative life that we all use the same set of myths, the same symbols derived from those myths. Yet some of us take possession of particular myths more convincingly, fulfilling symbolic ideals shared by all. Tamburlaine is obviously one of these powerful possessors. When, for example, Marlowe has Cosroe liken himself to Jupiter and claim a Jupiter-like outrage (I.2.6.4), the contrast with Tamburlaine is obvious. Cosroe's use of the myth seems weak and perfunctory, like poetry composed by phrasebook. Set against Tamburlaine's triumphalist adaptation of the exploits of "the eldest son of heavenly Ops," Cosroe's figuration pales, foreshadowing his defeat. Tamburlaine's martial prowess and his charismatic uncanniness coalesce in the myth. His entire speech to Cosroe becomes, after the identification with Zeus, a prising away of mythifications from the wider precincts of the cultural imagination.

Tamburlaine's colonization of myths occurs in tandem with his martial hegemony. Moreover, as his range of conquests expands geographically, Tamburlaine's charisma, best reflected in his rhetorical promiscuity, expands mythically and symbolically. For this reason, Tamburlaine's "earthly crown" speech becomes more important as a rallying of his followers than as a spurning of Cosroe. It constitutes a self-enclosing mystification, a putative revelation of mysterious forces in himself which his followers need to perceive in him (cf. Smith 1992, 177). His "thirst of reign" and his "aspiring" mind mirror the overawed ambition of others, who, on hearing him articulate his motives, can idealize (and ossify) his willful drive to reach "the ripest fruit of all." The speech is a kind of confession into which Theridamas, Techelles, and Usumcasane are able to project the authority and power lacking in themselves. This projection of omnipotence satisfies their charisma hunger while the language of the speech supplies them with new symbols that "give meaning to their experiences in terms of some fundamental cosmic, social, or political order" (Eisenstadt 1968, xxviii).

The new order is enigmatic, a charismatic kingship divine in inspiration but defined by earthly aspirations. Tamburlaine takes Zeus as an allegory only, an ideal. At this juncture he does not yearn to be a demigod but limits his desire as a means of manipulating his followers' ambition. Theridamas, acknowledging this deliberate limitation, declares it to be the very standard

> that made me join with Tamburlaine,
> For he is gross and like the massy earth
> That moves not upwards, nor by princely deeds
> Doth mean to soar above the highest sort.

> (I.2.7.30–33)

Later in the play Tamburlaine threatens Jove himself (I.5.1.453–54), realigning himself as a power beyond the pagan godhead. But, as is always the case, his rhetorical inflations reflect what his audience wants to hear—or what they need as a selfobject transference. When he threatens Jove, it will be remembered, he is speaking to the Soldan of Egypt, Zenocrate's father. He gloats, triumphs, scorns the recently dead (Bajazeth, Zabina, and the King of Arabia), and promises not only to spare the Soldan but also to "render all into your hands / And add more strength to your dominions / Than ever yet confirmed th' Egyptian crown" (I.5.1.448–50). He cannot take the rebellious son of Ops for his model here, not with his prospective father-in-law. Instead he shifts his symbols and remystifies himself once more, simultaneously aggrandizing himself and impressing the Soldan.

Bartels has suggested that Tamburlaine's "difference is a product not just of his own manipulative self-constructions, but also of those which others impose upon him. . . . While he builds his own incontestible singularity out of and against others' predilections, they validate their own constructions of difference upon him" (1992, 17). I would add that others also build their own constructions of identity out of Tamburlaine's manipulative self-constructions, and that identity more than difference drives the charismatic movement. But all of Tamburlaine's mystifications are self-enclosing, and the eventual result of any new structure of charismatic symbols will be the disengagement of the symbolic leader from the actual leader as a pragmatic force of change. Just such a gulf between the symbolic leader and the actual defines the tragic discourse of Part 2.

Marlowe frames Tamburlaine's speech to Cosroe with two myths from two different traditions, adding a *comparatio* on nature and the soul in the middle. Myth is the fitting vehicle for this expatiation not only because Tamburlaine habitually heightens his symbolic status with metaphors, but also because, as Ernst Cassirer once said, "in the critical moments of man's political and social life myth regains its old strength. . . . if the other binding forces of our social life, for one reason or another, lose their influence" (1979, 246–47). Marlowe chooses the two best-known myths of divine ambition to fill the void produced by the exceptional crisis of Tamburlaine's revolt against traditional social hierarchy. From the West comes the Greco-Roman tale of Zeus's deposition of his father; from the East, the Hebrew story of Eve's aspiration to godliness. The "ripest fruit" and "sweet fruition" are clear references to the forbidden fruit, but Marlowe carefully avoids any hint of a fall (in which context Lucifer would be conspicuous by his absence). Presumably Tamburlaine, "climbing after knowledge infinite," would approve Eve's aspiration just as he honors Zeus's successful overthrow of his father.

The ironies abound, however, because Marlowe detaches Tamburlaine as an agent of change from the more ominous implications of his speech. In contrast to both Zeus and Eve, who seek divine promotion, Tamburlaine aspires to an earthly crown. Does this make Tamburlaine more humble, and therefore more likely to succeed? Or is it just that the Tamburlaine of Part 1 still manages to balance his competing immoderations (cf. Battenhouse 1964, 228)? It is difficult to say. Perhaps Marlowe simply wants us to bear in mind that Zeus destroyed the Golden Age and then (according to Christian tradition) was himself eclipsed by the second Adam, while Eve destroyed something greater than, and antecedent to, the Golden Age. In the end these comparable but countervailing myths, like the "four elements / Warring within our breasts for regiment," cannot be resolved into a single status quo.

But that may be the point of juxtaposing the myths. Irresolution is at the heart of Marlowe's message regarding Tamburlainian rhetoric. Tamburlaine uses myths as contemplations of means or motives, never ends. His myths draw their metaphorical force from the mild chaos of irresolution, and, like his charismatic claim itself, they are always *in statu nascendi*. For this reason Tamburlaine mythologizes aspiration and "thirst of reign" as ideal states of coming-into-being. It is all part of his balancing of change and stability, his administration of the nonequilibrium system of his charismatic authority.[9] The trouble arises only later, when Tamburlaine himself wants to stabilize the idealizations of his nonequilibrium system—when, in Weberian terms, he starts to routinize his charisma, establishing a more or less traditional empire of contributory kingdoms and attempting to arrange for his succession.

Chaos and Conservatism

Even in his revolutionary fervor Tamburlaine tends to balance disruption and conservation of the existing moral standards of the social order, sometimes while in the very act of overthrowing the social hierarchy. He fits Charles Camic's description of an "omnipotent or excellent" figure whose relation to the social order fluctuates:

As Weber demonstrates in *The Sociology of Religion*, the potential consequences of satisfying extraordinary dependency needs—and here this can be extended to ego-ideal needs—are sometimes disruptive and sometimes conserving of the existing social order depending on the extent to which special (omnipotent or excellent) figures and their followers operate within the boundaries of that order to satisfy the specific variant of the needs in question. (1980, 20)

Tamburlaine ultimately replaces the existing social order while at the same time preserving its moral standards, as would a sacred figure like a prophet or a messiah. He is after all semisacred by his own lights, the "Scourge and wrath of God." As Ellis-Fermor describes him, he has "the force of Alexander with that steadfastness of vision that springs only from an inspiration, in its ultimate source religious" (1967, 38). That religious source is manifest in charismatic authority, which in turn manifests itself in the manipulation of existing social norms. He breaches the moral laws and the standards of decency, killing virgins or using Bajazeth as a footstool, but nonetheless adheres to a rigid set of moral principles in dealing with Zenocrate and his closest followers. Similarly, he destroys kings only to reestablish their kingships, sometimes taking the job himself, sometimes apportioning it out as a war prize. But he does not claim to destroy or to overturn the moral standards of the downed prince. On the contrary, his revolutionary ambition is to put himself, a mere shepherd, in the exact same moral and political position as that of lineage rulers, so that he might, in Camic's terms, "operate within the boundaries" of that now-fallen order. Tamburlaine represents a kind of hyperbolic class mobility, even though, as he and his shepherd peers precipitously ascend the social ladder, they turn out to be conservators of the social norms that dictate royal privilege and genealogical continuation.

There is a difference, however, between Tamburlainian kingship and the rulerships he overthrows—at least at first. Tamburlaine rules with the assent and the acclamation of his followers, and even when it appears most tyrannical his moral authority contains an element of mutual concord. For instance, after taking Cosroe's crown and putting it on his own head, Tamburlaine addresses his men as if he were suddenly in need of their sanction. He makes a speech at once hubristic and vulnerable:

> Though Mars himself, the angry god of arms,
> And all the earthly potentates conspire
> To dispossess me of this diadem,
> Yet will I wear it in despite of them
> As great commander of the eastern world,
> If you but say that Tamburlaine shall reign.

(I.2.7.58–63)

"If *you* but say"—this phrase hints at an uncharacteristic dependency in a man of Tamburlaine's fierce self-centeredness, coming only moments after his egotistical triumph over Cosroe. But his response to his followers' acclamation confirms the mutual dependency of their charismatic relationship:

All. Long live Tamburlaine, and reign in Asia!

Tamburlaine. So, now it is surer on my head,
Than if the gods had held a parliament,
And all pronounced me king of Persia.

(I.2.7.64–67)

The enthusiastic exchange demonstrates how Tamburlaine's calling to be a conqueror becomes the organizing principle of his charismatic authority. As with any "true" vocation, his calling brings with it both a revised symbolic order (new king, new divine models) and a new experience of subjectivity. His followers' acclaim makes him king of Persia, legitimating his rulership by acknowledging that, as Weber says, "it is the duty of those subject to charismatic authority to recognize its genuineness and to act accordingly" (1978, 1:242).

The notion of duty binds the charismatic leader to his followers' experience of him (or her). In Tamburlaine's case it puts him at the mercy of the promises both implied and explicit in his mirroring of his followers' transferences, his feeding of their charisma hunger. Just as it is their duty to recognize the genuineness of Tamburlaine's charismatic authority, it is his reciprocal duty to make his lieutenants potentates and kings. This reciprocity delineates the parameter of intrasubjectivity that he has set for the group, and the followers recognize it as such:

For as, when Jove did thrust old Saturn down,
Neptune and Dis gained each of them a crown,
So do we hope to reign in Asia
If Tamburlaine be placed in Persia.

(I.2.7.36–39)

Accepting Tamburlaine's charismatic symbols of Jove and Saturn, Usumcasane sets the pragmatic, highly rational goal of the Scythian rampage. In the name of dissension and revolt Tamburlaine's lieutenants seek to be tyrants themselves; with religious enthusiasm for Tamburlaine's gifts they follow him, expecting mundane rewards such as "earthly" crowns as their intrasubjective due. Given these blatant contradictions, it is no wonder Cosroe calls them "The strangest men that ever Nature made!" (I.2.7.40).

Like most groups, Tamburlaine's warrior band functions by means of a combination of what Weber calls value-rational (*wertrational*) and instrumentally rational (*zweckrational*) actions. These fundamental distinctions, to which are added traditional and affectual social action, help to clarify a plethora of apparently contradictory impulses:

> Examples of pure value-rational [*wertrational*] orientation would be the actions of persons who, regardless of possible cost to themselves, act to put into practice their convictions of what seems to them to be required by duty, honor, the pursuit of beauty, a religious call, personal loyalty, or the importance of some "cause" no matter in what it consists.

> Action is instrumentally rational (*zweckrational*) when the end, the means, and the secondary results are all rationally taken into account and weighed. (1978: 1:25–26)

In charismatic groups value-rational actions predominate because of the ethical dependence on honor and duty, loyalty and enthusiasm. But enthusiasm does not last and economic necessity tempers the idealism of causes. As a result, pure charisma must compromise with other forms of authority. When this begins to happen, instrumentally rational conduct tends to develop alongside the original value-rational impulses. For this reason the pure charismatic enchantment of Theridamas in act 1 ("Won with thy words and conquered with thy looks") can coexist with the rationalized outlook of Usumcasane in act 2. The incommensurates of Tamburlainian magic and Tamburlainian satrap imperialism converge in the ever-transforming person of the Scythian shepherd himself.

As Tamburlaine's successes multiply he surprises himself with the scope and the specificity of his ambition. When, for instance, he abruptly decides to turn on Cosroe's forces, Tamburlaine has a sudden prescience of himself as a king, and we share his surprise. Significantly, he first checks his vision in the mirror of his followers' minds. This is where Theridamas exclaims that "A god is not so glorious as a king" because "Such power attractive shines in princes' eyes" (I.2.5.57, 64). But when asked by Tamburlaine whether he would want to be a king himself, Theridamas replies "Nay, though I praise it, I can live without it" (I.2.5.66). Theridamas has only recently been integrated into the charismatic group, and his reply can be seen as proof that value-rational actions hold sway early in the charismatic relationship. So, at this critical moment of decision Tamburlaine ignores the regressive Theridamas, seeking proof of a metanoia in his followers' attitudes. He quickly turns to his older followers, nudging their ambition with the force of his own:

> *Tamburlaine.* What say my other friends, will you be kings?
>
> *Techelles.* Ay, if I could, with all my heart, my lord.
>
> *Tamburlaine.* Why, that's well said, Techelles, so would I.
> And so would you my masters, would you not?
>
> *Usumcasane.* What then, my lord?
>
> (I.2.5.67–71)

The drama turns on that last question. "What then, my lord?" contains both the expectancy of the followers' charisma hunger and the prelude to Tamburlaine's next step, his world conquests as a mirroring of his group's heretofore unrealizable ambitions. There occurs here a kind of paradigm shift in the circle of transference, a concurrence of metanoia and leadership. Reorienting himself toward kingship, Tamburlaine irrevocably transforms the charismatic experience of his followers:

> Why, then, Casane, shall we wish for ought
> The world affords in greatest novelty,
> And rest attemptless, faint and destitute?
> Methinks we should not: I am strongly moved
> That if I should desire the Persian crown
> I could attain it with a wondrous ease.
>
> (I.2.5.72–77)

Spurred by the assurance of mutual ambition, Tamburlaine flexes his charismatic strength, shattering one of the most sacred constraints of social order. His usurpation of the Persian crown satisfies the extraordinary dependency needs of his warrior band while subverting the norms of civic life. His betrayal of Cosroe, martial heroism, and oracular fulfillment combine to fashion a figurehead of pure charisma. At its most successful, Tamburlainian magic strikes a balance of pragmatic power and symbolic transcendence.

But even at this moment of high exhilaration—or in order to attain such a moment—Tamburlaine acknowledges the intersection of value-rational actions and instrumentally rational aims. "Why then, Theridamas," he astutely promises the man who would not be king,

> I'll first essay
> To get the Persian kingdom to myself;
> Then thou for Parthia, they for Scythia and Media.
> And if I prosper, all shall be as sure
> As if the Turk, the Pope, Afric and Greece
> Came creeping to us with their crowns apace.
>
> (I.2.5.81–86)

The incommensurates are enclosed in the charismatic "I," and the euphoria of the moment disguises the otherwise deflating necessities of imperial administration and economic stability. Later, in the banquet scene, Tamburlaine crowns Theridamas, Techelles, and Usumcasane "contributory kings" of Argier, Fesse, and Moroccus (I.4.4.114–20). At first the lieutenants are reluctant to accept these honors, pleading humility and insisting that such things as crowns are beyond their reach: "'Tis enough for us to see them, and for Tamburlaine only to enjoy them" (I.4.4.113–14). But Tamburlaine justifies his intentions by invoking the familiar sixteenth-century argument that favors advancement through individual merit over privileges accorded to aristocratic birth:

> You that have marched with happy Tamburlaine
> As far as from the frozen plage of heaven
> Unto the wat'ry morning's ruddy bower,
> And thence by land unto the torrid zone,
> Deserve these titles I endow you with,
> By valour and by magnanimity:
> Your births shall be no blemish to your fame,
> For virtue is the fount whence honour springs,
> And they are worthy she investeth kings.
>
> (I.4.4.124–32)

In addition to showcasing Tamburlaine's command of Renaissance ideals of the male ethos, this speech demonstrates his manipulation of charismatic factors toward the accomplishment of highly rational ends. Valor, *magnanimitas*, *virtú*, and honor are all terms descriptive of value-rational behavior, and all of them can be attributes of a charismatic relationship (cf. Waith 1971, 54, 64).

By reminding his audience of the connection between battlefield greatness (the Homeric *aristeia*) and the ideal aristocracy, Tamburlaine further justifies his creation of new royal lineages. In the course of doing so, however, he neutralizes somewhat the charismatic aspects of these sudden investitures by simultaneously instituting a rationalized economic relationship between himself and his three lieutenants. They are now "contributory kings," and, whatever the exact arrangements for their contributions, clearly some form of rational economic organization has replaced the economic irrationality of the pure charismatic band. No longer does Jove rain down gold in heaps from heaven. From here on, presumably, the contributory kings will provide a more or less regular income to the Tamburlainian war machine.

The full impact of this altered relationship never penetrates Tamburlaine's egocentric identification with the original symbols of his leadership. But his pseudosalvationistic mission will be irreversibly altered by his establishment of a permanent empire. In flagrant contrast to his charismatic origins looms the deadening structure of satrap imperialism, orderly economic organization, and governance by laws. Consequently, the practical outcome of Tamburlaine's promise to make his followers kings will be the routinization of his pure charisma. This gradual process begins at the end of Part 1, apparently set in motion by Tamburlaine himself but in fact forced upon him by the exigencies of sustaining the privileges of a charismatic warrior band in time of peace.

In the last lines of the play Tamburlaine crowns Zenocrate Queen of Persia, then makes her father ruler over "Egyptians, Moors, and men of Asia, / From Barbary unto the Western Indie" (I.5.1.518–19). Finally he turns to his closest followers:

> And now, my lords and loving followers,
> That purchased kingdoms by your martial deeds,
> Cast off your armour, put on scarlet robes,
> Mount up your royal places of estate,
> Environèd with troops of noble men,
> And there make laws to rule your provinces:
> Hang up your weapons on Alcides' post,
> For Tamburlaine takes truce with all the world.
>
> (I.5.1.523–30)

This is the incipiently patriarchal Tamburlaine, meant to replace the parricidal warlord. But Tamburlaine's truce, fraught with difficulties he does not foresee, contains a premonition of bureaucracy. "Cast off your armour," he says magnanimously, "put on scarlet robes"; he invites his warriors to become kings and to rule over courts filled with courtiers—"Environèd with troops of noble men." He now sees the future not in inspired charismatic terms but in terms antithetical to innovation and transcendent revolutionary force. Social order has suddenly become crucial to Tamburlainian triumph. "Charismatic authority," as Edward Shils summarizes it, "denies the value of action which is motivated by the desire for proximate ends sufficient unto themselves, by the wish to gratify personal affections, or by the hope of pecuniary advantage" (1982, 114). But Tamburlaine in an instant transgresses all these norms, replacing his highflown rhetoric of value-rational ideals with a new language of practicability. His final disbursements in Part 1 are made precisely for "proximate ends" and "to gratify personal affections," while he certainly means to promise "pecuniary advantage" to his "loving followers"—and the word *loving*, signaling the libidinal ties binding the group members together, will soon undergo a change in meaning too. In the routinization of Tamburlaine's charismatic band, irrational and emotional love arising from desire must eventually decay into the kind of rational relationship suggested by the word *love* when it means patronage in Elizabethan England.

At the end of Part 1, Tamburlaine envisions a new status quo which he expects his newly minted kings to maintain by means of what appears to be legal-bureaucratic authority: "make laws to rule your provinces." But Tamburlaine is probably not recommending legal authority in the strictest rational sense, that is, as a type of domination "resting on a belief in the legality of enacted rules and the right of those elevated to authority under such rules to issue commands" (Weber 1978, 1:215). The elevation of Theridamas, Techelles, and Usumcasane to provincial kingships, as well as that of the Soldan to his new contributory empire, does not rest on adherence to rules or laws but on Tamburlaine's imposition of will. He in effect shoehorns his charismatic band into what he considers a traditional form of authority through which princes are honored, are surrounded by retainers, and make laws in the arbitrary manner of a Solon or a Solomon. This merging of charisma and tradition, which are basically antagonistic, is nonetheless not unusual according to Weber, because both these forms of legitimate domination derive their power "from the belief in the sanctity of an individual's authority" rather than from "purposive-rational regulations" (1978, 2:1122). So Tamburlaine's revolution ends with the effacement of his absolute personal centrality. Traditional rulerships replace his revolutionary charismatic authority.

But Tamburlaine does not see this reapportionment of power as a personal loss. Rather, he regards his and his band's infiltration of the traditional hierarchy and their adoption of traditional methods of leadership as the most desired achievement of their bloody campaigns. At this juncture of social restructuring "charisma becomes a legitimation for 'acquired rights,'" a function "alien to its essence" (Weber 1978, 2:1122). But while Marlowe seems to be aware of the debilitating change in his hero's charismatic status, Tamburlaine himself remains oblivious to his incipient alienation from the essence of charisma and from the charismatic symbols that he sought to inculcate. As Part 2 shows, he will be trapped by those same symbols.

Zenocrate and Family Tragedy

Early in Part 1, after hearing Tamburlaine's paean to Zenocrate's icy beauty, Techelles asks, "What now? in love?" (I.1.2.106). Bartels has suggested that Techelles' startled question indicates his skepticism of Tamburlaine's sincerity (1992, 12). But I am not sure that that is the chief reason for his question. It seems more likely that Techelles means to express alarm or anxiety about the effect on the charismatic group of Tamburlaine's falling in love with a woman. Love interest outside the group, particularly when the revolutionary force is struggling to life, would represent a singular threat to the limitation of narcissism on which group cohesion depends. Freud warns that self-solicitousness precedes group breakdown, and Tamburlaine's sudden feelings for Zenocrate might well suggest to Techelles a self-solicitousness that would be deleterious to the aim-inhibited libidinal relationships already in place. If the group maintains cohesion by collectively inhibiting the actual expression of desire, then sexual love, which is by definition libidinally uninhibited, represents a significant disruption to the charismatic bonds.

Perhaps this antagonism between sexual love and group cohesion provides an explanation for the most anomalous aspect of Tamburlaine's character in Part 1, his sexual asceticism. Remarkably, he remains celibate throughout his conquests when comparable warlords would have availed themselves of the pick of the newly enslaved wives and daughters. But Tamburlaine restrains himself from this customary privilege just as, despite expectations, he refrains from forcing Zenocrate into his bed. Agydas speaks of Zenocrate's abduction as an "offensive rape by Tamburlaine," worrying that she will be "supposed his worthless concubine" (I.3.2.6, 29). He takes for granted the threat, if not the consummated act, of sexual violation (cf. Shepard 1993, 749), and he is stunned to hear of Zenocrate's "fancy" for Tamburlaine and of the warlord's unwonted refinement toward her. "Speak of Tamburlaine as he deserves," says the indignant Zenocrate,

> The entertainment we have had of him
> Is far from villainy or servitude,
> And might in noble minds be counted princely.

> (I.3.2.36–39)

Given Tamburlaine's repeated assertions that martial valor is the only measure of true nobility, it is ironic that he is called princely in connection with his good treatment of Zenocrate. But it is notable that his "princely entertainment" includes sexual restraint, which, in addition to crowning him a prince in Zenocrate's eyes, separates him from other conquerors, and even from his own behavior at other times.[10]

Indeed, Tamburlaine's sexual restraint is particularly striking when considered against the background of his habitual violence, his utter disregard for social norms, his neglect of chivalric ideals whenever it pleases him, and his figurative association with such ravishers as Zeus, Hercules, and Achilles. In the context of his cruelty and excess, Tamburlaine's behavior toward Zenocrate has a completely incongruous quality, like a splinter of asceticism in a sea of passions. For a man who denies himself nothing and whose ambition is beyond measure, there is something sublime in self-restraint. Whether or not we label it a charismatic gesture, there seems little doubt that the rare nature of Tamburlaine's conduct should be credited to his ability to surprise, to overturn norms, and to break everyday contraints.

Tamburlaine's sexual restraint also serves a definite tactical purpose with his followers. Zenocrate's lovelorn tears suggest no ambiguity in Tamburlaine's conduct, and Agydas' remarks on the subject are evidence of the public nature of the situation. It may seem perverse that Zenocrate, a captive, has fallen under the spell of her godlike captor. But she is living up to her name, which means "ruled by Zeus," and she has come to share Tamburlaine's identification with that god:

> higher would I rear my estimate
> Than Juno, sister to the highest god,
> If I were matched with mighty Tamburlaine.

> (I.3.2.53–55)

There is a curious commingling of sexual union and sexual taboo in these lines, "a hint of incest" in Kuriyama's phrase (1980, 29). Zenocrate refers to Juno as Jupiter's sister, but of course she was also his wife. The ambiguity, with its taint of improper desire, efficiently represents both Zenocrate's passionate desire for her captor and Tamburlaine's sudden shift from amorous to more brotherly affections.

Agydas misreads the change in Tamburlaine's attitude as the disdain of a parvenu Alexander for the daughter of a mere Soldan:

> You see, though first the king of Persia,
> Being a shepherd, seemed to love you much,
> Now in his majesty he leaves those looks,
> Those words of favour, and those comfortings,
> And gives no more than common courtesies.

> (I.3.2.59–63)

The reasoning may be faulty but the observation is important. Zenocrate too has noticed the cool restraint in Tamburlaine's behavior—"Thence rise the tears that so distain my cheeks" (I.3.2.64)—and, as Cunningham glosses, she later wonders "If any love remain in you, my lord" (I.4.4.70). Agydas thinks that the change in Tamburlaine's personality is a function of his change in social class, the great man having abandoned the open, warmhearted manners of a shepherd in favor of a chilly punctilio befitting his vertiginously high estate.

But this is probably a misprision. Newly acquired manners do not account for Tamburlaine's outward coolness, which in any case we know from the "fair Zenocrate" soliloquy conceals raging passions. Rather, the coolness constitutes a visible, public demonstration of Tamburlaine's sexual self-restraint, meant, I would conjecture, to impress his closest followers with his single-minded purpose. His coolness and restraint demonstrate the absence of libidinal self-solicitousness, confirming the increasing importance of Tamburlaine's ties to his lieutenants. Agydas correctly observes that once Tamburlaine became a king, and once he began seeking further crowns, his relations toward Zenocrate became less demonstrative. But, again, the elevation of Tamburlaine's social class alone does not cause this change. Instead the cause lies in the ongoing development of Tamburlaine's charismatic movement and the growing interdependence of the leader and his followers. As the martial crises build, the systemic mutuality of the group ties checks Tamburlaine's individuating actions, forcing him, for as long as he wishes to maintain a functioning charismatic group, to resist sexual demonstrativeness and to postpone marriage.

After the betrayal of Cosroe Tamburlaine reinvents himself as a king among kings-to-be. New emotional ties electrify the followers, confounding the causes with the effects of their revised, royally bound direction. As always (at least in Part 1) Tamburlaine manipulates the varieties of emotional stability among the people around him. His juggling of Zenocrate's love provides one example of this manipulation, and his tactical confirmation of his libidinal link to his men, another. Tamburlaine's sole objective in Part 1 is to maintain his group in functioning order, and therefore he must remain unmarried. When he finally prepares to marry, he reorganizes his charismatic band. In Tamburlaine's universe taking a wife is conceptually parallel to creating contributory kings among his closest followers. The shared charismatic experience, including the mutual limitation of narcissism and self-solicitousness, comes to an end when Zenocrate (or Tamburlaine's fulfillment of his desire for her) replaces the aim-inhibited libidinal ties that had held the group together. Economic organization follows the disruption of the shared experience because both Tamburlaine and his lieutenants want to sustain the privileges they came to expect at the height of their revolutionary success. But the changes obfuscate Tamburlaine's claim to charisma, blurring his mission. Moreover, after the tactical respite of his sexual self-denial, Tamburlaine's consummation of his desire for Zenocrate destroys his pure charismatic relationships.

Stephen Greenblatt has called Tamburlaine a "desiring machine" (1980, 195), but Tamburlaine's desire is not mechanical in the least. Repeatedly we see the Scourge and Wrath of God ruminating on and inwardly debating his impulsive desires, as when he decides to betray Cosroe (after reflecting on kingship with his men) or when he recognizes the depth of his feeling for Zenocrate. More than any other lines in the play, the "fair Zenocrate" speech confirms that Tamburlaine can be in conflict about his desires, revealing both the unruliness of his passions and his struggle to contain or to comprehend them:

> But how unseemly is it for my sex,
> My discipline of arms and chivalry,
> My nature, and the terror of my name,
> To harbour thoughts effeminate and faint!
> Save only that in beauty's just applause,
> With whose instinct the soul of man is touched—
> And every warrior that is rapt with love
> Of fame, of valour, and of victory,
> Must needs have beauty beat on his conceits—
> I thus conceiving and subduing, both,
> That which hath stopped the tempest of the gods,
> Even from the fiery spangled veil of heaven,
> To feel the lovely warmth of shepherds' flames
> And march in cottages of strèwed weeds,
> Shall give the world to note, for all my birth,

That virtue solely is the sum of glory
And fashions men with true nobility.

(I.5.1.174–90)

These lines capture Tamburlaine in the act of suppressing one passion to give vent to another, hardly the image of a machine. Rather, this speech provides a cross-section of Tamburlaine's will and a description of the strange asceticism with which he fuels his messianic status. The rhetoric of self-denial, of passion squelched, commands our attention more than many of Tamburlaine's excesses. He simultaneously conceives and subdues the instinct for beauty so that he can continue to pursue glory and nobility; and again his self-consciousness about his low birth demands an assertion "that virtue solely . . . fashions men with true nobility." As the end of the speech clearly shows, he resists Zenocrate's request not because he rejects its logic but to preserve his revolutionary mission. In reality it is not the request that he rejects but Zenocrate herself as an object of desire.

There are many ways to read Tamburlaine's soliloquy. But we should not overlook the importance of group survival to Tamburlaine's meditations. I have suggested that we might profitably interpret Tamburlaine's public resistance to Zenocrate as a sign of charismatic group solidarity. His self-restraint regarding beauty, which constitutes a kind of libidinal asceticism, confirms the intactness of the ties binding him to his followers. His claim that it is "unseemly" for someone of his sex, discipline, and nature to "harbour thoughts effeminate and faint" represents an act of decorum meant to impress his closest followers with his consistency. The killing of the virgins, therefore, furnishes an excellent example of Tamburlaine's handling of a leadership paradox: he adeptly manipulates the wanton killing, which in any reasonable judgment would signal the breakdown of humane law and chivalric norms, so as to conserve the status quo of the group. His refusal to give in at Damascus, like the equally misleading coolness toward Zenocrate, has more to do with his relationship to his own men than it has to do either with his power over the Egyptians or with his fear of effeminacy. Ultimately, for all its horror, the killing of the virgins merely defines another facet in Tamburlaine's mastery of the nonequilibrium system of his charismatic movement.

This mastery erodes in Part 2 largely because Tamburlaine is married and because his group functions under different economic constraints. No longer a revolutionary movement, the system has gained too much equilibrium. Although Tamburlaine himself institutes the permanent stability, he remains unconscious of the full implications of the shift toward routinization. As a result he confuses his own agency with petrified symbols of his charisma. His failure in his own family underscores this confusion. The family members remain outside the charismatic group; even if Tamburlaine at first awes Zenocrate, sweeping her along in his magnetic rise, after their marriage she represents the antithesis of group membership. She becomes the very pretext of Tamburlaine's libidinal individuation from the group and the harbinger of routinized charismatic administration. But Tamburlaine fails to perceive the symbolic nuances, and, trapped in his own symbolic ideal of himself, he mistakenly assumes all relations to be the same as relations to followers. This accounts for his awkward, not to say bizarre, treatment of his sons. He may not be mechanical in his desires, but once he routinizes his charismatic movement he becomes rigid and machinelike in his self-representations, a seized-up charisma machine unable to negotiate the balance between mild chaos and functioning order. Consequently, the vaunted Tamburlainian imagination cannot accommodate either the death of Zenocrate or the indifference and disobedience of Calyphas (cf. Proser 1995, 95; Bartels 1992, 17). Tamburlaine's excessive response to both events reveals a weakening (or misapplied) charismatic authority rather than the indomitable strength he is accustomed to shadowing forth.

Both the burning of the town where Zenocrate dies and the murder of Calyphas confirm the extent to which, in Part 2, Tamburlaine has become a prisoner of his own symbols. Both acts, to quote the Willners, "substitute symbolic action as ends instead of means" (Willner and Willner 1965, 87). The charismatic group cum group accomplishes nothing practical or tactical, either in the burning of the town or in the filicide; these acts symbolize ends in themselves, not means toward other ends. More to the point, Tamburlaine's followers play no part in these outbursts of rage and grief, and they stand to gain nothing. Tamburlainian agency, and the Tamburlainian symbolism that accompanies that agency, disengage from group function in these episodes, which shocks the group and threatens the interdependency of the charismatic experience.

The razed town and Tamburlaine's desire to preserve the destruction comprise an abuse of his own originating symbols. Nothing could serve as better proof of this abuse than Tamburlaine's belligerent, hamfisted self-symbolization when he orders a pillar erected on the site of the burned town in memory of Zenocrate, and has it inscribed with a multilingual edict: *This town, being burnt by Tamburlaine the Great,/Forbids the world to build it up again* (II.3.2.17–18).

The syntax is curious: the town itself forbids its own reconstruction, as if it were willingly participating in the observation of Tamburlaine's grief. But destroyed towns cannot be followers, and consequently the pillar rising in the ashes characterizes Tamburlaine's misguided sense of his own symbols of power. In its permanence and utter negation, the pillar is antithetical to the dynamism of flourishing charismatic power, reflecting instead the static condition of Tamburlaine's individual will in Part 2. Confined by the symbols of his power, he becomes increasingly unable to reconcile his acts to the group ideal that he himself once manipulated so successfully.

Descent and Dilution

In concluding this chapter I would like to return to Helen Gardner's observation that in Part 2 "the Tamburlaine spell is not working." Gardner cites the betrayal of Almeda as one of the signs of a change in Tamburlaine's powers, noting that such a situation, "in which a servant of Tamburlaine's is won over from him by the lure of money and glory, would be inconceivable in the first part" (1970, 204). Gardner does not offer a reason for the erosion of Tamburlaine's spell, but I would like to suggest that it occurs as a result of the change in Tamburlaine's charismatic status. In Part 2 his emotional hold on his followers has slackened, and Almeda's treason is emblematic of the less intensive emotional ties.

Betrayal often serves just such an emblematic purpose in tragedies involving charismatic figures, although it tends to affect the emotional structure of the plays more significantly than it alters the plot. In Marlowe's *Edward II*, for instance, Kent's defection and redefection cause no significant changes except to signal the ebb and flood of Edward's personal charisma. Similarly, in Shakespeare's *Antony and Cleopatra*, the defection of Enobarbus has little visible effect on events, yet it causes palpable damage to Antony's strength of mind. But whereas Enobarbus receives no censure from Antony, the treason of Almeda enrages Tamburlaine, inspiring an impressive string of threats and imprecations:

> Villain, traitor, damnèd fugitive,
> I'll make thee wish the earth had swallowed thee!
> Go, villain, cast thee headlong from a rock,
> Or rip thy bowels and rend out thy heart
> T'appease my wrath, or else I'll torture thee,

Searing thy hateful flesh with burning irons
And drops of scalding lead, while all thy joints
Be racked and beat asunder with the wheel:
For if thou livest, not any element
Shall shroud thee from the wrath of Tamburlaine.

(II.3.5.117–27)

This speech is curiously literal, the usual Tamburlainian hyperbole giving way to more or less realistic details of suicide and torture. Always the martial social climber, Tamburlaine first suggests suicide because that would be the noble Roman solution to treason; Brutus is the model (Enobarbus's odd death also comes to mind). His itemization of torture methods, coupled with the sheer breadth of attention he pays the subject, emphasize the significance for him of Almeda's treason. From a tactical standpoint Tamburlaine has reason to give weight to the betrayal; as a result of it Callapine has organized the Turkish host against him. But there is nonetheless something disproportionate in his fury at the all but simpering Almeda, who, scarcely responding to the threats, seems still to consider Tamburlaine his master.

As Cunningham notes, we find a bit of comedy in the lines following Tamburlaine's speech. Callapine offers Almeda a crown, but Almeda is reluctant to take it until he first asks Tamburlaine's permission to do so. This naturally infuriates Callapine—"Dost thou ask him leave?" (II.3.5.134)—but seems to appease Tamburlaine, who promptly urges Almeda to take the crown, as if killing King Almeda rather than merely Almeda the Jailer would raise his own martial stature. Significantly, the exchange ends with a mock-heraldic quibble:

Tamburlaine. So, sirrah, now you are a king and must give arms.

Orcanes. So he shall, and wear thy head in his scutcheon.

Tamburlaine. No, let him hang a bunch of keys on his standard, to
    put him in remembrance he was a jailor, that, when I take him,
    I may knock out his brains with them, and lock you in the stable
    when you shall come sweating from my chariot.

(II.3.5.136–44)

Even Tamburlaine's blazonry is hostile. But his fashioning of a new coat of arms reminds us how often his obsession with transforming low birth into aristocratic plaudits rises to the surface. Although in this passage he satirizes the custom of "creating" an armigerous knight, the undercurrent of the entire second part of the play belies his apparent scorn. His chief aim by the end of Part 2 has become the creation of a royal lineage, a dynastic succession based not on merit but on birth. And, despite his numerous crowns, he remains hysterically sensitive about his origins. In fact, the *flyting* that culminates with Almeda's scutcheon begins with a few contemptuous remarks from Orcanes regarding Tamburlaine's low birth. Orcanes, irate, speaks in response to a challenge of single combat:

> *Orcanes.* Now thou art fearful of thy army's strength,
> Thou wouldst with overmatch of person fight.
> But, shepherd's issue, base-born Tamburlaine,
> Think of thy end: this sword shall lance thy throat.
>
> *Tamburlaine.* Villain, the shepherd's issue, at whose birth
> Heaven did afford a gracious aspect
> And joined those stars that shall be opposite
> Even till the dissolution of the world,
> And never meant to make a conqueror
> So famous as is mighty Tamburlaine,
> Shall so torment thee and that Callapine
> That like a roguish runaway suborned
> That villain there, that slave, that Turkish dog,
> To false his service to his sovereign,
> As ye shall curse the birth of Tamburlaine.
>
> (II.3.5.75–89)[11]

A masterpiece of condensation, Tamburlaine's response in one sentence links his birth, his power, and Almeda's treason, for which he here blames Callapine. Once again he claims divine auspices for his mission, but unlike earlier opponents the Turkish kings seem unimpressed. They exhibit no awe of Tamburlaine, and consequently Tamburlaine's boasts echo hollowly, missing the resonance they had in confrontations with Mycetes or even Bajazeth. Tamburlaine continues to overcome his enemies by main force, but his violence and physical superiority have become empty symbols of his pure charisma. The routinization of his charismatic movement has diluted the symbolic effect of his physical power, still formidable but ironically carrying less meaning. Hence Tamburlaine's excesses tend to expose his vulnerability rather than confirm his strength.

The scene following the confrontation with Almeda, in which Tamburlaine murders his son, provides a case in point. The killing of Calyphas reflects Tamburlaine's two most paralyzing apprehensions in Part 2: fear of treason and anxiety regarding his succession. Almeda's obliviousness to Tamburlaine's wrath acts as a prelude to

Calyphas' insouciance. And it is crucial to recognize that the martial destruction of the Turkish kings does not satisfy Tamburlaine, as does, for example, destroying Mycetes, Cosroe, and the Egyptians. His apprehension only grows because his ambitions are now more symbolic than concrete. Not earthly crowns but immortality obsesses Tamburlaine; not a dynamic and charismatic administration of chaos but the permanent idealization of his mission, on multilingual pillars and in a dynastic lineage.

But pure charisma is finite. It does not survive its originator intact. For a charismatic movement to endure, its symbols must be separated from the human being at its center. Tamburlaine recognizes this necessity, but, for as long as he is alive, he remains trapped by those symbols. His behavior grows increasingly at odds with his own symbolic origins because, rather than seeking to overturn norms and to break down rational economic organization, the Tamburlaine of Part 2 becomes intent on establishing norms, protracting his satrap empire, ensconcing a lineage, and, paradoxically, making permanent his own symbols of destabilizing, revolutionary action. In Part 1 Marlowe aligns the identity of Tamburlaine with the symbols of his extraordinary martial mission. In Part 2 he shows us the alienation of Tamburlaine—or Tamburlainian agency—from the symbols of that mission. As Tamburlainian charisma becomes routinized, as followers learn to fend for themselves both economically and emotionally, Tamburlaine grows more and more isolated. In his frustration he resorts to his old methods and his old ethos, further alienating himself from the routinized form of his original charisma.

Calyphas offends the charismatic symbols, and for this reason Tamburlaine kills him. But the symbols have become ends rather than means and as such they are now unsynchronized with group function. If the killing of the virgins demonstrated Tamburlaine's libidinal solidarity with his group through his resistance to Zenocrate as an object of desire, then the killing of Calyphas reveals a nearly opposite characteristic. In killing his son, Tamburlaine confirms his alienation from his followers, his misunderstanding of what being made contributory kings has meant to their charismatic experience. For the first time in both parts of the play, Tamburlaine's followers oppose him. When Tamburlaine prepares to mete out "martial justice" with his "striving hands," Theridamas, Techelles, Usumcasane, and his son Amyras together entreat him to pardon Calyphas. They even kneel down to make their entreaty, which only angers Tamburlaine. "Stand up," he says, "ye base unworthy soldiers! Know ye not yet the argument of arms?" (II.4.1.99–100). A. D. Hope sees Tamburlaine's behavior in the scene as consistent with his destructiveness throughout the plays, governed by an absoluteness that knows no degrees in a world "in which what is not perfect is without meaning and without value" (1986, 51). But ironically Tamburlaine's very consistency is the alienating factor of Part 2. The absoluteness of the argument of arms cannot be reconciled with the compromised and diluted charismatic organization that follows Tamburlaine's marriage and the economic routinization of his forces. He may still see himself as the Scourge and Wrath of God, the violent upholder of absolutes, but the values he strives to enforce have already served their purpose. Tamburlainian symbolic justice has become unnecessary to the progress of the transformed charismatic group—indeed, the lieutenants-turned-kings even seem embarrassed by their leader's excesses. They apparently recognize that the lessons Tamburlaine wants to teach and the values he wishes to inculcate as symbols have already been established. To return to the physical enactment of those values at this late date is regressive and perhaps even detrimental to the preservation of the original (now ossified) charisma that serves as the foundation for routinized group function.

Tamburlaine's obsession with permanence blinds him to the gap between his absoluteness and his followers' experience of him. The systemic mutuality that the group so relied on is atomized, while Tamburlaine, as evidenced in his fanatical speech before killing Calyphas, no longer completes the circle of transference with his followers. His self-solicitousness and his narcissism individuate—and therefore alienate—his ambitions from theirs. "Here, Jove," Tamburlaine says, about to stab Calyphas,

> receive his fainting soul again,
> A form not meet to give that subject essence
> Whose matter is the flesh of Tamburlaine,
> Wherein an incorporated spirit moves,
> Made of the mould whereof thyself consists,
> Which makes me valiant, proud, ambitious,
> Ready to levy power against thy throne,
> That I might move the turning spheres of heaven:
> For earth and all this airy region
> Cannot contain the state of Tamburlaine.
>
> (II.4.1.111–20)

He excludes the group from this system, no doubt unthinkingly. They may well recognize, as we do in the concept of the "state of Tamburlaine," a case of symbolization run amok. For Tamburlaine is not talking about a state in the political sense so much as a state of being or perhaps a status. The social component of his quest has shifted from the hegemony of his warrior band to the immortality of his name and lineage, the transmigration of Jove's spirit through Tamburlaine to his sons. Demoting group function from its central importance in Part 1 Tamburlaine no longer satisfies the charisma hunger of his followers. Their objection to Calyphas' execution implies their incipient detachment. As Tamburlaine's emotional ties to the group and his economic power over followers become increasingly attenuated, his ambition narrows, turning inward. Ominously, by the end of Part 2 Tamburlaine has come to dwell exclusively on the genealogical continuity of an essence "whose matter is the flesh of Tamburlaine."

The play ends with the depersonalization of Tamburlaine's charisma as he attempts to pass on his extraordinary powers to his sons. Weber noted that "the most frequent case of a depersonalization of charisma is the belief in its transferability through blood ties" (1978, 2:1136). This is precisely Tamburlaine's belief:

> But sons, this subject, not of force enough
> To hold the fiery spirit it contains,
> Must part, imparting his impressions
> By equal portions into both your breasts:
> My flesh, divided by your precious shapes,
> Shall still retain my spirit though I die,
> And live in all your seeds immortally.
>
> (II.5.3.168–74)

Dying, Tamburlaine hopes to "impart" the "impressions" of his "fiery spirit" to the next generation. Once unique and subversive, Tamburlaine now endorses the traditional myth of lineage charisma, asserting the hereditability of his extraordinary powers by male members of his family. But, as Marlowe and maybe Tamburlaine himself recognize, charismatic authority becomes diluted when it is depersonalized and thereby transformed into an abstract hereditary quality. Theridamas feels the shock of this change when Tamburlaine insists on crowning Amyras; in some despair he exclaims, "A woeful change, my lord, that daunts our thoughts / More than the ruin of our proper souls" (II.5.3.181–82). Even in its routinized state Tamburlainian charisma depends on a personal component, and Theridamas, whose charisma hunger was so palpable in Part 1, feels the imminent absence of Tamburlaine to be irremediable. Divided from the symbols of his charismatic authority, Tamburlaine no longer mirrors his followers' ambitions, as his attempt to pass on his charisma confirms.

His alienation from his own symbolic value reminds us that Tamburlaine never manages the stages of routinization as expertly as he balances the chaotic forces of his revolution in Part 1.

The Scythian shepherd dies with the intuition of his tragedy on his tongue. His blindness to the different forms of charisma clashes with his prescience that his own extraordinary authority will fail in the next generation. Therefore he dwells on Phaeton in his last instructions to Amyras, urging his successor-son to "reign . . . scourge and control" the raw inherited power of Tamburlaine's authority as if it were akin to Apollo's "rebelling jades" (II.5.3.228, 238):

> The nature of thy chariot will not bear
> A guide of baser temper than myself,
> More than heaven's coach the pride of Phaeton.
>
> (II.5.3.242–44)

Tamburlaine's last words concern the management of unruly power. But Marlowe leaves open the question of whether Amyras will struggle more with vast unruly power or with the impotence of diluted lineage charisma. This same question vexes Tamburlaine in the last scene. His perceptible awareness of the decay from pure personal charisma to a depersonalized dynastic substitute imbues his dying with tragic pathos. Even while struggling against the implications of Theridamas's despair, he all but concedes that the shared experience of Tamburlainian charisma will die with him.

2

CHARISMAS IN CONFLICT

Richard II and Henry Bolingbroke

Shakespeare's *Richard II* is an anatomy of charismas in conflict. Pure personal charisma, lineage or dynastic charisma, and several kinds of office charisma confront each other throughout the play. But these charismatic manifestations do not remain in ideal forms. Instead, the different kinds of charisma interpenetrate and overlap, producing ambiguous figures of shifting status. The chief examples are Richard and Bolingbroke. The personally charismatic Bolingbroke rises to power partly through subversion of traditional hierarchy and partly through an appeal to traditional hierarchical and genealogical values. The paradox of this situation resounds in such self-defining speeches as

> I am a subject,
> And I challenge law; attorneys are denied me,
> And therefore personally I lay my claim
> To my inheritance of free descent.

$$(2.3.132-35)^1$$

This passage highlights the near-contradiction of making a personal extralegal claim—a charismatic challenge of the law—and at the same time invoking the traditional authority of genealogical privilege. Unlike the low-born Tamburlaine, Bolingbroke can claim a birthright to justify his rise to power. His ambiguous rationalizations tend to promise a restoration of aristocratic governance.[2] Treason dissolves into salvific heroism, defiance of law into institution-building, and charisma into traditional authority.

Richard's relation to his own charismatic claim is equally ambiguous, although from a different angle. Ruth Nevo once noted that "behind the regal bearing and the regal gesture is revealed Richard's dismal lack of that inalienable personal power which a later age would come to call charisma, and which alone could carry him through" (1972, 65). Nevo is referring to pure or personal charisma, the undiluted form that we see in Bolingbroke at crucial moments. But Richard's true charismatic claim is dynastic, a diluted but effective form of charismatic domination. As a lineage king Richard bases his authority on hereditary charisma and postfeudal convention. Yet, despite his evident belief in the permanence of kingship, Richard too makes ambiguous statements regarding his status, confusing and sometimes enraging his followers, as when the Bishop of Carlisle must admonish him that "wise men ne'er sit and wail their woes" (3.2.178). Richard's kingship keeps disappearing behind his human vulnerability, and his reactions to his fluctuating status are contradictory and manipulative:

God save the king! Will no man say amen?
Am I both priest and clerk? well then, amen.
God save the king! although I be not he;
And yet, amen, if heaven do think him me.

(4.1.172–75)

One critic suggests that Richard's ironic comments in this passage give him "a strange detachment from events, so that he seems not to know where reality lies" (Cowan 1981, 73). But I would say that his sense of reality is acute: anger and near hysterical frustration notwithstanding, he treads a difficult line with superb intuition of the group dynamic. His performance is charismatic despite his apparent weakness, personal rather than a product of his office. He is even rebellious in the circumstances, summoning his personal charisma in response to Bolingbroke's sudden legalism. But, like Bolingbroke's, Richard's personal claim is also paradoxical. While he asserts divine auspices ("heaven do think him me"), he also relies for his royal legitimacy on the antitheses of personal charisma—hereditary charisma and traditional authority.

The play abounds in this kind of liminality and paradox. We repeatedly encounter examples of enigmatic subjectivity challenging the law of subjecthood. Particularly where the kingship is concerned, Shakespeare contrasts the language of self-identification with the conventional symbols of identity: "I am a subject, / And I challenge law." As agents of change both Richard and Bolingbroke manipulate their different forms of charisma, and in the end both of them—from opposing angles—recognize the conflict between traditional and charismatic authority. Bolingbroke's subjecthood weaves in and out of the smoke of his parvenu kingship. Richard seems most kingly when stripped of royal trappings, when more clerk than priest (to use his own distinction). They are not interchangeable, yet they seem at times to occupy a similar imaginative space, a limbo between improvisational personal power and established traditional rule.

Before Shakespeare, Samuel Daniel was sensitive to this conflict of charismas and to the effect it can have on distinguishing Richard from Bolingbroke, both ethically and as a royal presence. In the *Civile Wars*, a likely source of *Richard II*, Daniel describes an unusual scene in which Queen Isabel mistakenly takes the usurper for her husband from a distance: "For nearer come, shee findes shee had mistooke, / And him she markt was *Henrie Bullingbrooke*," (bk. 2, st. 71). The rhyming of "mistooke" and "Bullingbrooke," literally a reference to Isabel's misrecognition, in a figurative sense links Bolingbroke to error while at the same time acknowledging the crisis of royal authority. The queen's confusion at the window increases as the "glittering troupe" draws closer, an irony Daniel uses to emphasize that Isabel's recognition of her husband, rather than resolving the confusion, only confirms and compounds the social disorder.

Once Isabel recognizes Bolingbroke, she curses him as a traitor and turns away, ordering her ladies to "looke you about, / And tell me if my Lord be in this traine" (bk. 2, st. 71). But the queen cannot bear not to look and soon turns back to the window. By this time "the chiefest traine of all was past" (bk. 2, st. 72), at which point a second, even more significant mistaken identity occurs:

> At last, her loue-quicke eyes, which ready be,
> Fastens on one; whom though she neuer tooke
> Could be her Lord; yet that sad cheere which hee
> Then shew'd, his habit and his woful looke,
> The grace he doth in base attire retaine,
> Caus'd her she could not from his sight refraine.

> What might be he, she said, that thus alone
> Rides pensiue in this vniuersall joy?
> Some I perceiue, as well as we, do mone:
> All are not pleas'd with euery thing this day.
> It may be, he laments the wrong is done
> Vnto my Lord, and grieues; as well he may.

> Then he is some of ours: and we, of right,
> Must pittie him, that pitties our sad plight.
>
> (st. 75–76)

Isabel thinks she is observing "some of ours," a Richard loyalist trail-
ing behind Bolingbroke's riotously celebrating train. But Daniel tips
off the man's identity with the key words "grace" and "pensiue," the
latter a term already applied to Richard. Now, somewhat aghast,
Isabel realizes her mistake:

> But stay: ist not my Lord himselfe I see?
> In truth, if 'twere not for his base aray,
> I verily should thinke that it were hee;
> And yet his baseness doth a grace bewray:
> Yet God forbid; let me deceiued be,
> And be it not my Lord, although it may:
> Let my desire make vows against desire;
> And let my sight approue my sight a lier.
>
> (st. 77)

The spectacle of grace shining through baseness captures the liminality of Richard's status and anticipates Shakespeare's ambiguous portrayal of his authority. The base appearance of a king inevitably suggests a shift, even an anarchy, of social class, and the instance of
mistaken identity in the *Civile Wars* resonates with the dread of just
such an anarchic situation.

We experience the dread through Isabel's wifely confusion, what
Daniel calls her "passion" (st. 74), but the implications of Richard's
new baseness reverberate beyond the anxiety of a wife for her disap-
pointed and unattended husband—implications which are not lost
even on Isabel. Although she does not articulate it, she seems aware
that her own progress at the window from complacent illusion to
grim reality recapitulates her husband's political fortunes, and her
sorrow drives her to the irresolvable core of Richard's plight: the conflict between his lineage charisma (or grace) and the base status of his
natural body. This is in part a conflict between the immortal body
politic and the mortal body natural, a relationship I will discuss further below.

But there is also a more palpable sphere of authority that concerns
Isabel, the kind of authority that must be recognized and experienced
by others, as opposed to the authority of rank or office. The shared
experience of leadership, with which Bolingbroke so smoothly manipulates the populace, is absent from the Richard we see through Isabel's

eyes. From her perspective, and from ours as well in this scene, the crisis of Richard's identity doubles as a crisis of his charismatic authority. Within moments Isabel's confusion regarding Richard's identity deepens to anxiety about the permanence of his royal authority:

> Let me not see him, but himselfe; a King:
> For so he left me; so he did remoue.
> This is not he: this feeles some other thing;
> A passion of dislike, or else of loue.
> O yes; 'tis he: that princely face doth bring
> The euidence of Maiestie to prooue:
> That face, I haue conferr'd, which now I see,
> With that within my heart, and they agree.
>
> (st. 78)

"Let me not see him, but himselfe; a King" is a line that ably characterizes Richard's new problematic identity: he has become both too much himself and not enough. The loss of his authority has transformed his physical presence: Richard is now "him" but not "himselfe; a King." This transformation is representative of the change that comes about when lineage charisma loses its outward proofs. Without a crown and sceptre, the living evidence of genealogical superiority, Richard is forced to rely on his personal charismatic attributes, which scarcely exist at this stage in the story. Indeed, having recognized her husband, Isabel at first refuses to acknowledge his new, unkinged identity: "This is not he: this feeles some other thing." Richard has suddenly become "other," alienated both from "himselfe" and from his wife and loyalists. His physical or natural body becomes the source of any power he can muster. (Ironically, his personal power will have a rebellious quality under the new circumstances, even though the aim of his resistance to Bolingbroke would be a retrenchment of the traditionally established lineage.)

The "grace" that Isabel senses beneath her husband's base appearance reflects the conflict of his new status. Such barely perceptible grace might be either a sign of a nascent personal charisma or merely the afterglow, in the queen's mind, of lineage privilege. Shakespeare develops the dialectic between Richard's personal charisma and his lineage authority more expansively than does Daniel. But Daniel's Isabel captures the emotional ambivalence of a follower caught between the personal magnetism of "him" and the erstwhile power of "himselfe." Her confusion and anxiety are emblematic of the effect that the instability of the cousins' identities has, not only on themselves but also on those others who share the changing charismatic experience of their leadership. Of course Isabel is more than just a group member. She is a wife who is also part of the lineage charismatic group, so her passions reach to the plane of tragic emotion, and her torn feelings reveal the pattern and the force of charisma in Richard's tragedy.

Lineage Charisma, or the Myth of the Vials

To analyze the conflict between Richard's personal charisma and his lineage authority—as well as that between his person and his office, which is a slightly different relation (though in kind the same)—it is important first to understand the properties and structure of lineage charisma. I will rely primarily on a Weberian definition, but again with adjustments to bring empirical data (mostly Shakespearean) to bear on the ideal type. Weber speaks of lineage charisma as a "depersonalization" of pure charisma (*Versachlichung des Charisma*), literally an "objectification" or perhaps even a "neutering" of a personal gift of grace (cf. Weber 1956, 2:679). "Depersonalization" is a signal concept, marking the transition in a charismatic movement from the often revolutionary personal management by a central figure to the administration of the movement after the loss of that figure: "From a unique gift of grace charisma may be transformed into a quality that is either (a) transferable or (b) personally acquirable or (c) attached to the incumbent of an office or to an institutional structure regardless of the persons involved" (Weber 1978, 2:1135). The need to depersonalize the original charisma and routinize it, making it available as a continuing benefit to the surviving followers, causes inevitable conflicts between forms of authority. Because of later-generation dependence on traditional or bureaucratic authority, or a mixture of the two, depersonalization can lead to a diminution of charismatic authority—a problem we see threatening Tamburlaine at the end of both Parts 1 and 2. Charisma obviously loses its original and originary force when integrated with traditional or bureaucratic authority. Rather than a power of disruption and change, transformed charisma becomes an institution-builder. And lineage, especially aristocratic lineage, is one of its most successful institutions.

"The most frequent case of a depersonalization of charisma," according to Weber, "is the belief in its transferability through blood ties" (1978, 2:1136). The charisma of a house replaces the individual inheritance of an original charisma, at the same time diluting it and preserving it in succeeding generations. Logically charisma cannot be heritable, since a unique gift of grace—and particularly one that

manifests itself in the management of nonequilibrium systems—
should die with its possessor. Thus Weber explains that charisma is
hereditary "only in the sense that household and lineage group are
considered magically blessed, so that they alone can provide the
bearers of charisma" (1978, 2:1136).

> Because of its supernatural endowment a house is elevated above
> all others; in fact, the belief in such a qualification, which is unat-
> tainable by natural means and hence charismatic, has everywhere
> been the basis for the development of royal and aristocratic power.
> For just as the charisma of the ruler attaches itself to his house, so
> does that of his disciples and followers to their houses. (Weber
> 1978, 2:1136)

Aristocratic power is not exactly charismatic power. Although charisma provides the supernatural endowment of elite families, the
power which that endowment helps to maintain tends to be traditional or legal rather than heterogeneously charismatic. Thomas
Spence Smith has noted that in Weber's theory "social life beyond the
charismatic circle was founded on ways not of retrieving charisma
but of preventing its return, or, perhaps more accurately, of filtering it
out" because rationality and traditionality "were incompatible with
the radically dependent, subjectively fused, unstable and incalcula-
ble forms of personal charisma" (1992, 185). Lineage charisma provides a clear example of this filtering-out process inasmuch as stability and permanence are its chief reasons for being. It depends on
depersonalization to obviate those "subjectively fused" and "incal-
culable" elements that kept the original charismatic group in disequilibrium, dependent on a unique supernaturally endowed leader.
Lineage replaces the unique leader with the impersonal—and presumably more stable—authority of a family.

But as *Richard II* demonstrates, the stability of lineage claims can
be challenged, albeit at great cost both to the general political stability
and to the myth of hereditary charisma. Lineage and the offenses
against it furnish a moral backdrop to the play. Within the first hundred lines of act 1, Bolingbroke calls attention to his blood lines, deliberately separating royal descent from violence. "There I throw my
gage," he challenges Mowbray, "Disclaiming here the kindred of a
king, / And lay aside my high blood's royalty" (1.1.69–71). He implies
that there is a moral conflict between being a king's cousin and want-
ing to fight "arm to arm." Replying to Bolingbroke, Richard puns on
the subject of blood descent, at the same time acknowledging the
moral gravity of the accusation:

What doth our cousin lay to Mowbray's charge?
It must be great that can inherit us
So much as of a thought of ill of him.

(1.1.84–86)

The king does not overtly refer to Bolingbroke's "disclaiming" of
kindred, but the word *inherit*, here meaning "make us heir to," marks
his recognition of the several related subtexts of the challenge:
the succession to the throne, the king's unkindredlike treatment of
uncles and cousins, and particularly his part in Gloucester's death.[3]
"Inherit" also contains a bit of a dig at Bolingbroke, who is in no position to bequeath anything to Richard and indeed would very much
have liked the Lancastrian line to have inherited the throne. At a
supersubtle level Richard may be taunting Bolingbroke with his possession of the crown, acknowledging the subtexts of his cousin's disclaimer while playfully inverting the roles of bequeather and heir. But
the playfulness, if that is what it is, serves chiefly to emphasize
Richard's birthright (and Bolingbroke's subjecthood vis-à-vis that
birthright). It is difficult to determine whether Richard or Shakespeare is in control of the language in these lines, although Richard
seems pointedly conscious of his royal authority. The scene ends with
his stern and deeply resonant statement, "We were not born to sue,
but to command" (1.1.196); and the punning reversal of "inherit us,"
which cannot withstand the finality of Richard's succinct description
of his birthright, has the force of a conscious taunt when read in tandem with the king's last remark.

That Bolingbroke invokes the royal blood line only to reject it in
favor of his own actions, his unaffined moral agency, provides a clear
picture of the conflict between charismas. The lineage charismatic
authority represented by Richard will not suffice to accomplish true
justice, so Bolingbroke dissociates himself from his "kindred of a
king." Courtesy or public humility may require that he characterize
his challenge of Mowbray as morally inconsistent with royal blood.
But the implication of Bolingbroke's attitude is somewhat different: he
probably dissociates himself from his royal cousin not because arm to
arm combat is anathema to kingship per se, but rather because—and
this becomes the Lancastrian position—proper justice is alien to
Richard's rulership.[4] From this early scene Bolingbroke casts his personal charisma into conflict with Richard's lineage claims, even
though the Lancastrian line itself depends on similar claims to sustain
its ascendency. Bolingbroke declares, "what I speak /My body will
make good upon this earth" (1.1.36–37), suggesting that his natural
body will provide the source and sole limit of his power—another

disclaimer regarding hereditary charisma. Bolingbroke here exhibits the personal charisma with which he will capture both the public imagination and the throne. But his natural-body claim is ultimately disingenuous despite its charismatic force since, as is soon clear, the ostensible criterion for his triumphant return from France will be outrage over his abused lineage privileges.

As the play progresses the conflict of charismatic claims seems to motivate the action. Nothing can stem this conflict, not even the reversal of power. Even after the challenge to Richard's lineage rights has become a fait accompli at Flint Castle, the ambiguities of charismatic authority continue to multiply. Perhaps, indeed, the ambiguities become more pronounced after the deposition. As Louise Cowan has pointed out, "in being deprived of the power of the crown, [Richard] begins to feel himself all the more genuinely a king in the hidden recesses of his soul" (1981, 73). Because those around Richard also sense this incipient conviction of genuineness, there is confusion regarding the source of kingly and ex-kingly power. In the end the demystification of Richard's vested authority—accomplished in part by neutralizing his depersonalized charismatic claim—serves only to remystify the myth of lineage charisma, clouding rather than resolving the relation of traditional to charismatic rulership.

The myth of the transferability of charisma through blood ties is the foundational myth of aristocracy. Its prevalence in Elizabethan culture is so wide as to be something of a commonplace, a form of *consensus gentium* reaching to every level of society.[5] Shakespeare exploits the myth in *Richard II* and, as so often in his writing, also manages a metacommentary on the myth while remaining inside it. Bolingbroke's disclaimer of royal kinship and Richard's taunting use of the word *inherit* suggest this dual approach. Still more revealing is the itinerary of the imagery of blood ties, the stock in trade of genealogical myth. The first elaboration of this imagery comes from the Duchess of Gloucester. She invokes and superbly mystifies the dynastic blood lines when urging Gaunt to avenge her husband's murder:

> Finds brotherhood in thee no sharper spur?
> Hath love in thy old blood no living fire?
> Edward's seven sons, whereof thyself art one,
> Were as seven vials of his sacred blood,
> Or seven fair branches springing from one root.
>
> (1.2.9–13)

This speech is a good illustration of lineage as moral backdrop. The Duchess castigates Gaunt for disregarding the supernatural—and charismatic—unity of the patriarchal blood line. Her image of Edward's blood passed on in seven filial vials, along with the image of the family tree (cf. Shakespeare 1984: 17n. 13–21), reflect a working definition of lineage charisma. The peculiar amalgamation of blood and tree celebrates the myth of the transferability of charisma through blood ties. And Gloucester's death folds back metaphorically into the institutional fiction:

> One vial full of Edward's sacred blood,
> One flourishing branch of his most royal root,
> Is crack'd, and all the precious liquor spilt,
> Is hack'd down, and his summer leaves all faded.
>
> (1.2.17–20)

This is a normative moral allegory, and one which Gaunt will remember. It operates on ascending levels of figuration. At a nearly literal level, Gloucester's blood (inherited from Edward) has been spilled, thus weakening the generational connection; more figuratively, the lifeblood of the nation is lost in the cracking of the vial. The alternating lines of the speech, which suggest a scribal transposition, link sacredness to earthly rootedness. The depersonalization of Edward's charisma could not be more explicit: his blood thrives in seven other bodies, thus preserving the charismatic magic but filtering out the subjectivity of the original bearer.

The Duchess's mystification of Edward's blood may have its source in the anonymous play *Woodstock*. In the first scene of that play, during an unfavorable comparison of Richard to his father (the Black Prince Edward), an embittered Lancaster invokes his brother's royal blood:

>   heaven forestalled his diadem on earth
> To place him with a royal crown in heaven.
> Rise may his dust to glory! Ere he'd 'a done
> A deed so base unto his enemy,
> He'd first have lost his royal blood in drops,
> Dissolved the strings of his humanity
> And lost that livelyhood that was preserved
> to make his (unlike) son a wanton king.
>
> (1.1.37–45)

Lancaster is complaining about an attempt to poison the uncles. The burden of his theme is heredity, specifically the failure of his brother's "unlike" son to inherit the warlike virtues and the ethics of killing. He calls Richard "so wild a prince /So far degenerate from his noble father" (1.1.28–29). The drops of the Black Prince's blood, which "He'd first have lost" before stooping to poison, owe their royalty to Edward III since "heaven forestalled [the Black Prince's] diadem on earth." In this respect the drops are comparable to the cracked vial of the Duchess's speech, whose sacred properties also go back to Edward III.

The author of *Woodstock* recognized the potency of that imagery. Later in the play he deliberately omits the blood myth from a scene in which Richard ruminates on his connection to Edward III. It is a somewhat chilling scene, in which Bushy urges Richard to take his grandfather's example and execute his own protector, Woodstock, just as Edward

> Although but young, and under government,
> Took the Protector then, proud Mortimer,
> And on a gallows fifty foot in height
> He hung him for his pride and treachery.
>
> (2.1.62–65)

Richard responds as expected, with a childish blend of enthusiasm and ruthlessness:

> Why should our proud Protector then presume
> And we not punish him, whose treason's viler far
> Than ever was rebellious Mortimer?
> Prithee read on: examples such as these
> Will bring us to our kingly grandsire's spirit.
>
> (2.1.66–70)

Richard's command "Prithee read on" refers to the "monument of English Chronicles" from which Bushy is reading aloud. The scene consists of a series of passages from the chronicles followed by Richard's reaction and the encouragement of his sycophants. After hearing the story of the unfortunate Mortimer, Richard declares that "examples such as these" will unite him with Edward's "spirit," presumably supplying what he lacks in political imagination while providing a script for his conduct. But his connection to his grandfather's "spirit" seems intellectualized and bloodless in this passage, a function of reading or reflection rather than of spontaneous action. The charismatic inheritance so prominent in blood-ties imagery does not seem a part of Richard's eagerness to identify his kingship with Edward III's. Somehow he has to make too self-conscious an effort to recapture his grandsire's spirit, and the effort (or the self-consciousness) defeats its own purpose of establishing a natural connection with the past. As a result, part of Richard always seems illegitimate in this play, particularly in terms of charismatic lineage authority. Another example occurs further on in the same scene. Still listening to the English Chronicles read aloud, the king interrupts to compare himself to his father, declaring "as we are his body's counterfeit, /So will we be the image of his mind" (2.1.93–94). He has identity in mind again, but the word "counterfeit" undermines his filial ambitions. The double meaning of the word characterizes Richard as, at once, a genuine reproduction and an illegitimate or phony copy.[6] Again there is no mention of blood ties, as if the *Woodstock* author were calling attention to the absence of the myth from Richard's own conception of hereditary greatness.

It is difficult to know what Richard's silence on the subject means. But in Shakespeare's play as well, where the myth has a central metaphorical role, Richard himself scarcely alludes to it except in passing reference to his "sacred blood" when proclaiming his impartiality to Mowbray (1.1.119). Both plays rely on somewhat peripheral, older speakers to remystify the past and preserve tradition, the significance of which fact should not be overlooked in regard to charisma. But as Ure has noted (Shakespeare 1984, xxxix–xl) it is impossible to determine whether *Woodstock*'s uncles influenced Shakespeare's Gaunt, or vice versa, or whether both authors were merely following Holinshed and Froissart. Nevertheless, both *Woodstock*'s Lancaster and Shakespeare's Gaunt bring together similar themes in similar imagery. Lancaster speaks of "royal blood in drops" and calls Richard an "(unlike) son" and a "wanton king." Comparably, in his pelican speech Shakespeare's Gaunt comments on Richard's wantonness while invoking the blood imagery:

> O, spare me not, my brother Edward's son,
> For that I was his father Edward's son;
> That blood already, like the pelican,
> Hast thou tapp'd out and drunkenly carous'd.
>
> (2.1.124–27)

The Duchess's image of Edward's blood as "precious liquor" reappears in revised form here. Richard has tapped it out of the keg and drunkenly "carous'd" it, notionally a wanton grandson ruining the family cellar. However, the image of the young pelican Richard sucking dry his nurturer's blood has a shock value beyond royal gluttony. Not only has the sacred vial been cracked, but also, thanks to Richard's delinquency, the sacred myth of the vials has lost its immutability and coherence. Gaunt's rhetorical manipulation of the myth implies a parallel between fact and figuration, an almost Cratylan contiguity, as if Richard's moral failure had caused a sympathetic faultline in the mythification of aristocratic blood ties.

As the itinerary of the blood-ties imagery leads from the Duchess's myth of the seven vials through Gaunt's rhetorical manipulations in the pelican speech, the mythical status of Edward's blood remains the same. And in this sense Shakespeare operates exclusively from within the myth of dynastic blood ties. But the metaphorical shifts—from sacred vials to quaffed tankards—also suggest a temporary detachment from mythological orthodoxy, a brief experience of myth as malleable fiction. This temporary detachment is what I earlier referred to as Shakespeare's metacommentary, although the term is not crucial. More important is the effect that the inside-outside shift can have on our perception of Richard's lineage charisma.

Both the Duchess and Gaunt historicize the myth of blood ties, introducing a diachronic element into the synchronic field. But Gaunt's historicization contains an internal contradiction. It pits the hereditary ruler against the hereditary ideal, and, ironically, it enhances the importance of Richard's actions. The king's moral agency and his natural body become necessary to the continuity of his charisma—and to others' experience of him—even though his charisma is supposed to be depersonalized and inherited. I doubt that it is Gaunt's intention to weaken the validity of lineage charisma; his aim seems to be simply to make Richard more accountable to tradition for his actions. But by mutating the myth Gaunt distinguishes Richard's natural body from both the corporate body he heads and from the lineage charisma he should unproblematically inherit. The obvious contrast is Gloucester, who in the Duchess's historicization inherits his father's blood without any requirement of action for validation, as is normal in the transferrance of blood ties. On the other hand, Gaunt's manipulation of the myth tends to suppress the depersonalized quality of Richard's charismatic authority while activating its subjective element.

Body Natural, Body Politic, and
Corporate Ambiguity

The subjective element of Richard's authority, as opposed to what might be called the objective reality of lineage rulership, is manifest in the subtle relationship between the king's natural (or mortal) body and the immortal body politic. I would characterize this relationship as interdependent, even intrasubjective. In the Introduction I noted that subjectivity should be redefined to accommodate the charismatic experience because the natural body of the charismatic leader functions on two levels at once, acting as the center not only of the disposition of individual power but also of the mythification of group power. Richard's gradual isolation from his political cohort provides a glimpse of this double function, confirming rather than annihilating the interdependence of the king's two bodies. It may be true that, in contrast to the ongoing group myth of lineage privilege, Richard's personal magnetism fails to bind his group or to satisfy extraordinary group needs. And it may also be true that as a result of his increasingly subjective outbursts Richard's mind and natural body seem to be separate from his inherited political being. Yet that separation is less than meets the eye—to inflate its definitiveness is, in my view, a sign of Lancastrian optimism. In point of fact, the two interdependent king's bodies constitute a sort of corporate ambiguity.

But corporate ambiguity blurs the clean structural lines associated with *de casibus* tragedies. In consequence there is a tendency among critics to overpolarize the body natural and the body politic, despite Ernst Kantorowicz's careful tempering of the polarities in *The King's Two Bodies* (1957). It is indeed tempting to see these two bodies as somehow discrete, one natural and mortal, the other supernatural and immortal. But our conception of kingship in general—and Richard's kingship in particular—suffers if we insist on excessive polarization of the body natural and the body politic. Moreover, if we confuse the opposition between kingship and subjecthood in English discourse for the independence of one from the other, we will incorrectly characterize Richard's subjectivity as an aberration, rather than as an integral, if temporarily unsynchronized, component of his authority. Kingship and subjecthood should be seen as interdependent, both in the wider social sphere and in the king himself. One of many proofs of this interdependence, as Kantorowicz aptly notes, is found in Richard's "duplications" in "the King, the Fool, and the God": "Those three prototypes of 'twin-birth' intersect and overlap and interfere with each other continuously," he observes, concluding that in the crucial scenes of the play—in Wales, at Flint Castle, and at Westminster—we encounter a "cascading: from divine kingship to kingship's 'Name,' and from the name to the naked misery of the man" (1957, 27).

This "cascading," which really is a manifestation of interdependence, is especially visible in the operation and transformations of the king's charismatic authority. Charisma connects kingship to subjecthood ambiguously but inextricably. As the play progresses the lineaments of Richard's authority dodge and shift, as if his subjectivity were spontaneously activated in response to martial defeat, deposition, and imprisonment. Indeed, charismas are in conflict in *Richard II* not only because Richard's lineage clashes with Bolingbroke's personal force, but also because different forms of charismatic authority coexist in Richard's body—or bodies.

Richard himself characterizes the revelation of his subjectivity either as moral weakness or as a species of vocational confusion. For instance, at one point he remarks:

> I live with bread like you, feel want,
> Taste grief, need friends—subjected thus,
> How can you say to me, I am a king?

(3.2.175–77)

And at another point he asks, "Am I both priest and clerk?" (4.1.173). Both questions concern essential identity, and both polarize the relations of group leader to group membership. Neither Richard nor anyone else in the play can satisfactorily determine whether he is ever *not* a king, because all questions of royal identity are also questions of group function. Members of the group cannot detach themselves from the group without destroying it, and the group's destruction would on some level mean their own destruction as well. This situation creates a version of the subject-object dilemma so often discussed in sociological theory, but with a rather Pauline difference. Because Richard is the head of a lineage charismatic group, his rejection or deposition consititutes a dismemberment of the group, creating an interesting conundrum: how can the lineage group function or even continue to exist without a hereditary leader?

The solution is a powerful abstraction, specifically, that there exists an absolute distinction between the office and the person of the king, and that the two can be separated without damage to the permanent glory of the former. This argument resonates in the legalistic justifications for Richard's deposition and, most significantly, in metaphors alluding to the myth of the bodies natural and politic. But Shakespeare is at pains to show that there can be no absolute separation of the two bodies, nor, as I will discuss below, of person and office. If there could be an absolute separation, then the impact of Richard's tragedy would be diluted by the idea that some aspect of his being eludes suffering and death in the abstraction of ongoing "kingship." Yet nothing of the kind seems to happen. Richard "tastes grief" and the rest of us certainly encounter, in Kantorowicz's phrase, "the naked misery of the man" (1957, 27). It may well be a conscious objective of Shakespeare's tragedy to expose the limits, even the futility, of mutually exclusive political categories in human drama.

The categories themselves are quasilegal fictions. Citing Edmund Plowden's *Reports*, Kantorowicz illustrates how in English law a king's mortal body could be seen as separate from his immortal political being:

> The King has two Capacities, for he has two Bodies, the one whereof is a Body natural, consisting of natural Members as every other Man has, and in this he is subject to Passions and Death as other Men are; the other is a Body politic, and the Members thereof are his subjects, and he and his Subjects together compose the Corporation . . . and he is incorporated with them, and they with him, and he is the Head, and they are the Members, and he has the sole Government of them; and this Body is not subject to Passions as the other is, nor to Death, for as to this Body the King never dies, and his natural Death is not called in our Law . . . the Death of the King, but the Demise of the King, not signifiying by the Word (*Demise*) that the Body politic of the King is dead, but that the Body politic is transferred and conveyed over from the body natural now dead, or now removed from the Dignity royal, to another Body natural. (1957, 13)[7]

There is no mention of heredity in this passage, or of the safeguarding of succession. The body politic is simply "transferred and conveyed over from the natural body now dead . . . to another Body natural." We can see how such a thesis would support dynastic claims, but also how it might foster confusions, particularly when, as in *Richard II*, there is no "Demise of the King" before the body politic is conveyed over. The miraculous transition from dead body to living may confirm the immortality of the mystical body politic, but it does little to resolve political and moral crises such as the one that leads to Richard's deposition.

The use of the human body as a metaphor for a political entity has a long history, beginning with Greek analogies of the *polis* to the individual body and continuing through Menenius Agrippa's fable of the belly and beyond that to medieval adaptations (see Hale 1971, esp. 11–47). Christian culture merged Greek and Roman versions of the metaphor with Paul's memorable use of it in 1 Corinthians 12, a passage discussed in the Introduction. To some extent the Pauline text trumps all others. As Edward Forset puts it in the preface to *A Comparative Discourse of the Bodies Natural and Politique* (1606), "The like

comparison [of the body natural to the body politic] is most divinely
enlarged by a much better Orator, and in much more important poynt
of the inseparable union of the members of Christ with their head,
and of the necessary communion of their distinct gifts and works
amongst themselves" (n.p.). Forset's orator is Saint Paul, and those
"distinct gifts" are the nine charisms; moreover, the "necessary communion" of the charisms should remind us that there is a systemic
mutuality—a shared charismatic experience (cf. McIntosh 1970,
902)—at the core of this kind of group function. (Incidentally, Forset's
"works" do not appear in Paul, and probably have a Protestant gene-
sis). Kantorowicz does not consider charismatic authority or group
function per se in his discussion of the two-body metaphor.[8] But
given the importance of 1 Corinthians in the legitimation of the concept we would be well-advised to recognize that charisma has a pivotal relation to idealizations of the bodies natural and politic. Thus
when Plowden speaks of the political "Corporation" composed of a
king as head and his subjects as bodily members, he is in essence
describing a charismatic group relationship.

As I suggested at the beginning of this section, the corporate
charismatic relationship in *Richard II* is ambiguous. Partly because
Richard is not himself a forceful charismatic figure and partly
because his authority derives from diluted forms of charisma such as
lineage and kingship, it becomes impossible in the play to separate
the bodies natural and politic from their dependence on the mutuality of group function. Richard must be seen as a representative simultaneously of divine order and of what Edward Shils calls "institutional charisma" (1982, 131). Shils explains the origins of the highest
authority in this way: "Great earthly power has a manifold, obscure
affinity with the powers believed to inhere in the transcendent order.
Those who believe in divinely transcendent orders also believe that
earthly powers, to enjoy legitimacy, must have some connection
with transcendent powers, that rulers are necessarily involved in the
essential order of things" (131). This connection to the "essential
order" is a charismatic sanction. It makes the ruler a separate and
unique figure, while at the same time establishing his or her dependence on group membership to survive. Likening the ruler to the soul
and the ruled to the body, Forset characterizes the functioning mutuality of the ideal monarchy as "the surest bond of human societie":

> so both the ruler should wholy indeuour the welfare of his people,
> and the sujiect ought (as in loue to his owne soule) to conforme
> vnto his soueraigne; that both of them mutually like twinnes on

one wombe may in the neere and deare nature of relatiues, main-
taine vnuiolate that compound of concordance, in which and for
which they were first combined. (1606, 3–4)

The notion of twins in one womb is difficult to reconcile with the kind
of kingship we encounter in *Richard II*, and not just because Richard
has tyrannical tendencies. The king's royal authority rarely if ever
seems a matter of concordance with his subjects.

Richard enjoys legitimacy, in Shils's terms, above all through his
"connection with transcendent powers"—the blood-ties myth is supposedly the proof positive of this connection. As Larry Champion
points out, the king "touts himself as an embodiment of the religio-
political principle of divine right, constantly invoking God and legal
doctrine to validate his political power" (1990, 101–2).[9] He gets a good
deal of support from others in this area. Gaunt calls him "God's substitute, /His deputy anointed in His sight" (1.2.37–38), translating the
Latin *vicarius Dei.* And Carlisle asserts transcendental auspices, saying
to the apprehensive Richard, "That Power that made you king /Hath
power to keep you king in spite of all" (3.2.27–28). Bucked up by
Carlisle's speech, Richard himself declares his divine charisma:

> Not all the water in the rough rude sea
> Can wash the balm off from an anointed king;
> The breath of worldly men cannot depose
> The deputy elected by the Lord.
>
> (3.2.54–57)

Shakespeare sets these last two speeches against the onslaught of bad
news Richard receives after landing on the Welsh coast. There is consequently something strained about the assertions of divine connection, as if when other forms of authority have failed, when the relation between leader and led has begun to break down, the king and
his close followers must invoke the irrational and patently disproved
notion that Richard has a privileged connection to the order of things.
Everyone protests too much in this scene, with the result that the so-
called divine deputation, faced with the fact of revolt, seems little
more than hollow rhetoric.

The painful and embarrassing oscillations in act 3, scene 2, between
the puffed-up, royal Richard and the defeated, "subjected" Richard
are reflected in stark contrasts between the immortal body politic of
the realm (now escaped from the king) and the feeble natural body of a
man who talks "of graves, of worms, and epitaphs" (3.2.145). Kan-
towicz argues regarding this scene that "the kingship itself seems to

have changed its essence. . . . Gone is the oneness of the body natural with the immortal body politic" (1957, 30). If we take "oneness" to mean interdependence, resting on mutual concordance and group function as legitimating criteria, then Kantorowicz is probably right about the changed essence of the kingship. If, on the other hand, we understand "oneness" to mean a quasilegal theological autonomy that eschews group function or is superior to group needs, then I think we are in danger of positing a condition that never really exists in Shakespeare's play. Despite the apparent autonomy of Richard and Bolingbroke in their decisions, changes in group status in fact supply the barometer of their political successes and failures. On the coast of Wales with Richard and his entourage, the barometer is falling precipitously. The cohesion of Richard's forces is breaking down: York has betrayed him, the Welsh army has abandoned him, and he soon learns that his favorites have been executed. Unable to use this moment of severe disequilibrium to his charismatic advantage, Richard himself breaks down, draining what little personal authority he commands and relying erratically on his diluted lineage claims to confront the overwhelming threat of Bolingbroke's rebellion.

Richard's palpably self-indulgent narcissism in the scene at Wales, whether we regard it as a cause or an effect of the crisis, is emblematic of "oneness" or theological autonomy hoist with its own petard: the king's poetizing individuality is clear evidence of political isolation (as Carlisle and Aumerle recognize). The veneer of intrasubjective group dependency has peeled off, leaving only the weak king and a few followers loyal not so much to Richard as to the myth that his kingship represents. Richard suffers a disengagement from his royal image, and in his desperation he counts more heavily than ever on the rhetoric of anointment and divine connection. But the disengagement is deadly, not only separating the twin bodies of the king but, more significantly, dividing Richard from the traditional (and somewhat ossified) symbols of his charismatic claim to authority. Thus the decay of group cohesion leads to a breakdown in group meaning itself, heightening the conflict between the kinds of charisma that Richard has relied on and presaging tragedy in the failure of the shared charismatic experience of his rulership.

The breakdown in meaning confuses the question of the king's two bodies, since both the natural man and the political body have significance to the royal supporters. There is a curious irony in this: Richard does not become less a king merely by becoming more a man. Rather, he becomes less a king by relying too much on himself as a symbolic figure—by seeing himself too exclusively as a product of chrism—asserting for instance that "For every man that Bolingbroke hath press'd ... God for his Richard hath in heavenly pay / A glorious angel" (3.2.58, 60–61). In other circumstances, coming from a different monarch, such language might be inspiring. In Richard's mouth, and given the present logistical difficulties, it is pathetic and absurdly impractical (as Aumerle tries to suggest earlier in the scene). The recourse to symbolic rather than personal authority reveals a gap between the needs of Richard's group members and their leader's ability to fulfill those needs.

Missing from Richard's authority is the institutional charisma with which the modern ruler maintains power. Although Richard, "in the Elizabethan sense, is secure" (Palmer 1948, 138) in his indisputable lineage claim to the throne, he loses his rights (and life) in a confrontation with a superior charismatic movement. Paradoxically, his best defense would have been not less but more diffusion of charismatic authority. Richard lacks a corporate organization in which he as the incumbent in the role of authority would be "enveloped in the vague and powerful nimbus of the authority of the entire institution" (Shils 1982, 131). This would constitute institutional charisma, a diffused form of charismatic organization considerably more stable than lineage charisma, since it demands a wider membership: "it is not a charisma deduced from the creativity of the charismatic individual. It is inherent in the massive organization of authority. The institutional charismatic legitimation of a command emanating from an incumbent of a role in a corporate body derives from membership in the body as such, apart from any allocated, specific powers" (Shils 1982, 131). The only membership Richard actually shares is that of his lineage group. But while the aristocratic bond of the blood-ties myth has enormous force in early modern culture, as does the providentialism with which it is associated, in pragmatic political terms the lineage group is too easily fragmented and reduced in size.

Richard himself causes the first cracks in his lineage bond when he steals the dead Gaunt's estate, a mistake whose far-reaching implications York immediately recognizes: "Take Herford's rights away," he warns, and Richard will "Be not thyself. For how art thou a king / But by fair sequence and succession" (2.1.195, 198–99). Shakespeare exposes the fragility of dynastic charisma in this episode, particularly ᵛulnerability. Richard is both the author and the prisoner of bility. He has neither the personal resources nor the polit- ʿuntil it is too late) to achieve the legitimation of power embership in a corporate body "apart from any allo- ᵛers." Such a form of corporate authority will have nonarchs, or so we infer from Richard's tragic iso- ngbroke is the first evolutionary step toward that new ideal, a creative charismatic individual who is also the harbinger of institutional charisma.

Person and Office

Wolfgang Iser recently remarked that *Richard II* contains a "vehement" clash between person and office in which "the norms by which the ruler's position is defined are made subservient to the quest for the self" (1993, 69). There is a large nugget of truth in this statement but also a bit of overpolarization. As Nicholas Brooke put it some time ago, "Shakespeare does not [in *Richard II*] . . . make a simple distinction between the man and the office: the office is the necessary concomitant of the man" (1968, 133). Philip Edwards appears to concur with Brooke, observing that only as Richard's authority slips away does the king "begin to learn the true nature of his person and his office, that true nature being the identity of those two things" (1972, 100). Perhaps Brooke's "concomitant" is a better word than Edwards's "identity," but the fundamental point is the same. Only at the risk of destroying the concept of kingship can we separate person and office.

Indeed, this is exactly the risk taken by the Lancastrian side, the seed of the civil strife to come in the fifteenth century. But that is historical, not "tragicall" discourse (to quote Marlowe). The focus of the tragic experience of the play is Richard, not Bolingbroke or his heirs. The tragedy emanates from Richard's recognition of his self-division, an appalled and appalling recognition compounded of the horror of impotence and the horror of acquiescence. "Mine eyes are full of tears," he says, asked to "confess" his crimes during the deposition:

> I cannot see.
> And yet salt water blinds them not so much
> But they can see a sort of traitors here.
> Nay, if I turn mine eyes upon myself,
> I find myself a traitor with the rest.
> For I have given here my soul's consent
> T'undeck the pompous body of a king.
>
> (4.1.244–50)

Here, at his nadir, Richard acknowledges complicity in the deposition, his own treason against the "pompous body of a king." Kantorowicz calls this passage Richard's "self-indictment," in which "the king body natural becomes a traitor to the king body politic" (1957,

39). Yet it is also the moment in which Richard realizes the interdependency of those two bodies, along with the "concomitant" nature of person and office.

The opposition of person and office, like that of body natural and body politic, tends to oversimplify the structure of Richard's authority. Such polarized or binary categories ignore the various forms of authority that constellate in *both* person and office. For instance, we have already explored the importance of lineage charismatic authority in the play. But it is impossible to say whether lineage authority belongs entirely with the king's office or partly with the king's person. By its depersonalized nature, lineage charisma seems to belong with office charisma. Yet Weber makes a distinction between the two. He speaks of office charisma (*Amtcharisma*) as a form of depersonalization distinct from lineage charisma, in a sense adding a third variable to the opposition of person and office in *Richard II*.[10] Weber maintained that charisma "may be transferred through artificial, magical means instead of through blood relationship": "The apostolic succession secured through episcopal ordination, the indelible charismatic qualification acquired through the priest's ordination, the king's coronation and anointment, and innumerable similar practices among primitive and civilized peoples all derive from this mode of transmission" (1978, 2:1139). It might be recalled that the term for anointment in the Septuagint is *chrism*. And in connection with *Richard II* one wonders whether charismatic qualification can be neutralized by the inverse of anointment, which would be deposition, or indeed whether the symbolic power of coronation has any lasting meaning at all. Weber suggests that it does not, explaining that the concept of office charisma has a more functional value than its ritual occasions:

> Most of the time the symbol has become something merely formal, and in practice is less important than the conception often related to it—the linkage of charisma with the holding of an *office*, which itself is acquired by the laying on of hands, anointment, etc. Here we find that peculiar transformation of charisma into an institution: as permanent structures and traditions replace the belief in the revelation and heroism of charismatic personalities, charisma becomes part of an established social structure. (1978, 2:1139)

In other words, the symbolic anointing of a king, the coronation ceremony, belongs to a superseded world of charismatic authority. It can be seen as vestigial and preinstitutional, reduced in many social structures—such as the collapsing one portrayed in *Richard II*—to an ossified symbolic formality. Like the original heroism of an aristocratic house, the "artificial, magical means" of transferring charisma become less important than the institution into which the charisma has been transformed.

This last fact adds myriad complications to our understanding of Richard on his own as well as Richard's charismatic claim in confrontation with Bolingbroke's. Shakespeare's play often seems to be acting as a reluctant witness to the obsolescence of both original charisma (in regard to bloodlines) and artificial symbols of magical endowment. Yet Richard, for all his qualities of *roi fainéant* or *rex inutilis*, reveals an affecting and nearly persuasive virtuosity in the defense of both these kinds of symbols.[11]

The deposition (or abdication) scene may be the best example. In this scene we witness not only Richard's witty manipulations but also a socially determined phenomenon involving the royal charisma. As Edward Shils explains, as if with Richard in mind (though he does not mention him in a list that includes the twentieth-century Duke of Windsor):

> All effective rulers possess charismatic qualities, that is, have charismatic qualities attributed to them, unless it is known that they are *fainéants*, who have abdicated their responsibilities out of moral weakness or are otherwise incompetent. Even then, it is not easy to divest failed incumbents of the charismatic qualities attributed to them during their sovereignty. . . . What was attributed to the person in the role adheres to him in attenuated form after he has ceased to occupy it, or even when by his own weakness he diminishes the expected effectiveness of the role itself. (1982, 128)

Richard is certainly *fainéant*, both morally weak and "otherwise incompetent." But certain charismatic qualities adhere to him even when he officially renounces them, and even when he is confronted with Bolingbroke's strong personal charisma. It is not possible for Richard fully to divest himself of his royal charismatic attributes; he retains them in what Shils terms "attenuated form." Consequently his enemies cannot leech all royal authority from him, despite their rationale to withdraw political support. This imperfect divestiture energizes the abdication scene, ultimately frustrating Bolingbroke's (and Northumberland's) wish for a smooth exchange of power.

Cowan has pointed out that "Richard is unmistakably the master of [the] abdication scene, unpredictable in his speech and action and no doubt acutely embarrassing to Bolingbroke" (1981, 74). Being "unpredictable in speech and action" might well signal a resurgent personal charisma capable of reinspiring group cohesion, evidence of undivested authority. But there is a conflict between Richard's unexpected mastery and his deflating sentimentality, as is seen in his morbid attachment to the symbols of his (erstwhile) authority.[12]

The deposition begins in act 4 when Richard is led into the Parliament chamber by York. They are accompanied by "Officers *bearing the regalia*"; the sceptre and the crown immediately become catalysts for Richard's self-examination, all the contradictions of royal symbolization flooding his speech. When York reminds him that the attending lords are expecting "The resignation of thy state and crown / To Henry Bolingbroke," Richard responds with mock-complicity:

> Give me the crown. Here, cousin, seize the crown.
> Here, cousin,
> On this side my hand, and on that side thine.
>
> (4.1.179–81)

His playfulness is false and brittle, verging on hysteria: "Now is this golden crown like a deep well . . . That bucket down and full of tears am I, / Drinking my griefs, whilst you mount up on high" (182, 188–89). We notice that Richard refers to himself in the first-person singular, "me" and "I," while he addresses Bolingbroke with the polite form "you" as if referring to a social superior. Nevo suggests that Richard's use of first-person singular pronouns calls attention to his "fully exposed personal existence," especially in his "graves, worms, and epitaphs" speech (3.1.145–77) and after his descent to the base court at Flint Castle (3.3.190–210) (1972, 78). She maintains that the pronouns "chart a spiritual progress" (84) from king to person. A similar "progress" is in evidence in the deposition scene, although Shakespeare has deliberately undermined the progressive decline of Richard's pronouns by holding back Bolingbroke from any sort of progessive ascent. As a result there is a confusion of address that reflects the conflict of charisma in the scene and indicates how awkwardly royal authority changes course.

Yet Richard seems to use the first-person singular pronouns with more calculation in the deposition scene than earlier, exhibiting a self-consciousness about his and Bolingbroke's liminal (or very nearly shared) status that was absent from both his speech in Wales and his conduct at Flint. Like the metaphor of the bucket of tears, the pronomial demotions mix accusation and self-pity. But Richard is finally a shade too manipulative to win full sympathy for his decline—literally manipulative in that he uses his hands to fashion a pose in which his rival will appear to "seize" the crown and become a living sculpture of violent usurpation. Bolingbroke will not be drawn, however.

He merely questions the practical implications of Richard's display, addressing him with the formal pronoun and referring to himself not prematurely as "we" but still as "I":[13]

> *Bol.* I thought you had been willing to resign.
>
> *Rich.* My crown I am, but still my griefs are mine.
> You may my glories and my state depose,
> But not my griefs; still am I king of those.
>
> *Bol.* Part of your cares you give me with your crown.
>
> (4.1.189–94)

Richard's attitude toward the regal objects, its morbid quality aside, stands in marked contrast to Bolingbroke's. Both see the crown as symbolic, but Bolingbroke regards it as a public symbol of power, responsibility, and authentication, whereas Richard cannot help but regard it as a symbol of self—that is, of personal identity indivisible from such mystifications as lineage charisma, anointment, and the role of *vicarius Dei.* To an extent, the regalia represent a third protagonist in the deposition drama, a ghostly symbolic ideal trapped between waning lineage authority and nascent charismatic authority.

The scene continues with Richard's self-deposition. As has been recently observed, Shakespeare "understood more than merely the 'pangs' involved in royal abdication"; he also understood that deposition, "like death, is a formal process with clearly defined stages" (Merrix and Levin 1990, 2). The control and scripting of these stages is not, however, entirely in Bolingbroke's command. After Richard's initial hesitation—and following a bit more wordplay in which Bolingbroke asks if he is "contented to resign" and Richard answers, in the original spelling, "I, no; no, I; for I must nothing be" (4.1.201)—the king abruptly declares himself no longer in possession of the salient royal attributes, which he itemizes in stark sequence:

> Now, mark me how I will undo myself.
> I give this heavy weight from off my head,
> And this unwieldy sceptre from my hand,
> The pride of kingly sway from out my heart;
> With mine own tears I wash away my balm,
> With mine own hands I give away my crown,
> With mine own tongue deny my sacred state,
> With mine own breath release all duteous oaths;
> All pomp and majesty I do forswear.
>
> (4.1.202–11)

He goes on to list less symbolic privileges, "manors, rents, revenues
... acts, decrees, and statutes" (4.1.212–13) in the same pseudo-official
rhetoric. But the emphasis should be on the *pseudo* and on Richard's
almost taunting utterance of a litany that probably has more to do
with mastery of the moment than with the necessities of abdication.

It is by no means clear whether Richard's itemization of the symbols of his kingship—I hesitate to use the word *office*—was required
or expected by the Parliament or the Bolingbroke faction. That particular anatomy, excruciating in the deepest sense of the word, seems to
be Richard's idea, perhaps with a glance by Shakespeare at Holinshed's elaborate description of the young Richard's coronation (cf.
Holinshed 1807, 2:713–14). In fact, Bolingbroke and the others have
something quite different in mind for Richard's resignation speech,
as Northumberland's insistence on the confessing of the articles
makes clear.

Shakespeare may have taken the pattern for Richard's speech from
Daniel's version of the deposition, although the speech is reported
rather than rendered directly in the *Civile Wars*. Daniel notes that the
king is brought before the assembly and, apparently without irony,
confesses his abuses and willingly abdicates, "Protesting, if it be for
their good, / He would gladly sacrifice his blood" (bk. 2, st. 110). The
reference to blood is notable in that it invokes both the blood-ties
myth and Richard's actual lifeblood, apparently putting in the service
of the usurpers both the king's natural body and the symbol of his
royal lineage charisma. But the reference also echoes a passage a few
stanzas earlier in which Richard uses the double imagery with
exactly the opposite intention. Trapped and confronted by Bolingbroke he declares, "*Henrie* do thy worst, / For, ere I yeeld my Crowne,
I'le lose my blood; / That blood, that shall make thee and thine
accurst" (st. 107). Daniel seems to refer to this threat in the last stanza
of book 2 when he speaks of "Our fieldes ingrayn'd with bloud" (st.
117) in the succeeding age, but Richard suppresses any hint of a threat
in his renunciation speech (as reported):

> There, he his Subiectes all (in general)
> Assoyles and quites of oath and fealtie,
> Renounces interest, title, right and all
> That appertaind to kingly dignitie;
> Subscribes thereto, and doth to witnesse call
> Both heauen and earth, and God, & Saints on hie,
> To testifie his act, and doth professe
> To do the same with most free willingnesse.
>
>   (bk. 2, st. 111)

The contrast with Shakespeare is more in spirit than in substance, a difference of tone that provides what Cowan calls Richard's mastery of the deposition scene.

That difference of tone translates into a difference of posture and agency in *Richard II*, for which Holinshed might well have supplied a model. In contrast to Daniel's, Holinshed's Richard not only does not resign willingly but in fact plays no active role in the renunciation. He *is renounced by* the Parliament: "Iustice William Thirning, in name of the other [i.e., 'king Henrie'], and for all the states of the land, renounced vnto the said Richard late king, all homage and fealtie vnto him before time due, in maner and forme as apperteined" (1807, 2:868). Note the word "apperteined," which Daniel picks up but puts into the mouth of a contrite Richard. Holinshed continues: "Which renuntiation to the deposed king, was a redoubling of his greefe, in so much as thereby it came to his mind, how in former times he was acknowledged & taken for their liege lord and souereigne, who now (whether in contempt or in malice, God knoweth) to his face forsware him to be their king" (2:868). Surprisingly, there is more psychological and emotional depth in Holinshed's portrayal of the king than in Daniel's—and more sense of tragedy. The king suffers "a redoubling of his greef" and (presumably along with the chronicler) bafflement in regard to the contempt and malice with which his former subjects forswear him. The seeds of Shakespeare's brittle, embittered Richard are found here in the *Chronicles*, as are the roots of the ex-king's unique relation to the symbols of his rulership.

The importance of those symbols to Richard's idea of himself—to his increasing awareness of his own subjective reality—points to a pivotal conflict in his exercise of authority. This conflict illustrates the difficulty in simplifying the division of person and office in the play, while at the same time it complicates Richard's relation both to his rival and to his followers. For all his dependence on the depersonalized charisma of the blood-ties myth, Richard rejects—or finds repugnant—the concept of office charisma. In his mind the kingship does not inhere in the office per se, which may be the underlying message of his reaction to Bolingbroke on Roan Barbary:

Rich. Rode he on Barbary? Tell me, gentle friend,
How went he under him?

Groom. So proudly as if he disdain'd the ground.

Rich. So proud that Bolingbroke was on his back!
That jade hath eat bread from my royal hand;
This hand hath made him proud with clapping him.

Would he not stumble? would he not fall down,
Since pride must have a fall, and break the neck
Of that proud man that did usurp his back?
Forgiveness, horse! why do I rail on thee,
Since thou, created to be aw'd by man,
Wast born to bear? I was not made a horse,
And yet I bear a burthen like an ass,
Spurr'd, gall'd, and tir'd by jauncing Bolingbroke.

                                        5.5.81–94)

In this passage the horse is emblematic of the kingship, and its apparent disloyalty symbolizes the interchangeability of kingship when it is conceived of as an office. After alluding to the link between his own natural body and the royalizing of Roan Barbary—"That jade hath eat bread from my royal hand; / This hand hath made him proud with clapping him"—Richard forgives the horse as a mere creature. But his contempt for Bolingbroke's facile assumption of royal privileges reflects an ingrained superiority to the function of office, and by extension his particular dissatisfaction with the notion of kingly office. When he declares "I was not made a horse" he not only introduces the irony that he has been treated like a beast of burden, but also emphasizes his radical differentiation from the emblem of office charisma. Thus we can say that he rejects not only Bolingbroke's specific claim but also what is (to the rightful heir) effectively the bureaucratization of English monarchical authority.

Consider in this context Weber's statement regarding the office charisma of the Catholic church, and the priest's *character indelibilis*: "The bureaucratization of the church was possible only if the priest could be absolutely depraved without endangering thereby his charismatic qualification; only then could the institutional charisma of the church be protected against all personnel contingencies" (1978, 2:1141). Gaunt, Bolingbroke, Northumberland, and the rest of that faction consider Richard utterly depraved. Moreover, they think he believes his charismatic qualification is protected by his office, by a divine right *in addition to* an institutional form of charismatic authority that persists regardless of his behavior. But in fact Richard does not believe in this extreme form of office charisma. He instead believes that a modicum of personal charisma mixed with lineage endowment (which, in his view, is inseparable from the person) go into the making of a ruler. Ironically, it is the members of the Bolingbroke faction who actually support the notion of office charisma. For all their dependence on the personally charismatic duke, they come by expediency to accept a version of office charisma comparable to Weber's description of the bureaucratized church.

Bolingbroke and Group Function

Critics have often described Bolingbroke as a Machiavellian politician, a practitioner of *realpolitik* (cf. Champion 1990, 146n. 10). His attitude toward the crown as a material possession rather than as a magical, divinely imbued symbol of anointment, seems to confirm such a view. But we should bear in mind that Bolingbroke too depends on other-worldly auspices. He is not so much a normal male figure in the play as he is a charismatic experience. His supernatural authority simply has not yet been solidified into a set of symbols, as Richard's has, so that Bolingbroke's followers can count on an identity between the aims of their leader and the meaning of his charismatic rebellion.

The most striking description of Bolingbroke's personal charisma comes from Richard himself. The king claims to have watched the banished duke setting out from London toward foreign exile. "Ourself and Bushy," he announces,

> Observ'd his courtship to the common people,
> How he did seem to dive into their hearts
> With humble and familiar courtesy;
> What reverence he did throw away on slaves,
> Wooing poor craftsmen with the craft of smiles
> And patient underbearing of his fortune,
> As 'twere to banish their affects on him.
> Off goes his bonnet to an oyster-wench;
> A brace of draymen bid God speed him well,
> And had the tribute of his supple knee,
> With "Thanks, my countrymen, my loving friends"—
> As were our England in reversion his,
> And he our subjects' next degree in hope.
>
> (1.4.23–36)

Richard's speech contains equal parts of jealousy and contempt, although it is difficult to say how worried he really is about Boling-broke's becoming "our subjects' next degree in hope." The burden of Richard's description is Bolingbroke's craftiness, his calculated and (to Richard's mind) patently insincere populism. Yet even Richard, who sneers at the duke's "supple knee," seems quietly awed by the way in which "he did seem to dive into their hearts / With humble and familiar courtesy." The sources of this passage in Froissart, Holinshed, and Daniel all describe the people's behavior toward Bol-ingbroke (Shakespeare 1984, 43n. 24–36). In contrast, using Richard's bias as a fulcrum, Shakespeare describes Bolingbroke's "wooing" of the masses as though the duke had somehow engineered the group bond. There is more threat and perhaps more delusion in the Shake-spearean version, and therefore greater capacity for drama. But no amount of royal bias can mask the group experience of Bolingbroke's charismatic presence. Richard's negative characterization of the peo-ple's response to the departing duke only underscores the bond between Bolingbroke and his followers—"my countrymen, my lov-ing friends."

Bolingbroke's charismatic appeal to the common people need not be seen in opposition to his appeal to aristocrats. In the best Pauline sense the duke is "all things to all men"; moreover, the right to free-dom against tyranny developed in England mainly as the freedom of noble peers against royal tyranny, as the Magna Carta reflects.[14] Bol-ingbroke never attempts to bring on a popular revolt. He succeeds not as a populist but consummately as an aristocrat. "As I was ban-ish'd, I was banish'd Herford," he says on returning from exile, "But as I come, I come for Lancaster" (2.3.112–13). The followers upon whom he depends are also aristocrats, and he casts his rebellion in terms of shared privilege and family rights. "Wherefore was I born?" (2.3.121) he asks York, who has just accused him of "gross rebellion and detested treason" (2.3.108). Bolingbroke invokes the protection of the lineage charismatic group, describing an analogous situation in which Aumerle might have been deprived of his rights and inheri-tances: "Had you first died, and he been thus trod down, / He should have found his uncle Gaunt a father" (2.3.125–26). Fatherhood, blood ties, and dynastic charisma all meet in Bolingbroke's justification as the duke marshals the most powerful myths of his milieu to organize a group of followers, finally declaring himself a subject who chal-lenges law: "And therefore personally I lay claim / To my inheritance of free descent" (2.3.133–34). Yet, as so often happens in the play, dif-ferent kinds of charisma conflict in the Bolingbroke experience. His rebellion is justified as an instrument of the retrenchment of tradi-tional authority, whose laws and tenets Richard has abrogated in stealing Lancaster's property. At the same time, however, Boling-broke displays a magnetic personal charisma, a disruptive force which is essentially antagonistic to traditional authority. It is to this latter disruptive force that York responds in condemning the man who would "Be his own carver, and cut out his way, / To find out right with wrong" (2.3.143–44).

The balancing of these conflicting forms of authority distinguishes Bolingbroke as a leader. His abilities come to light in crises of group cohesion, a fact that should remind us of Thomas Spence Smith's observation that some charismatic groups may be unable to function without an element of decay. As will be recalled from the Introduction,

such groups thrive in dissipative structures, and their leaders, like Bolingbroke, capitalize on the entropy of the social structure to achieve
and maintain ascendency (cf. Smith 1992, 110–11). But Bolingbroke
publicly eschews socially dissipative situations, representing himself
as the hero of homeostasis. His rebellion paradoxically offers political
stability, official respect for lineage authority, and a return to traditional rulership. The governmental chaos which he helps foment—
and which parallels Richard's emotional state—provides Bolingbroke
with the opening to appear "as a double-visaged Janus, projecting
himself on the one hand as the omniscient repository of ancient wisdom and on the other as the new man of the people" (Willner and Willner 1965, 87).

The double visage and its political implications are particularly
clear in Shakespeare's main source. According to Holinshed, Bolingbroke addressed Parliament after Richard's deposition with these
words:

> I Henrie of Lancaster claime the realme of England and the crowne,
> with all the appurtenances, as I that am descended by right line of
> the blood comming from that good lord king Henrie the third, and
> through the right that God of his grace hath sent me, to recouer the
> same, which was in point to be vndoone for default of good gouer-
> nance and due justice. (1807, 2:865)

Even in the *Chronicles* the figure of Bolingbroke thrives on the threshhold of different kinds of charisma that are not so much in conflict as
in hopeful tandem. In this passage he invokes both his lineage and
his personal charismatic claim. He offers to restore "good gouer-
nance" and "due justice," in Weberian terms fulfilling extraordinary
social needs by transcending the sphere of everyday routines. This
he will accomplish "with the helpe of my kin, and of my freends,"
(2: 865) an acknowledgment of group function, or more precisely,
the cooperation of two different groups: one the product of lineage
connections, the other of personal bonds. In claiming the crown, Bolingbroke calls attention to his charismatic leadership while simultaneously presenting himself as a scion of traditional authority, a legitimate hereditary ruler.

Ironically, the contradiction implicit in these appeals to different
forms of authority works to Bolingbroke's tactical advantage. In
Holinshed's account Bolingbroke stands up in a literally kingless
meeting of Parliament: Richard has refused to attend the session and
in his absence the "speciall commissaries" list his crimes against the
realm and "depriue him of all kinglie dignitie and worship, and of

any kinglie worship in himself" (Holinshed 1807, 2:864). They depose him *in absentia*, his personal resignation to take place the following day. At this point in the proceedings the Parliament, indeed all England, has no head. An extreme crisis of political disequilibrium faces the assembled house, providing the ideal moment for an intervention of charismatic management:

> Immediatlie as the sentence was in this wise passed, and that by reason thereof the realme stood void without head or gouernour for the time, the duke of Lancaster rising from the place where before he sate, and standing where all those in the house might behold him, in reuerend manner made a signe of the crosse on his forhead, and likewise on his brest, and after silence by an officer commanded, said vnto the people there being present these words following.
>
> The duke of Lancaster laieth challenge or claime to the crowne. (Holinshed 1807, 2:865)

Bolingbroke's response to the situation—even if we reckon the crisis to have been stage-managed by him[15]—places him at the focal point of the dissipative government structure, a heroic institution-saver. Yet as solemnly as he invokes his genealogical descent, the valence of his authority nevertheless leans toward personal charisma, a form of leadership "specifically salvationist or messianic in nature" (Tucker 1968, 743). This valence, necessary to Bolingbroke's political survival, results from the weakness of his lineage claim. Although he can trace his bloodline beyond Edward III to Henry III and he is at the same first-cousin level as Richard in the kinship group, he is not the first son of a first son and therefore does not have the same mystified claim to the family's charismatic endowment.[16] Consequently he must count on integrating a combination of destabilizing elements with the highly stable idea of a kingly office to effect the political homeostasis he implicitly promises when he "laieth challenge or claime to the crowne."

Despite his personal charisma, or because of it, Bolingbroke remains a genealogical compromise. Thus in reading *Richard II* it is impossible to decide whether Richard can justifiably be deposed, whether "God's substitute" can be replaced by someone chosen on earth. This problem supplies the content of the play's political debate. Richard himself provokes the issue when he is brought before Bolingbroke for his abdication. "God save the king!" he exclaims blackly, "although I be not he; / And yet, amen, if heaven do think him me" (4.1.174–75).

But, both specifically in the deposition scene and generally throughout the play, Shakespeare does more than merely oppose the anointed
to the unanointed. Bolingbroke's charismatic presence has the force
of a divine gift, if not a Tamburlainian superiority then at least a
fresher sanction than Richard's lineage claims. As Weber suggests in
one of his more extreme characterizations of pure (i.e., personal)
charisma, "Instead of reverence for customs that are ancient and
hence sacred, [charisma] enforces the inner subjection to the unprecedented and absolutely unique and therefore Divine" (1978, 2:1117).
Although, as we have seen, Bolingbroke pays reverential lip service
to old and sacred customs, his disruptive, revolutionary mission
demands of his followers what Weber calls an "inner subjection"
(innere Unterwerfung) to the divine (cf. 1956, 2:666). Consequently
Richard's anointed status must confront the divinity of his chal-
lenger's charismatic auspices.

Because Bolingbroke has better administrative skills, not to mention a better strategic imagination, he manages his charismatic claim
more perceptively, taking less for granted regarding his followers'
duty to him. We might say (with due acknowledgment to Pierre
Bourdieu) that Bolingbroke possesses charismatic capital, and that
experiencing his charisma means sharing in a process of its distribution. Perhaps it is worth recalling in this context that Paul speaks of
distribution, "diaireseis de charismaton," when describing the human
manifestations of the nine charisms, a sense that is lost in the English
translation (cf. Introduction n. 2). But the Bolingbroke experience
restores the original notion of charismatic distribution, which tends
to be effaced by such diluted forms of charisma as those associated
with lineage and office. Simultaneously conserving and disrupting
the social equilibrium (cf. Camic 1980, 20), Bolingbroke measures his
individual power against group satisfaction and enhances his personal aggrandizement with the distribution of charismatic capital.

Bolingbroke's word for this distribution is love. At the end of act 2
he meets Northumberland in Gloucestershire and travels with him to
link up with other allies. Northumberland is unctuous, apparently
enthralled by Bolingbroke's very presence:

> I bethink me what a weary way
> From Ravenspurgh to Cotshall will be found
> In Ross and Willoughby, wanting your company,
> Which I protest hath very much beguil'd
> The tediousness and process of my travel.
> But theirs is sweet'ned with the hope to have

The present benefit which I possess,
And hope to joy is little less in joy
Than hope enjoy'd.

                                                              (2.3.8–16)

These words seem uncharacteristically effusive for Northumberland.
His hyperbole echoes the language of courtly love: he "protest[s]"
that Bolingbroke's company has "beguil'd / The tediousness and
process of [his] travel," the hendiadys doubling not only the difficulty
but also presumably the "present benefit" that he possesses—hope
and joy combined in "hope enjoy'd." There is little doubt, I think, that
Shakespeare means for us to recognize this scene as a demonstration
of Bolingbroke's magnetism, the root and controlling factor of his
charismatic authority. An undercurrent of religious, and maybe
amorous, devotion resonates in the words "hope" and "joy," and in
Northumberland's fantasy that Ross and Willoughby, like the biblical
Magi, are traveling in "sweet'ned" anticipation of the epiphany to
come when they will meet the savior-duke.

Bolingbroke's return fulfills the salvationistic promise of the charismatic bond, satisfying his followers' charisma hunger and instantly
reorganizing the symbolic order around his charismatic mission. His
followers, of whom Northumberland is emblematic, begin to experience their own idealizing transferences, their own unattainable ambitions, through Bolingbroke's leadership. Like the suborned Theridamas with his new lord in *Tamburlaine*, Northumberland promptly
fits the returning duke into an idealized symbolic scheme. His lover's
enthusiasm, hinting at the aim-inhibitied libidinal ties of group cohesion, animates the scene and provides the proof of Bolingbroke's ability to satisfy extraordinary needs and to feed charisma hunger while
managing the functional disequilibrium of a rebellious movement.

Bolingbroke's response to Northumberland's enthusiasm is properly humble, as un-Tamburlainian as it could be: "Of much less value
is my company / Than your good words" (2.3.19–20). This is the Bolingbroke of the supple knee, acknowledging the interdependence of
his relationship to Northumberland. His magnanimity continues
when Harry Percy rides up, at which point we glimpse an exchange
of vows between political lovers. After his father has introduced the
duke, Percy begins:

Percy. My gracious lord, I tender you my service,
Such as it is, being tender, raw, and young,
Which elder days shall ripen and confirm
To more approved service and desert.

> *Bol.* I thank thee, gentle Percy, and be sure
> I count myself in nothing else so happy
> As in a soul rememb'ring my good friends,
> And as my fortune ripens with thy love
> It shall be still thy true love's recompense.
> My heart this covenant makes, my hand thus seals it.
>
> (2.3.41–50)

Once again, as in Tamburlaine's battlefield meeting, talk of happy souls, true love, hearts, and hands echoes the language of courtly *fin' amors*. Moreover, as H. R. Coursen has pointed out, Bolingbroke also invokes the "reciprocal nature of the feudal oath" (1982, 78), promising to reward Percy as his "fortune ripens with thy love." It has been repeatedly noted that the promises made here are later condemned by Hotspur as the "candy deal of courtesy" (cf. *I Henry IV* 1.3.251–55). But the feudal character of the meeting in *Richard II*, and of the reciprocity implied, confirms the charismatic status of Bolingbroke's authority. Feudal relations tend to have a charismatic basis insofar as fealty contravenes economic rationality. Feudal lords grant rewards and distribute spoils as it pleases them. The bond between Percy and Bolingbroke has traces of this same kind of irrational economic conduct, this same charismatic management of payment. Thus the unspecific, easily misinterpreted promise to give "thy true love's recompense," while speeding Bolingbroke on his way, also causes problems later when the routinization of his charismatic movement has begun in earnest.

The magnanimous duke repeats the same vague promises to Ross and Willoughby, with the same emphasis on their love:

> All my treasury
> Is yet but unfelt thanks, which, more inrich'd,
> Shall be your love and labour's recompense.
>
> (2.3.60–62)

"Your presence makes us rich," answers Ross. "And far surmounts our labour to attain it," chimes in Willoughby. For the third time we hear the same attitude toward Bolingbroke's "presence" and witness an identical staging of his charismatic experience. Through it all Bolingbroke continually speaks of love as a service rendered that deserves recompense. He vows to distribute the capital he gains, presumably both material and honorific, as his fortune "ripens" and fills his treasury with more than "unfelt thanks." In this sense, as I mention above, Bolingbroke manages the accumulation and distribution of charismatic capital. The duke may speak airily of such tangibles as exchequers and fortunes, treasury and enrichment, but at this point in the play his value to his followers is primarily symbolic.

Bolingbroke's value as a bearer of charismatic symbols remains more or less in suspension throughout *Richard II*. The strain of routinization does not occur until the Henriad. Given the conflicting forms of authority which Bolingbroke exploits in his rise to power, it is no wonder that his charismatic idealization increasingly suffers damage as he establishes himself as a traditional ruler. But that conflict is not the tragedy of Richard's play, if indeed it can be termed a tragedy at all.

3

INDIVIDUATION AS DISINTEGRATION

Hamlet and Othello

In both *Hamlet* and *Othello*, group experience contributes less than individual revelation to the tragic force of the catastrophes. Yet both Hamlet and Othello are charismatic figures, and both suffer as a result of their individuation from a group. In the broad picture Hamlet is right (Claudius committed regicide) and Othello is wrong (Desdemona did not commit adultery). They kill for utterly different reasons and they are victims of patently different kinds of betrayal. Moreover, one of them is a prince of the blood while the other is a Moorish soldier in a Continental capital; that is, one of them is a consummate insider while the other is an exotic. Nevertheless, Hamlet and Othello are comparable in their failure to sustain charismatic hegemony in their spheres of social action. Both Hamlet and Othello mismanage their authority; both become disengaged from their own charismatic symbols and thereby cease to satisfy the extraordinary psychological needs of their followers. These failures, different as they are in detail, result in analogous individuations of the protagonist-leaders from their groups and in the subsequent disintegration of group, group ideal, and charismatic mission.

Hamlet

Let me begin by establishing the place of charisma in the play and identifying the status and character of Hamlet's charismatic claim. This section provides an overview of Hamlet the character with reference to charismatic authority, rather than offering a complete reading of the play. Consequently I concentrate more on Hamlet's relation to his charismatic father, and his relation to the routinization of his father's charisma, than on the complications surrounding his relations with his uncle. As in other chapters, I am concerned here with charisma as a functioning group experience, although I have paid close attention to the definition of Hamlet's charisma in relation to his father's charismatic authority. The temptation to regard charisma as a zenith of individuality (see Introduction) can be very strong when analyzing Hamlet. The Danish prince has been, for many readers and critics, the supreme model of subjective awareness: thus Hazlitt's famous remark, "It is we who are Hamlet." But fascination with the individual psyche, whether his or ours, tends to divert attention from the collective sensibility. As a consequence even Hamlet's charisma has been romanticized. Harold Bloom, for example, asserts that "the character of Hamlet is the largest literary instance of what Max Weber meant by *charisma*, the power of a single individual over nature, and so at last over death" (1990, 1). Bloom exuberantly misrepresents both Hamlet and Weber, largely at the expense of charismatic group experience. In point of fact, Marlowe's Tamburlaine is a better (or "larger") literary instance of charisma than Hamlet in terms of group experience.

But it almost seems counterintuitive to suggest a more charismatic figure than Hamlet, which may tell us less about Hamlet than about our misunderstanding of charisma and group function. Hamlet's political isolation, his soliloquies, his originality, and his personal suffering all militate against our perceiving him in the context of group experience. His charisma seems to separate him from others rather than bind him to a group. Yet it is precisely as the center of a group experience that Hamlet exerts his authority in the Danish court. Group function may not be as obvious an emphasis in the play as it is in *Richard II* or *Antony and Cleopatra*. But it is nonetheless an invaluable, if subtle, indicator of tragic development. Hamlet's failure in managing his own charismatic symbols causes a breakdown of group function— a collapse of the dissipative structure in which the returned prince at first seems to thrive. For this reason, it is worth exploring group function even when the experiences of the group seem to contribute less to our understanding than does individual revelation.

It is an irony of the play that Hamlet's intellectual magnetism obscures his function—or dysfunction—as a group leader. In the early acts, despite (or because of) his distraction, Hamlet demonstrates remarkable skill in creating group homeostasis by effecting a balance between stabilizing and destabilizing elements. But the balance lasts only as long as Hamlet restrains himself from violent action.

Shakespeare shrewdly links the delay of violent revenge ("the basic *donnée* of the play" [Nevo 1972, 130]) to charismatic group homeosta- sis. Once the violence begins, however, with the killing of Polonius, Hamlet's relation to the dissipative structure of the Danish court starts to change. He becomes increasingly individuated from his group, and increasingly isolated. The shared experience which is Hamlet alters as the balance of nonequilibrium forces decays toward chaos. Inevitably, as the chaos deepens, the audience is drawn into the vortex of Ham- let's emotional and political isolation. But the center of the vortex is not the best vantage point for analysis and interpretation of the action, nor should isolation be regarded as a heroic norm in Hamlet's case. Indeed, to identify solely with the individuated Hamlet is tantamount to ignoring the effect of Hamlet's isolation on his charismatic group.

The available experiences of Hamlet bifurcate after the violence begins: on one side, that of audience or readers and on the other, that of the other characters. These experiences would seem easy enough to keep apart, but in fact Hamlet's overwhelming psychological pres- ence tends to marginalize all except transcendental human bonds, masking the vicissitudes of charisma and group function. (For exam- ple, most people would probably say that Hamlet's charisma remains the same or even increases throughout the play, which is patently untrue.) Therefore, to analyze the relation between individuation and group disintegration, as well as the effect of that relation on tragic dénouement, the experience of *Hamlet* the play must remain distinct from the shared experience of Hamlet the charismatic figure, this lat- ter experience being confined to the *dramatis personae*. Ruth Nevo, speaking of Shakespeare's dramaturgy, has characterized the play as a chain reaction of uncertainties "felt sometimes by Hamlet, some- times by the audience that is watching Hamlet, sometimes by the stage audience that is watching Hamlet, sometimes by all the watch- ers at once" (1972, 137). I would like to resist conflation of these dis- tinctive watchers and concentrate on Hamlet's stage audience. As much participants as watchers, the stage audience forms the charis- matic group at the center of which Hamlet performs a balancing act of stabilizing and destabilizing forces.

Some time ago John Holloway observed that "Hamlet pursues his course as revenger, scourge and minister, within a social group; but that group is not stable, it is itself disintegrating" (1961, 29). Holloway quotes G. Wilson Knight, who thirty years earlier had written, in regard to Hamlet's responsibility to avenge his father, "good cannot come of evil: it is seen that the sickness of [Hamlet's] soul further infects the state—his disintegration spreads out, disintegrating" (1930, 20). Knight does not mention Hamlet's social group, but his implication is that the prince's spreading disintegration itself causes the disintegration of a previously coherent entity of some sort. Knight's statement suggests that what Rosencrantz says of kingship generally can be applied to Hamlet's magnetic force at court, his delicate group relations:

> The cess of majesty
> Dies not alone, but like a gulf doth draw
> What's near it with it.
>
> (3.3.15–17)[1]

This is a political black hole theory, replete with "stinging irony," according to Holloway, because "Claudius is not the prop of the social weal" but "the very man who knocked that prop away" (1961, 31). The deeper irony of Rosencrantz's somewhat obsequious observation—it will be recalled that he is replying to Claudius's "commission" to accompany the mad Hamlet to England—is that the "cess of majesty" applies better to Old Hamlet on one hand and to his son on the other. Young Hamlet's election may have been blocked, but in the structure of the tragedy his charismatic hegemony has the far-reaching effect of majesty, its collapse palpably more threatening to the drama's social groupings than Claudius's removal. It is not necessary to be part of a politically informed Elizabethan audience, cognizant of both the Essex and the Mary Queen of Scots controversies in the background, to recognize Hamlet's rights and to perceive a superior element of *maiestas* in his attitudinizing. His power over the collective stability reflects his hegemonic charismatic authority. Consequently, the disintegration of Hamlet's management of collective relations, the breakdown of charismatic mutuality and interdependence, produces a Charybdislike gulf that "doth draw what's near it with it."

It can be difficult, however, to identify specific members of a charismatic group responsive to Hamlet. At times, in fact, all of the Danish court make up this group, and the young prince's authority creates (and eventually destroys) a collective expectancy which has a deceptively binding effect throughout the play. Hamlet is a curiously pivotal figure at the Danish court, even while he remains outside the daily routine of diplomacy and rule. His centrality reflects a unique charismatic claim, combining lineage rights with ambivalence about traditional symbols of ascendancy. Even if that ambivalence is a pose, Hamlet's negative status—not being a king and also not being an avenger—predicates a continual anticipation that he will manage to inherit Old Hamlet's mantle, thereby overthrowing the current regime. His every move after his return from Wittenberg is imbued with a noticeable antagonism to the norms of courtly decorum; every action he takes or refuses to take confirms his rebellious posture, from the black color of his clothing to his initial delay of revenge to his feigned madness. In this rebellion, most specifically in the restraint of action, Hamlet's charisma is manifest. His charismatic claim, by the very nature of court life, fosters and is fed by a mutuality of experience, an interdependent relationship not only with such prominent figures as Ophelia and Horatio but also with the faceless court members whose loyalty has recently switched from Old Hamlet to Claudius.

HAMLET'S CHARISMA

Hamlet's tragedy provides proof of the generational limits of pure charisma. The difficulty, as Shakespeare poses it in this play, lies in how Hamlet can harness the charismatic power of his predecessor without diluting his own power, particularly when the force and originality of his charisma depend to a degree on the rejection of that predecessor. To be sure, Hamlet is inconsistent in his attitude toward lineage charismatic claims. Despite his frank (if snide) opposition to the existing order, he never forms a dissident group nor does he assume the leadership of a distinct cohort. Moreover, he seems at critical times to plead the dynastic rights of a hereditary king, Denmark's so-called elective monarchy notwithstanding. Yet—and here the inconsistency is most pronounced—his charisma has a revolutionary force in confrontation both with his father's warrior code and with the defense of the status quo offered by Claudius and Gertrude (structurally it does not seem to matter that their status quo is freshly established). The effect of this inconsistency on Hamlet's intellectual equilibrium has been well documented. But its effect on his social authority has received less attention. The delimitation of Hamlet's charisma has suffered in consequence, so that many critics ignore Hamlet's group relations entirely while others imagine that he could out-Fortinbras Fortinbras. The reality of his effect on group function falls somewhere between those extremes.

Delimitation should begin at the beginnng, I think, with the establishment of the source of Hamlet's charisma. In the early acts, his charismatic authority combines generational resistance, dynastic outrage, and Davidic restraint of violence, all overlaid with the unique and compelling aura of a revolutionary intellectual in exile. But Hamlet's ambivalence toward his father is probably the predominant source of his charisma. It is an ambivalence both pragmatic and temperamental, originating in whatever repugnance first led Hamlet to become an exile and culminating in his tentativeness in regard to revenge. Harold Goddard suggested that Old Hamlet polarizes his son's feelings, representing two different fathers in young Hamlet's mind:

> One, his sun and the source of his inspiration, is the product of that idealization of the older generation by the younger which ensures the continuity and, in so far as it is justified, the uplifting of life. This father Hamlet worships. The other is a type of that authority and violence that the racial father always represents and that his own father as renowned warrior (pirate in the original version) specifically incarnates. This father, however unconsciously, Hamlet abhors. (1951, 1:346–47)[2]

In daily life this overarching dichotomy—generational versus racial fatherhood—would have played itself out in less obvious binarism. The more abstract elements would have been manifest in Old Hamlet's active participation as a father (in contrast merely to a father figure), a husband, a ruler, and a court figure. And in all likelihood it would have been at this social level that Hamlet's ambivalence first developed. His idealization and abhorrence (if we can call it that) after his father's death do not spring full-blown from his grief, but are products of long brooding on the charismatic experience of Old Hamlet. His extended sojourn in Germany should be seen as a voluntary exile from Denmark, an evasion of social and familial constraints as much as an intellectual venture.

Norman Austin notes that, in revising Saxo and Belleforest, "Shakespeare plays down the most blatant aspects of King Hamlet's piratical character" and "gives the old pirate a semblance of respectability . . . since the ghost takes the form of the old king as he was remembered by those completely submissive to his charisma" (1990, 157). Young Hamlet cannot be numbered among such a group. As his voluntary exile to Wittenberg implies, his opposition to his father antedates the play's action by many years. But that opposition is as profoundly a struggle for *original* authority as it is the clash of two different personality types and of two epochs, in which "Wittenberg—the University—is face to face with the heroic past" (Alexander 1955, 35). We should bear in mind Barbara Everett's point, in connection with Hamlet's advanced age for an undergraduate, that "the university is the characteristic anteroom or waiting-place for the life of mature years: the life of power" (1989, 19). If Hamlet was waiting, then he must have been waiting for his father's death. If he was waiting in Wittenberg—and not at court under his father's wing, as an acolyte—then perhaps his ambitions for authority failed to coincide with his father's idea of dynastic continuity.

In any case, there does not seem to have been much love lost between father and son while Old Hamlet was alive. Austin remarks that "through a play dominated by the image of the father, Hamlet never recalls a single gesture of his father's love"; concomitantly, Austin asks, "Does the ghost recall so much as one hour when father and son had enjoyed each other's company?" or "Do we hear one word . . . to indicate [the ghost's] interest in his son's well-being, or see one gesture that, by the broadest definition, could be construed as affection for the son whose love he commandeers to his own ends?" (1990, 170, 168, 162). These may seem anachronistically sentimental, even bourgeois, concerns, but they call attention to an emotional starkness at the personal level (contrast Yorick, the surrogate father figure). Hamlet idealizes and therefore depersonalizes his father— and his father's charisma as well. His resistance to Old Hamlet doubles as a resistance to the routinization of Old Hamlet's charismatic claim: a claim to warrior honor, violent revenge, and, most significantly, to utter obedience from young Hamlet, the putative follower.

Hamlet's temporizing allows him to hedge in regard to filial obedience. Delay serves as a pocket veto of his father's emblematic charismatic attributes, preventing Hamlet's absorption into his father's charismatic sphere. For as long as it lasts, this resistance provides Hamlet with his own charismatic claim, his own revolutionary disregard for routinized constraints. Moreover, if Hamlet's resistance to his father's authority nurtures his delay in executing the command to wreak vengeance, then the delay becomes a charismatic gesture in its own right. It reflects more than the tension between the older and the younger generations. It further reflects Hamlet's successful displacement of his father's overshadowing charisma with a new and antithetical charismatic claim.

In terms of charisma, however, the delay of revenge is not coterminous with Hamlet's resistance to his father. David Scott Kastan has suggested that the ghost "demands the radical identification of son with father that their undifferentiated name suggests," while "to deserve the name, at least as far as the ghost is concerned, is to be a revenger" (199). This may characterize the ghost's limited interests in his son. But Kastan concludes that "what differentiates *Hamlet* from the Ur-*Hamlet*, as well as what differentiates Hamlet from Old Hamlet, is that Shakespeare's prince can never fully credit the impulse to revenge" (1995, 199). This statement is less persuasive. There is no proof of the equation, no binding relation between Hamlet's troubled self-differentiation from his paternal imago and his attitude toward revenge. His delay has personal charismatic value, allowing him simultaneously to resist his father's authority and to foster a manageable dissipative structure at Elsinore. Thus his dilatoriness may have less to do with his unwillingness to "credit the impulse to revenge" than with his inner drive to differentiate himself from his father's charisma and, however instinctually, to establish his own original authority among a group of followers.

As is well known, Hamlet never says anything specifically against revenge, although his delay has often been taken as proof of his aversion. There is some justice in this assumption. Even if we accept that delay is a dramatic necessity of revenge tragedies (cf. Nevo 1972, 130), such plays, as James Calderwood observes, "do not normally make the hero himself the major obstacle, and they do not have him repeatedly announce that nothing impedes his revenge but himself" (1983, 27). Still, this is not to say that Hamlet necessarily has ethical scruples, whether as a sign of Christian conscience or of modern morality, nor that his reasons for delaying the revenge are available to his consciousness at all (cf. Crutwell 1963; Prosser 1967; Montano 1985, 226; Gottschalk 1972, 54–66; Goddard 1951, 1:346). The most we can really say, as William Kerrigan has observed, is that "Hamlet at some level resists the ghost," despite the transfer of power from one to the other by the end of the play (1994, 45). This resistance energizes Hamlet's charismatic presence against a background of unstable social and affective forces. But it is better to allow the resistance to remain value-free, a dynamic rather than a moral condition.

The prince's authority garners strength from the exploitation of unstable social forces—what Smith terms "far-from-equilibrium" systems. In the early acts he holds together a charismatic circle by resymbolizing the destabilized social structure in which he finds himself (especially after his conversation with the ghost). The resymbolization takes a number of forms. For instance, even Hamlet's objection to drinking has a charismatic importance, reorganizing the somewhat chaotic wassails of the Claudian court around a new symbol of ascetic authority. Horatio asks, "Is it a custom?" in regard to the flourish of trumpets, the celebratory cannon blasts, and the racket of the king's carousing. "Ay marry is't," answers Hamlet,

> But to my mind, though I am native here
> And to the manner born, it is a custom
> More honour'd in the breach than the observance.
> This heavy-headed revel east and west
> Makes us traduc'd and tax'd of other nations—
> They clepe us drunkards, and with swinish phrase

Soil our addition; and indeed it takes
From our achievements, though perform'd at height,
The pith and marrow of our attribute.

(1.4.12–22)

Introducing a political element, a form of dissent in fact, Hamlet at
the same time presents himself as a new kind of leader. He deliberately rejects the custom of his nation. This attitude is particularly
interesting in that the ghost's appearance interrupts his speech. There
seems little question that, although Hamlet is complaining about
Claudius in this scene, the complaints more properly are aimed at
prior rulers, Old Hamlet supplying the readiest example to Hamlet's
experience. Thus, just instants before Hamlet is to meet the ghost and
receive his portentous commands, he disparages the practice of ex-
kings and exhibits a revolutionary impulse to break the constraints of
custom. In other words, the ground for resistance is well-prepared
and thought-out, notably in terms of national pride—the kind of
preparation one might expect of a politically ambitious prince.

HAMLET AND HOMEOSTASIS

It makes little sense to discuss charisma except in terms of leadership.
But Hamlet's leadership can seem anomalous. At times he appears to
be a leader without followers, a charismatic ideal without imitators.
His presence in scene after scene both mesmerizes the members of his
stage audience and simultaneously repels them. This is because
Hamlet is caught between leading and following. Whether we call his
resistance to revenge a matter of Christian, Wittenbergian conscience
or a liberal-intellectual misinterpretation out of joint with the facts, as
Kerrigan suggests, there can be no doubt that Hamlet is on the horns
of a dilemma (Kerrigan 1994, 158n. 39; cf. Crutwell 1963, 184). He cannot freely follow the ghost's commands, nor can he confidently reject
them. This dilemma paralyzes him for a time, allowing him alter-
nately to manifest signs of charismatic leadership along with signs of
being led. In his resistance to being led, which is also a rejection of traditional authority and conventional expectation, Hamlet appears
most creative and original, most powerfully charismatic in the genuine sense.

Yet at different times Hamlet seems to satisfy contradictory charismatic criteria. He is at once an outsider at Elsinore and the consummate court insider around whom much attention swirls, "an
outsider-within" as Calderwood puts it (1983, 103). This ambiguous status bridges the dichotomous sociological conditions associated with charisma: "Charisma may . . . be characteristic of socially

marginal individuals, coming into society in the role of strangers, perhaps even legitimating their authority by virtue of this strangeness. But charisma may also be a trait of individuals located at the center of the institutional fabric in question, a power of 'radicalization' from within rather than challenge from without" (Berger 1963: 950). Hamlet fits both descriptions. He comes into the Claudian court pretentiously playing the role of moral stranger. He declares himself to be "more than kin, and less than kind" (1.2.65), the reluctant family member "too much in the sun" (1.2.67) whose strangeness legitimates his charismatic authority. But Hamlet also radicalizes the court from within. His pouting indignance in the early acts may give him the force of an outsider, but no court member can forget for long the rank and connectedness of the crown prince. As Laertes reminds the infatuated Ophelia, "His greatness weigh'd, his will is not his own. / For he himself is subject to his birth" (1.3.17–18).

The implication is that there are two Hamlets, the lover and the inevitable prince—the would-be royal outsider, an effigy of true human subjectivity, and the "subject" to royal birth. Perhaps, as Laertes thinks, Hamlet's outsider's posture has gulled the suggestible Ophelia into loving a counterfeit figure. On the other hand, it may be that Ophelia experiences the charismatic Hamlet more fully than Laertes, both in his role as marginal stranger and also as royal radicalizer. Perhaps we should see her as the court barometer of Hamlet's ambiguous charismatic presence, a sensitive instrument caught in a maelstrom. Swept up in the bifurcated Hamlet experience, she embodies the most profound and inexpressible metanoia of the stage audience, her disintegration twinned with that of group homeostasis.

The disintegration of group homeostasis, like Ophelia's sad ruin, results from Hamlet's fluctuating subjectivity, which by turns defines both a shared experience and a detached individuation that alienates his prospective followers. As a leader he fosters disorder, sometimes deliberately and sometimes inadvertantly, and his shifting identities confound the best efforts of the stage audience to idealize him. What, after all, is the expectation of the court in regard to Hamlet? This question is rarely asked, yet the answer is critical to understanding group function in the play. If Gertrude's marriage seems hasty and incestuous to Hamlet, would it not seem so to the others as well? Similarly, if Hamlet feels that Claudius has come between the election and his hopes, then the court no doubt suspects the same. And wouldn't they expect some reaction from the crown prince? Hamlet's refusal to act organizes those expectations, creating a manipulable bond for as long as the question of his reaction remains unanswered.

The court and indeed the populace all function as Hamlet's charismatic group, bound in an intersubjective structure by the anticipation of Hamlet's action.

The killing of Polonius dispells the anticipation, however, and deflates Hamlet's symbolic idealization, not so much because he uses violence but because he does not take appropriate credit for it. He issues no challenge behind which his partisans might rally, nor does he satisfy the court's anticipation of his reaction. He kills and, like a half-hearted criminal, tries to hide the body. The hiding-place sequence is farcical—"if indeed you find him not within this month, you shall nose him as you go up the stairs into the lobby" (4.3.35–36)—a ridiculous episode at once trivializing Hamlet's secret mission and deflating the anticipatory structure of his charismatic authority.

Claudius, on the other hand, is a more astute politician than his nephew. He recognizes the potential charismatic force of Polonius's murder, although he does not seem to realize that Hamlet is incapable of using it to his political advantage. Claudius fears that Hamlet could portray the murder as an indication of fiery purpose, in which case any punishment meted out by the king would heighten the polarization between the prince and his uncle, very likely making a martyr out of the young murderer. With these eventualities in mind, I think, Claudius calls together his closest advisors and notes that, despite the danger of letting Hamlet run loose, he must not "put the strong law on him" (4.3.3). His justification for holding back, he claims, is Hamlet's popularity:

> He's lov'd of the distracted multitude,
> Who like not in their judgment but their eyes,
> And where 'tis so, th' offender's scourge is weigh'd,
> But never the offence.
>
> (4.3.4–7)

Ostensibly sending Hamlet away to avoid executing him, Claudius in fact plans to have him killed in England. His fear, he says, is that the multitude love Hamlet and will object to his execution without giving due consideration to its justice. This is another way of saying that Hamlet has charismatic power with the populace and that their bond to him is irrational—which is the meaning of "distracted"—and therefore dangerous to Claudius' rulership. Claudius fears revolution at this juncture just as much as he worries about his own exposure as a murderer. Fortuitously for him, by concealing Hamlet's death from the multitude he would also conceal his own homicidal act—a fact on which Hamlet does not have the tactical attentiveness to capitalize.

I suggested earlier that Hamlet's charisma had the characteristics of Davidic restraint. I was referring in particular to the David of 1 Samuel who, like the Danish prince, feigns madness and spares a helpless enemy. David and, to a degree, Hamlet are both anointed crown princes, but both refuse at first to kill the reigning monarch; in fact, David never kills King Saul. Although Hamlet eventually kills Claudius in retaliation for both his father's and his mother's murders, his prior resistance to that regicide bears an interesting relation to David's sparing of Saul. As Gene Edward Veith has noted, the relation is especially provocative if we compare David in the cave at Engedi to Hamlet in the chapel scene (1980, 74–75). In the biblical story David flees with his men to the wilderness of Engedi, but Saul "toke thre thousand chosen men out of all Israél, and went to seke Dauid and his men vpon the rockes *among* the wilde goates" (1 Samuel 24:3). A strange encounter occurs inside one of the caves:

> And he came to the shepecoates by the way where there was a caue and Saúl went in to do his easement: and Dauid and his men sate in the inward partes of the caue.
>
> And the men of Dauid said vnto him, Se, the day is come, whereof the Lord said vnto thee, Beholde, I wil deliuer thine enemie into thine hand, and thou shalt do to him as it shal seme good to thee. Then Dauid arose and cut of the lappe of Sauls garment priuely.
>
> And afterward Dauid was touched in his heart, because he had cut of the lappe which was on Sauls *garment*.
>
> And he said vnto his men, The Lord kepe me from doing that thing vnto my master the Lords Anointed, to lay mine hand vpon him: for he is the Anointed of the Lord.
>
> So Dauid ouercame his seruants with these words, and suffred them not to arise against Saúl: so Saúl rose vp out of the caue and went away.
>
> (1 Samuel 24:1–8)

The scene is reminiscent of Hamlet and Claudius in the chapel, but David's reluctance is more John of Gaunt's than Hamlet's. While David and his men, hidden in the dark recesses of the cave, sit and watch Saul "do his easement" (move his bowels, presumably), David slips over to cut a swatch from Saul's garment. This small act proves to David what his men have said, that the Lord has delivered his enemy into his hands—and the swatch will later prove the same to Saul, who embraces David when he realizes that he has been spared. But first David must convince his men not to strike down their pursuer in the cave. He accomplishes this extraordinary feat by assuring them that his unwillingness to kill Saul—what Veith refers to as David's "radical forbearance" (1980, 80)—has divine sanction.

David's leadership depends on his production of mild disorder. In refusing to kill his enemy despite what seems to be the ideal tactical opportunity, he destabilizes expectations regarding his next move and prepares the ground for his charismatic intervention as a bearer of supernatural knowledge. He buttresses his act of radical forbearance by seizing the role of *sacer interpres*, and he confidently reads a heavenly sign in his cutting of the garment: "The Lord kepe me from doing that thing vnto my master the Lords Anointed," he announces, referring by "that thing" to using his knife on the king. He thus mystifies his forbearance, confirming the divine auspices of his leadership. By means of a charismatic reversal the warrior leader now wields an ascetic authority, and he is able to organize the mild disorder of his men's disturbed expectations around a new symbol of divine mission. The Geneva Bible translation says that David "ouercame his seruants," and I think it is fair to conclude that this "overcoming" constitutes an example of charismatic leadership, a shared experience of David's uniqueness that ultimately enthralls the men in the cave. David's behavior has an irrational, even revolutionary quality in the context of the bloody strife with Saul. It is truly a radicalizing gesture; and through such gestures David continues to foster a nonequilibrium dynamic among his followers and to maintain the ascendancy of his charismatic claim.

Hamlet too demonstrates a radical forbearance when presented with a chance to kill his royal enemy; and, for as long as his forbearance lasts, he also protects his charismatic claim. But his forbearance is shortlived, and he thwarts the irrational radicalizing impulse of his resistance to his father's code with rationalizations for revenge. Whereas David spares Saul for the sake of mercy, Hamlet spares Claudius "not from mercy, but from a most chilling malice" (Veith 1980, 74). Sword drawn, he reasons himself out of murdering his uncle at prayer:

> A villain kills my father, and for that
> I, his sole son, do this same villain send
> To heaven.
> Why, this is hire and salary, not revenge.

> (3.4.76–79)

Hamlet's rationalization for forbearance indeed reflects a profound hostility, a putative wish to guarantee Claudius's postmortem suffering. Mere earthly death, it would seem, does not satisfy the scourge and minister. Although Hamlet prolongs his resistance to revenge for a few moments by not killing Claudius, his rationalizing indicates the extent to which he acts with dispassion and calculation where the subject of revenge is concerned.

REVENGE AND RATIONALIZATION

Throughout *Hamlet*, revenge encourages conduct inimical both to charismatic authority and to the collective dynamic. Not only Hamlet but also Laertes neutralizes his charismatic claim by abandoning irrational revolutionary conduct for the dispassion and calculation of personal revenge. Of course Laertes' charisma does not depend on radical forbearance, but, to the contrary, on a storming violence. He returns to England accompanied by followers, a man with a genuinely revolutionary mission. And although he is supposedly "in secret come from France" (4.5.88), his return captures the public imagination as well as alarming the court in advance of his arrival. Claudius is worried both about "the people muddied, /Thick and unwholesome in their thoughts and whispers /For good Polonius' death" (4.5.81–83) and about the possibility that Laertes will hold him responsible for the old man's death (90–94). The messenger's speech heightens the sense of anxiety in the scene. "Save yourself, my lord," he says to Claudius,

> The ocean, overpeering of his list,
> Eats not the flats with more impetuous haste
> Than young Laertes, in a riotous head,
> O'erbears your officers. The rabble call him lord,
> And, as the world were now but to begin,
> Antiquity forgot, custom not known—
> The ratifiers and props of every word—
> They cry "Choose we! Laertes shall be king."
> Caps, hands, and tongues applaud it to the clouds,
> "Laertes shall be king, Laertes king."
>
> (4.5.98–108)

The speech describes a charismatic figure in action, down to the remarkably subtle detail of "Antiquity forgot, custom not known—/ The ratifiers and props of every word." This qualification confirms precisely what Weber means when he says that charisma and tradition are antithetical forms of authority. Laertes, in his impetuosity and overbearing physical force, rejects the form of authority represented by Claudius and the Switzers—his brief charismatic movement "forgets" antiquity and ignores custom. This kind of conduct, in addition to its irrationality in the present social context, also breaks the everyday routine constraints imposed on Danish subjects. Thus Laertes is for the moment more than an impassioned individual. He has become the center of a shared group experience of unique authority, innovation, and finally revolution—"Choose we! Laertes shall be king."

But the movement falters as a result of Laertes' individuation from the group. He comes violently into the castle—"The doors are broke," remarks the king (4.5.111)—but immediately, and ill-advisedly, separates himself from his followers. Significantly, Shakespeare records the exchange between them (after the stage direction "*Enter* Laertes *with* Followers"):

Laer. Where is the king?—Sirs, stand you all without.

Followers. No, let's come in.

Laer. I pray you give me leave.

Followers. We will, we will.

Laer. I thank you. Keep the door.

(4.5.112)

Although these lines seem innocuous, they in fact have ominous implications for Laertes' authority over Claudius. The physical separation of the followers from their leader, which the group instinctively resists, anticipates both the disintegration of the rebellion and the isolation and destruction of Laertes himself.

Claudius clearly recognizes the importance of isolating Laertes. He asks, not without cunning, "What is the cause, Laertes, / That thy rebellion looks so giant-like?" (4.5.120–21), the inference being that the situation calls for solitary rather than group action. Any king would protect himself in this way if he could, but Claudius demonstrates particular skill in reducing Laertes' rebellion to a circumscribed personal plot for revenge. He tells Laertes that the "general gender" have great love for Hamlet, though in fact we have already witnessed (4.5.102ff) that the "rabble" have switched allegiances and now want Laertes to be king. It would seem that Hamlet has been replaced since his departure—or perhaps since his murder of Polonius. But Claudius does not acknowledge the shift. Instead, as when talking to his advisors, he uses Hamlet's erstwhile popularity to justify not having punished the prince for Polonius's murder. This is an astute rhetorical tactic, at once refocusing Laertes' anger on Hamlet alone (rather than on the king's authority) and also deflating the group imperative of Laertes' return. The irrelevance of group function to personal revenge appears with sudden clarity. And there is a foretaste of tragedy in Laertes' deterioration from charismatic revolutionary leader to revenge conspirator, a nearly absurd decline from public, Bolingbrokean outrage to the perverse, secretive calculations of a Vindice or an Orgilus. The meanness of participating in a murderous conspiracy, unbating and poisoning the sword, trivializes the authority Laertes commands in the messenger's speech, just before he bursts through the doors with his band of followers. As with Hamlet, the dispassion and calculation of revenge stifle the irrational element of Laertes' group appeal. Willing as he might be to cut Hamlet's throat in a church (4.7.125)—a prime example of "antiquity forgot, custom not known"—his revolutionary charismatic force is neutralized by Claudius's rationalizations regarding revenge.

Laertes' failure as a group leader sheds light on Hamlet's predicament. Revenge and its rationalizations destroy Hamlet's forbearance, thereby undermining the basis of his mystery and authority. The killing of Polonius strips Hamlet of his Davidic aura, and he sacrifices his radical forbearance to resolve the ethical conflict he has felt between conscience and "the name of action." Just as Laertes, in an instant, switches from rebel leader to individuated conspirator, Hamlet, when he kills, instantly alters his relation to the court members who have been held in suspense anticipating his response to Claudius. Whereas David maintained his charismatic hegemony by resisting retaliation of any kind, thus destabilizing expectations in order to manage the resulting nonequilibrium of his social group, Hamlet negates the "nonequilibrium" bond he—chiefly by means of his forbearance—has already established at court.

Hamlet's violence reflects a highly rationalized choice, and in all likelihood it would satisfy rather than confound the expectations of the court (although Polonius might seem an odd target). We should not mistake Hamlet's harried emotional state for the irrational social conduct inherent in acts of charismatic leadership. Gertrude's presence makes Hamlet seem irrational in the closet scene, but he is actually more impassioned than irrational in regard to social authority and conventional moral imperatives. Indeed, his first injunction to his mother is both rational and rather sternly moralistic:

Come, come, and sit you down. You shall not budge.
You go not till I set you up in a glass
Where you may see the inmost part of you.

(3.4.19–21)

To "set [her] up in a glass" is only a figure of speech; he does not plan to drag a mirror into the room. Rather, he will act as a mirror himself and explicate her behavior, ruthlessly parsing her "inmost" parts. He is angry and upset, but also coldly rational in his method. No doubt the sheer extravagance of his emotions blurs the character of the killing to follow. And Hamlet's surprise at finding anyone at all behind the arras makes his reaction seem impulsive.

But the impulsiveness can be misleading. In actuality, Hamlet's murderous action results from a lengthy calculation, as well as his desire to fulfil a command from the grave. The prince after all thinks Polonius is the king: "I took thee for thy better," he says to the old man's corpse (3.4.32). The sudden thrust through the arras is more than a consequence of Hamlet's flaring ire, ignited by the confirmation of the Mousetrap. It is also the culmination of months of plotting, maneuvering, weighing, and internal argument, added to the proximate calculation that the king, no longer at prayer, is ripe for slaughter. Despite the apparent spontaneity of Hamlet's sword thrust, the murder is predicated on laboriously rationalized motives. It is consummate vengeance, and it marks what Calderwood has termed the shift from "Hamlet the complex individual into that generic entity, Hamlet the revenger" (1983, 105). That he kills the wrong man, and that no vengeance is served by dispatching Polonius, underscores the tragic misdirection of Hamlet's violence. The killing represents a signal moment of *hamartia*, which in Greek drama tends to mean mistaken identity and which is also a term derived from the word for missing the mark in archery.

Ironically, the replacement of the complex individual by the generic entity also brings on Hamlet's individuation from his group of followers. Appearances to the contrary, the entire closet scene serves to reunite Hamlet with his parents, thus stifling the rebellious son and unconventional political aspirant. Hamlet allows himself to be reintegrated into the traditional structure of authority: he abandons his charismatic delay and accepts his lineage responsibility to avenge his father. This rationalized acceptance causes the emptying-out of Hamlet's personal charismatic claim. Although his individuality might have seemed paramount before the killing, it is in fact afterward that Hamlet loses his group orientation. His restraint, or radical forbearance—or perhaps simply the mystery of his nonaction—had bound the stage audience to him as a charismatic group, in the same way that David's restraint in Engedi binds his followers to him. The revolutionary stance at Elsinore is the passive one, but after killing Polonius Hamlet no longer can count on that particular charisma of broken conventions and shattered constraints. If, as a revenger, he becomes a generic entity, then he also becomes a predictable genealogical one. The pocket veto of his father's warrior code disappears in the thrust of his sword.

That sword thrust also reveals the narrow limits of Hamlet's irrational imagination as it had been manifest in his shortlived defiance of convention. He fails in the end to radicalize the Danish court largely because he is unable to shrug off the rational social constraints of his milieu: dynastic rights, warrior honor, filial (or familial) codes of vengeance, and all the other accoutrements of a depersonalized charismatic claim.[3] When Hamlet suppresses his personal emotions and obeys the ghost, subordinating his own charismatic claim to that of his father's and in effect accepting revenge as a routinized condition of lineage charisma, he inevitably abandons his personal authority over the dissipative structure of the Claudian court.

As we have seen, that authority rests on Hamlet's ability in the early acts to balance the stabilizing expectations of court members against his destabilizing mystification of his actions. Hamlet's charismatic symbols, the idealizations with which group members instinctively identify, derive from this resistance to expectations. As soon as Hamlet's actions coincide with the expectations of the court, as soon as Hamlet behaves like a typically offended crown prince outraged by the affront to his lineage privilege, he loses his centrality as a charismatic leader. Because of the way he mismanages the violence, his actions separate him both from group members and from the symbols of his charismatic claim.

Consequently, after the killing of Polonius Hamlet becomes Claudius's enemy, a threat to the court, and a liability to his friends. This is exactly as it should be, and even as it should have been from the beginning of the play, if Hamlet were to be taken as his father's son. But the organizing charismatic ideal of *Hamlet* is that Hamlet is not his father's son. Having dedicated his thirty years to pursuits and interests incompatible with the patriarchal warrior code, Hamlet had positioned himself to resist absorption into the traditional authority of Denmark. His delay, fleeting as it may be, reflects his skill in balancing his rebelliousness against the putative status quo. His authority derives from and controls the nonequilibrium system that his very presence at court brings about. And this system functions as long as he maintains his radical forbearance. But the catastrophe unfolds when the system breaks down, when Hamlet inadvertently separates himself from the very symbols of resistance he himself *charismatically* fostered in his first months in Denmark. Hamlet's neglect of those symbols and his consequent individuation from potential group members does indeed cause a spreading disintegration at court, as Knight and Holloway suggest. But it is not so much that Hamlet's "soul . . . infects the state" as that he misconstrues and abandons the symbolic restraint of action by which he, like David at Engedi, first "ouercame his seruants."

Othello

In the Introduction I suggest that, for charismatic protagonists, tragedy might be seen as a fall into ordinary social life from the heights of those powerful abstractions by which cultures mythicize authority. Othello's fate is an excellent example of this kind of fall. He is (or, better yet, was once) the bearer of impeccable charismatic credentials: an utterly unique, physically superior martial hero, racially exotic, without debt to traditional or bureaucratic authority for his power, who maintains his ascendancy among his followers by adherence to such charismatic ideals as honor, reputation, and magnanimity. Othello has the virtues of a tamed Tamburlaine, and both his person and his legend inspire belief in his supernatural endowment (cf. McAlindon 1991, 134). Stephen Greenblatt once remarked that what the sociologist Daniel Lerner calls "empathy" Shakespeare calls "Iago" (1980, 225). In a similar vein we might note that what Weber calls "pure charisma" Shakespeare calls "Othello."

But let me hasten to add that I am not suggesting the play is predominantly about charisma or group homeostasis. Othello is about sexual jealousy if it is about any one subject. Nevertheless I think that by recognizing the sudden changes in Othello's charisma and in the dynamic of his charismatic group we can experience more fully the way in which his jealousy unfolds and becomes dangerous. Moreover—and this in itself might be worth the candle—an analysis of shifting charismatic authority sheds some new light on Iago's inscrutable hostility toward Desdemona.

Othello's tragic failure reveals the central paradox of charismatic group function: emphasis on a charismatic group ideal tends to destroy the individuality of the human being at the group's center. In this context Othello's wooing of Desdemona might be seen as an attempt to assert his individuality and to redefine himself apart from his followers. But, just as the group ideal is inimical to individual agency, the assertion of individuality can be disastrous, too, because the autonomy of a group leader tends to destroy the group ideal. In Othello this latter tendency presents a threat to which Iago seems particularly sensitive. Othello's individuation through marriage, which may allow him to fulfill himself as a human being while perhaps providing a form of traditional legitimation, also isolates him from his group. His isolation causes both the group's disintegration and his own catastrophic fall into social life from the symbolically laden heights of charismatic generalship.

MARRIAGE AND GROUP METANOIA

The play opens with Iago's plans for betrayal, suggesting that by the time we meet the Moor the lineaments of his pure charismatic appeal have already shifted and his status as a leader has already changed for the worse. It is not too farfetched to conclude that a significant change in charismatic status has been brought on by Othello's marriage. By seeking a tie to Desdemona Othello has disturbed the aim-inhibited libidinal ties that bound his army group together (cf. McIntosh 1970, 905, 911). A proof of this disturbance might be that although the tie to Desdemona is (in theory) libidinally *un*inhibited, the group conspires to inhibit Othello's libidinal aim, interrupting his lovemaking both on the wedding night and again when the brawl breaks out on Cyprus. By marrying, Othello has altered and disturbed the charismatic symbols associated with his authority, and consequently the mode in which his followers participate in those integral symbols has also begun to change (cf. Eisenstadt 1968, xlv–xlvi).

We can infer from Othello's early speech that his charisma in fact has been diluted by the marriage. At the moment that he achieves a new and higher class status, he effectively lessens the force of his personal charisma. Replying to Iago's report of Brabantio's angry response to news of the secret marriage, Othello defends his love for his new wife:

> for know, Iago,
> But that I love the gentle Desdemona,
> I would not my unhoused free condition
> Put into circumscription and confine
> For the sea's worth.
>
> (1.2.24–28)[4]

The word "unhoused," glossed by most commentators as "unconfined" or "uncircumscribed," also can refer to Othello's being without an aristocratic house or lineage before marrying "gentle" Desdemona.[5] Yet, in contrast to Othello's own implicit claim, his marriage was not entirely a matter of his own will. As Peter Stallybrass has shown, Othello's status begins to change precisely because his role as master of his own fate is reduced by his future wife's aggressiveness: "Desdemona is portrayed not as passive beloved but as 'half the wooer'" (I.iii.176). Desdemona's active choice is the seal on Othello's incorporation as Venetian and on his repudiation of the 'unhoused, free condition'" (1986, 136). The term "incorporation" should remind us of Kantorowicz's category of the corporate body, the union of the king with his subjects; in Othello's case, his union is with the lineage of Brabantio, an incorporation that separates him from his charismatic claim. In Weberian terms, his becoming housed constitutes a diminution of his pure charisma, his magical and supreme otherness—whether we take "housed" in the solely domestic sense or in the sense of being absorbed into the ranks of traditional authority (recall that Desdemona's father, Brabantio, is a senator in Venice). Unwittingly Othello becomes the victim of a compromise with the constraints of less pure forms of charisma.

As if to emphasize what is being sacrificed, however, moments later in the same scene Shakespeare provides a demonstration of Othello's charismatic force. As it turns out, this demonstration is his swan song, the last time in the play he and his men act as a group in support of Othello's charismatic mission. Challenged by Brabantio and a ragtag bunch of minions, Othello utters the deservedly celebrated line, "Keep up your bright swords, for the dew will rust 'em" (1.2.59). To all appearance his superhuman presence is enough of a threat to freeze the aggressors in midaction. But perhaps there is more to Othello's power in this scene than individual force. Without trivializing the sublimity of the line, it should be noted that Othello has little to fear in the challenge, and that his warning can apply to the uneven match as well as to his own formidable strength. His threat carries especial force because it expresses the collective will of his group, a homogeneity of intent for the moment unaffected by Iago's self-solicitousness. Authority and obedience are mutually solicitous in defense of honor, and, at this early juncture, the group honor remains utterly bound to Othello's personal honor, to his "prestige" (cf. Freud 1960, 17–18).

The result of this collective will to fight can be nothing short of awesome under the circumstances. Consider the two sides in the brawl: Othello, Cassio, and Iago have all three drawn their swords on Brabantio, Roderigo, and a few servants, which is to say that three professional soldiers—indeed, the three highest-ranking soldiers in the Venetian army—have risen to an impulsive challenge from a middle-aged senator, a silly gallant, and whomever (of his household?) Brabantio could gather up in the middle of the night. Cassio and Iago may not be Theridamas and Usumcasanes, but their superiority to their opponents is obvious. Taking their stand with their general,

Cassio and Iago are suddenly in revolt against Brabantio, who, as a member of the Venetian governing council, is officially their civil head. This is more than simply military discipline. It constitutes voluntary group affirmation, a moment of homeostasis in a nonequilibrium situation. The charismatic unity of Othello and his officers presents an overwhelming opposition to the feeble coalition of Brabantio's people. Othello's threat has a thrilling veracity when we contrast one group with the other, when we see an energized charismatic band facing a hastily assembled group without emotional links. The power of Othello's threat—maybe even the possibility of his uttering it without overweening pride—depends on the presence of his charismatic group. The libidinal ties which he thinks are intact (and which the reader knows are breaking down) furnish him with physical support against the challenge, as well as with the psychodynamic latitude to lead.

Significantly, the proof of Othello's charismatic generalship lies in his resistance to violence, as his next gesture in the scene confirms. Rather than allow Cassio and Iago to fight Brabantio's men, Othello agrees to be taken:

> Were it my cue to fight, I should have known it,
> Without a prompter; where will you that I go,
> And answer this your charge?
>
> (1.2.83–85)

Such passivity is unexpected and therefore revolutionary in the narrow sphere of the play's social action; by such small revolutions a charismatic claim is sustained. Othello's sense of his own power is uncanny, and his self-denial is sublime. The ascetic reversal of unexpected passivity reorganizes the unstable forces at play in the interaction: Othello's charismatic presence becomes the sole guarantor of continued stability. The almost palpable self-denial enhances our awe of Othello's strength, in the same way that the asceticism of charismatic orders of monks deepens our appreciation of their human appetites. Typically, Othello also eschews any element of theatricality in his conduct, as his scorn for the prompter indicates. Despite all doubts to the contrary, such as those fueled by the knowledge that Othello is already "housed," he dominates this scene as a charismatic, and his domination depends entirely on his intuition to break the everyday constraints of the code of honor by remaining passive.[6]

More than his raw power, Othello's self-restraint in the encounter proves his pure charismatic claim, creating, in a few lines, a gifted leader from a fuming colossus. Given the unnevenness of the sides, one supposes that the soldiers are about to make short bloody work of their opponents when Othello unexpectedly decides not to fight. Although the dispute is a matter of personal honor rather than a national cause, Othello nevertheless dominates as a general, as if to remind us that charismatic criteria, such as honor, form the basis of his power to command. Moreover, in contrast to his coming distortions of honor ("An honourable murderer, if you will: /For nought did I in hate but all in honour" [5.2.295–96]), Othello responds circumspectly, dispassionately, and without the slightest indignation that such lowly physical specimens should dare to challenge him. One need only imagine, say, Bussy D'Ambois, or for that matter, Hamlet, in a similar situation: there would be a good deal of *flyting* followed by bloodshed. Othello, on the other hand, seems to have nothing to prove. At this point in the play, in Nevo's words, he has an "unflinching sense of his own worth" (1972, 185; cf. Adamson 1980, 116)

The scene turns on Othello's manipulation of the loyalty and shared dissent of his troops, recalling Paul's manipulation of the dissenters at Corinth. Of course, Othello is deluded in trusting the health of the aim-inhibited libidinal ties between him and his men, not only because the two-faced Iago has begun to plot against him but also because his marriage has altered the purer form of charisma with which he previously had dominated the group. Still, his delusion regarding the group's integrity and his ignorance of its inward metanoia permit him in this scene to give the play's only demonstration of his charismatic generalship in action. His charisma and the charismatic symbols of his power are synchronized. The homeostasis of Othello's band depends on the threat of sudden chaos and dissolution, a balance of destabilizing expressions of power. At his most charismatic, Othello controls the disorder skillfully, retaining his power and his men's bond to him while evading the absolutism of traditional order which would rob him of his exceptional stature. His manipulative gesture serves to shore up his command by advancing a newly dissipative structure, while at the same time he manages to repress any (overt) dissent from within the ranks.

The irony of the encounter, however, is that Othello's charismatic accomplishment might easily be construed as a sign of nascent uxoriousness. Personal honor aside, the Moor can hardly allow his father-in-law to be killed on his wedding night. His effort to preserve the old senator ultimately undermines his own antitraditional authority, despite its charismatic execution. Othello is in a bind, whether he knows it or not: he now must divide his authority to satisfy the countervailing needs of his army group and, simultaneously, of his lineage group. Insofar as these groups represent antithetical forms of authority, Othello would have little choice but to effect a compromise between charisma and tradition, in the manner of Bolingbroke, for example. Unfortunately, neither group accepts Othello's leadership. The senator rejects the idea outright, while the soldiers, through disobedience and betrayal, ruinously withdraw from group membership.

OTHELLO'S ARM, OR DISCIPLINE AND DISMEMBERMENT

Without ignoring the murder of Desdemona, we might connect the catastrophe of the play to Othello's inadvertant detachment of his personal power from the group bond. His individuation as a married man leads to the disintegration of his charismatic band. The newly "housed" Moor is already a man whose strength of mission has faltered. Consequently the play does not explicitly trace the development of Othello's loss of charisma. Rather, Shakespeare uses the subsequent acts to pull away a series of veils, in turn revealing what has always (in the time period of the plot) been true: Othello has compromised his charismatic status by marrying Desdemona.[7]

That Othello is not aware of his compromised status is amply clear throughout the play—and inexpressibly redolent of pathos. He argues:

> I fetch my life and being
> From men of royal siege, and my demerits
> May speak unbonneted to as proud a fortune
> As this that I have reach'd.
>
> (1.2.21–24)[8]

Othello's accomplishments, in the discourse of meritocracy which undergirds his assertion, give him parity with the house of Brabantio, justifying the fate he has attained (and probably striven for). But Othello's blindness is telling. True, he may be worthy of Desdemona's social background as a result of his services to the signiory. But in claiming parity with traditional authority (represented by both the aristocratic Brabantio and his own royal ancestors), rather than recognizing his own revolutionary or charismatic superiority to traditional power, Othello has allowed the traditional force of class domination—and perhaps racial domination as well—to stifle his pure charismatic claim. Because this irony remains hidden to him, one of the more excruciating aspects of the action is the ever-widening gap between Othello's mistaken belief in himself as intact and the observer's suspicion that his charismatic force is ebbing and he is permanently and irrevocably altered.

The breakdown of Othello's band of officers, which begins to occur in the first act, anticipates the loss of power which Othello is last to recognize in himself. By the time he reaches Cyprus his grip has definitely loosened. Iago and Cassio, who are emblematic of Othello's followers, turn out to be monumental liabilities. One gets drunk on watch in a foreign port during wartime—perhaps the most serious breach a soldier can commit[9]—and the other, a traitor to his general, is as *other* as a human being can be. Even Montano, the ex-governor now attached to Othello's command, cannot resist the call to defend his personal honor in a brawl, against all the rules of military discipline. The result of these deviations is a fragmenting of group membership, a dismembering of the charismatic body. Figuratively, this is an example of *sparagmos*, the frenzied climax of Dionysian tragedy— a dismemberment perhaps linked in Shakespeare's imagination to the destruction of the "one body" of Christ.

Othello's separation from his charismatic band is subtle at first because it is punctuatated by powerful, charismatic gestures. That such gestures are vestigial, that Othello's charisma is all but moribund, remains temporarily cloaked behind the pomp and occasion of the Cyprus campaign. One must glance away from Othello himself and resist the vortex of his jealousy to recognize the change in his charismatic status. Cassio provides a useful alternative to Othello's perspective, serving as an on-stage model of what Maynard Mack refers to as engagement and detachment, the two psychological states whose fluctuations account for "most of the transactions that take place between an audience and a play" (1993, 13). Cassio's single-minded sense of the libidinal ties that link him to Othello, and his pain in their dissolution, provide a corrective both to Othello's self-contradictory attitude regarding charisma and military discipline and to Iago's deliberate obfuscations of charismatic duty (as when in act 2 he derides reputation).

The cashiering of Cassio is the first overt sign of Othello's waning charismatic influence. It is bitterly ironic that Othello should expose the weakness of his charisma in a justifiably strict act of military discipline. But the time is out of joint and Othello's attempts at discipline are misguided, chiefly because he is unable on Cyprus to balance his personal charismatic power with the rational components of military discipline. Weber notes that "the most irresistible force is *rational discipline,* which eradicates not only personal charisma but stratification by status groups" (1978, 2:1149). Discipline is impersonal, while charisma depends on personal devotion to a leader. It is certainly possible, and even necessary, for status groups like Othello's officers to adopt strict discipline—Napoleon, for example, created a large and enduring organization to complement his charismatic mission. But Othello has sacrificed his pure charismatic status by the time he reaches Cyprus. And his entire exchange with Cassio in 2.3 communicates a contradictory message.

To start, he urges Cassio to perform well on his watch, not for the sake of maintaining strict discipline but for the sake of honor—honor being a measure of charismatic status: "Good Michael, look you to the guard tonight: /Let's teach ourselves the honourable stop, /Not to outsport discretion" (2.3.1–3). Yet when Cassio fails to learn the "honourable stop" Othello punishes him as an officer rather than as a member of a charismatic group. Jane Adamson sees the scene as a conflict between the personal and the professional, pointing out that Othello, while justifiably angry with his lieutenant, is torn between "real fondness of Cassio, and his determination not to let his personal affection and sense of disappointment overrule his judgment as a soldier, which dictates that the culprit must be sacked, not excused" (1980, 55). While I generally agree, I would add that sacking is itself a sign of compromise with more inspired forms of judgment (cf. Weber 1978, 2:1115). Just imagine, in contrast, how Tamburlaine might have dealt with Cassio's disobedience. Indeed, Othello threatens a Tamburlainian response, claiming to be on the verge of violence:

> Now by heaven
> My blood begins my safer guides to rule,
> And passion having my best judgement collied
> Assays to lead the way. Zounds, if I stir,
> Or do but lift this arm, the best of you
> Shall sink in my rebuke.
>
> (2.3.195–200)

Perhaps he should have lifted his arm. The control of passion reveals the extent to which Othello now represses the irrational component of his power. The cashiering of Cassio signals a decline in power, a recourse to depersonalized formulae, which, ironically, Desdemona tries to circumvent by an appeal to personal rather than professional assessment.

As if in response to that personal appeal, Othello does not allow himself to act violently until he strikes Desdemona in front of

Lodovico. From the perspective of charismatic leadership, one might argue that Othello does to Desdemona in act 4 what he should have done to Cassio in act 2—but of course striking Desdemona cannot have the same effect, since she is not a group member. Moreover, the repression of the irrational component in the exchange with Cassio does not constitute a revolutionary self-denial on Othello's part, as does his passivity in 2.1 when he allows Brabantio to arrest him. To the contrary, Othello's attempt to impose military discipline reveals his new association with traditional, rather than charismatic, forms of authority.

Othello's reference to his arm in 2.3 ("if I stir, /Or do but lift this arm") recalls what we must suppose to have been an earlier cohesion of charisma and military discipline. It also resonates with his earlier mention of the same bodily member in his defense before the duke:

> Rude am I in my speech,
> And little blest with the set phrase of peace,
> For since these arms of mine had seven years' pith
> Till now some nine moons wasted, they have us'd
> Their dearest action in the tented field.
>
> (1.3.81–85)

The "pith" of his arms is a measure of the precocious manliness of his boyish body. *Pith* means *strength* or *vigor* in this passage, but, as Martin Elliott notes, "with perhaps some nuance, lingering from its Old English meaning of 'pith of a tree or vegetable,' of 'central' or 'essential'" (1988, 62). Primarily a boast regarding the early and ongoing strength of Othello's sword arm, the speech links physical action to the very core of Othello's being. In other words—in case we doubted the fact—Othello *is* his sword arm (and the pith of the sword arm is essence of Othello). The "arms" of Othello's body, through the word's double sense, can also be the arms he wields as a soldier. His sword arm and his sword merge, and the site of Othello's charismatic power is revealed to be a miraculous union of his natural body and his weapon.

Linking supposedly genuine, uncalculated speech to ideal manhood, Othello's entire performance in the council chamber, if "performance" is what it is, reveals a systematic economy of masculinity.[10] Shakespeare establishes a direct line between irrational (or antirational and anticonventional) conduct and Othello's sense of himself as a man and a warrior-leader: his personal sense of what Weber would call a charismatic mission. Yet generalship, discipline, strategy, and the other accoutrements of military organization have no part in the essential formula. To the contrary, if we think of tree limbs when recalling the "pith" of his arms, Othello's martial activity is now associated with nature: he is all but a vegetal deity towering amid the Venetians, an exotic with divine auspices. As A. C. Bradley put it, Othello holds "a volume of force which in repose insures pre-eminence without any effort, and in commotion reminds us rather of the fury of the elements than of the tumult of common human passion" (1991, 148).[11] Othello gives the impression that he is a being composed of extra-human materials, the product of a virtual symbiosis of nature and war. Together, these disparate components tally up to form a supremely charismatic personality, displaying, to quote Bradley again, "something colossal, something which reminds us of Michelangelo's figures" (148).

In a figurative sense, Othello will lose his arm by resorting to dispassionate measures with Cassio. His act constitutes a dismemberment of his own charismatic group, as Cassio himself implies. He pleads with Desdemona,

> I do beseech you,
> That by your virtuous means I may again
> Exist, and be a member of his love,
> Whom I, with all the duty of my heart,
> Entirely honour.
>
> (3.4.107–11)

The desire to be "a member of [Othello's] love" accurately characterizes the libidinal tie that binds a group. Cassio even mentions his duty to honor his leader, which Weber emphasizes as a fundamental component of charismatic group function. After his excision from the group, Cassio ceases to exist: a member, as Saint Paul says, cannot survive without the whole body. But the body also suffers in such excisions; so the loss of Cassio is ominous, suggesting not the vertical discipline of a newly installed government but, rather, evidence that the center is not holding, that the warrior-god is on the wane. If we need proof beyond Cassio of Othello's diminished charisma and crippled group, then Iago's usurping of Cassio's place supplies it.[12]

The Pauline metaphor of the "one body" seems to hover around Cassio. The stunned lieutenant himself, moments after Othello fires him, laments to Iago that he is "past all surgery" (3.2.252). Here he speaks figuratively, but his remark is very nearly prophetic of a material reality. After being attacked in act 5 (by Iago, though he does not know it), Cassio cries "I am maim'd for ever" (5.1.27), and suddenly there is a coincidence of the figuratively maimed group member and the literally maimed bodily member. Similar associations occur throughout the drama, linking group membership, bodily members, and dismemberment. For instance, in 3.4, once Cassio renews his "former suit" (107), Iago and Desdemona, with particular reference to bodily members, both ruminate on Othello's "strange unquietness" (as Emilia terms it [130]). It cannot be an accident that Iago mentions Othello's arm:

> Can he be angry? I have seen the cannon,
> When it hath blown his ranks into the air;
> And (like the devil) from his very arm
> Puff'd his own brother.
>
> (3.4.131–34)

Deliberately miscontruing the reason for Othello's mood, Iago torments Cassio with the unlikelihood of the general's being angry over the mere loss of his lieutenant; as dismemberments go, Iago reasons, losing a brother on the battlefield far outweighs anything that has happened in Cyprus. The "very arm" that held the brother, who in the tale is literally ripped from Othello's body, once again acts as a barometer of charismatic force. In the presence of a martial mission, leastways in the past, no dismemberment deterred the brave Moor— or, better yet, no loss dismembered him. Now that things have changed, however, Othello cannot but feel the pain.

Desdemona, unwitting cause of the change, empathically senses the impact of the group metanoia on Othello's natural body. Forgiving his jealous mood as a displacement of concern over affairs of state, she compares the incipient social (and domestic) breakdown to the phenomenon of pain in the body:

> for let our fingers ache,
> And it indues our other healthful members
> Even to that sense of pain; nay, we must think
> Men are not gods.
>
> (3.4.143–46)

It is difficult to say exactly what Desdemona's metaphor refers to: Is the aching finger the putative state problem? Or is it the jealous mood? Or, finally, is it the loss of Cassio, expectantly standing by for a word of encouragement? And are the "other healthful members" Cassio, Desdemona, Iago, and others? Or are they Othello's own deeds, the outward proof of his erstwhile gifts of grace? I doubt that we can find a suitable single answer to these questions, but perhaps we are not meant to try. With wifely indulgence Desdemona shares the evidence that Othello's supernatural gifts, his charisma, and his professional dispassion have all begun to decay. "Men are not gods," she says innocently, not realizing that to say such a thing about Othello is to utter his death sentence (and her own). There is no resignation in her observation that her husband is made up of human, rather than divine, parts. It is as though she is telling her auditors that she is no longer under the influence of his spellbinding presence. To the contrary, she is proud to be able to endure his all-too-human moodiness, proud to be seen as a bride waking into a wife. The irony, lost to everyone but Iago, is that the intimacy which her dutifulness reveals is the root cause of Othello's pain and, consequently, of all the destruction attendant on it.

If we view Cassio's cashiering as a dismemberment of Othello's extended body—his Pauline body politic, which is emphatically not immortal—then it foreshadows the murder of Desdemona as well as the dismemberment of Othello's body natural. This final, physical dismemberment occurs in the last scene, when Montano disarms Othello. Montano not only removes the great warrior's weapon, but, more importantly, he also neutralizes the arm which has been the symbol of Othello's power from the first act. Even in utmost distress Othello sees the symbolic import of the disarming:

> I am not valiant neither,
> But every puny whipster gets my sword;
> But why should honour outlive honesty?
> Let it all go.

> (5.2.244–47)

The enervation of Othello's will is unbearable. Yet his observation has a clear-eyed accuracy, which, despite the drag of immutable loss, seems irresistibly refreshing after five acts of myopia and distortion. The humiliating martial exchange with Montano should probably strike us as final proof of the dismemberment that has been occurring all along to Othello's group. It is fitting somehow that Othello's natural body along with its metonymical extension, his weapon, should suffer the final dismemberment. The disarming may not be a *sparagmos* exactly, but the horror of this ultimate stage of individuation confirms the absoluteness of Othello's tragedy.

There is, however, a notable anticlimax, Othello's rearming. Moments after being humiliated by a puny whipster, Othello finds the Spanish sword and, praising the weapon, boasts of his onetime prowess with it:

> I have seen the day,
> That with this little arm, and this good sword,
> I have made my way through more impediments
> Than twenty times your stop.

$$(5.2.262–65)$$

Again Othello's arm, this time characterized as "little" (and clearly differentiated from his weapon), serves as the symbol of his glory. In the repeated synechdoche a little member stands for the whole man, for both the spirit and deeds of the supernatural warrior. We cannot but follow the play's sad progress from the "pith" of Othello's youthful arm to the arm he nearly raises to punish Cassio to this "little arm," which he proffers with a mixture of distraction, impotence, and nostalgia. Yet even in this terrible moment there is something redeeming, some glint of honor in Othello's ability to recognize the vanity of his boast ("O vain boast, /Who can control his fate?" [265–66]). To my mind, however, his fluctuating sense of his own importance coupled with his weakened threats and flawed execution of them (he wounds but does not kill Iago with a surprise thrust) only further emphasize his humiliation as a warrior and a general.[13] The "vain boast," the failure to kill Iago, and even his suicide constitute searing proof of Othello's irreparable decline from a charismatic zenith to a nadir of separation and self-indulgence.

MAGIC, SEXUALITY, AND IAGO'S RATIONALISM

The final scene empties Othello of the last of his charismatic symbols, his exoticized and enigmatic sexual authority. The sexual sorcery that Brabantio (helped by Iago) imputes to Othello and which, despite Othello's deprecations of "young affects" (1.3.263), must be counted as part of his charisma, collapses, leaving an isolated human body without libidinal ties and very nearly devoid of libido. If the "arm" Montano takes from the Moor can be a metonymical extension of his physical arm, then it can also figure his penis, as swords and daggers so often do in amorous contexts. Thus his final disarming might also be seen as a castration, linking a symbolically charged physical mutilation to the destruction of Othello's reputation. There may be a resurgence of Othello's manhood in his rearming—the "little arm" is a fairly obvious double entendre—but the self-indulgence of the moment turns his sexual impulse inward. He impales himself on the sword of Spain in a furor of masturbatory self-immolation, and dies kissing a corpse. Any valedictory surge of manhood that the rearming or the suicide might promise appears ineffably mean when we recognize the extent of Othello's self-obsession in the last scene.

With group ties forgotten, charisma emptied out, and will destroyed, Othello is reduced to blustering irrelevance; as Auden says, "we feel pity for him but no respect" (1968, 247).

The knot of magic, sexuality, and charisma begins to unravel as early as the first act. Brabantio alleges in scenes 2 and 3 of the play that Othello has used magical powers rather than fair means to win Desdemona as a sexual partner. "Thou hast enchanted her," he cries, insisting that Othello has bound his daughter in "chains of magic" (1.2.63, 65):

> Judge me the world, if 'tis not gross in sense,
> That thou has practis'd on her with foul charms,
> Abus'd her delicate youth, with drugs or minerals,
> That weakens motion.
>
> (1.2.72–75)

He arrests Othello as "an abuser of the world, a practiser /Of arts inhibited" (78–79). Wrong as it may be in specific details ("drugs or minerals"), there is great value in this perception of Othello as the possessor of powers beyond those of normal Christians. His half-wooing of Desdemona had pied-piper qualities, compounding his charismatic uniqueness with a powerful sexual magnetism (Newman 1983, 206). The Othello Brabantio knew—that is, the unmarried and unhoused Othello—was an enchanting figure, wielding a pagan prerationalist claim to authority. Brabantio rejects the claim precisely because it is pagan and exceptional in Venetian society and, moreover, because it carries a revelation of sexuality and sexual magic heretofore confined to the masculine aim-inhibited libidinal ties of Othello's military band. But his rejection should not undercut the accuracy of his perception that the Moor somehow fulfills extraordinary human needs by magical, apparently supernatural means.

Othello, in contrast, scornfully dissociates himself from magic. His mention of it drips with sarcasm.

> I will a round unvarnish'd tale deliver,
> Of my whole course of love, what drugs, what charms,
> What conjuration, and what mighty magic,
> (For such proceedings I am charged withal)
> I won his daughter.
>
> (1.3.90–94)

Othello's denial of any magical component to his sexual conquest, while understandable from the perspective of what the duke refers to as "poor likelihoods /Of modern seemings" (1.3.108–9), clashes with the history and the exotic authority of his generalship. It may be that Othello would not himself associate his military superiority with witchcraft, but his "unvarnish'd tale" of mythological adventures and miraculous escapes nonetheless encourages such an association. And the imminent Turkish threat heightens the expectation that Othello will rescue Cyprus by means of a martial magic only he can muster, feats beyond the merely arithmetical skill (by Iago's measure) of his first lieutenant.

This salvationistic mission connects Othello's unique personal gifts to his charismatic centrality as a group leader and links his manipulations of sexual energy to his public role. Here again we find evidence of the systemic mutuality of group function. As Newman puts it, "the sexual flow of energy comes from the group to the leader as well as from the leader to the group. It is in all ways a joint enterprise" (1983, 206). Consequently, imputations of magic, and particularly sexual magic, are inseparable from Othello's ability to fulfill extraordinary needs—both physical and psychological—and from his unique authority. As Weber noted, societies have always associated shamanism and magical powers with charisma, setting aside the "practisers" of such arts as leaders in periods of crisis even if their social influence is weak under normal cirmumstances: "the charisma of the hero or the magician is immediately activated whenever an extraordinary event occurs: a major hunting expedition, a drought or some other danger precipitated by the wrath of the demons, and especially a military threat" (1978, 2:1134). Robert Tucker speaks of this as "situational charisma": "a leader-personality of non-messianic tendency evokes a charismatic response simply because he offers, in a time of acute distress, leadership that is perceived as a source and means of salvation from distress" (1968, 744). In just such a time of acute distress the duke "activates" Othello with a promise that he will "straight employ" the Moor against the Ottomans. So Othello already knows when he begins his repudiation of magic that he is needed precisely because he has extraordinary powers: "he knows," as Elliott puts it, "the Council's need of his military expertise, and he spends some time, very subtly, not in defending himself against the charge, but in mentioning—incidentally as it were—the depth of that expertise" (1988, 61).

He actually does more defending than he needs to do, and he attempts rather too earnestly to strip himself of his exotic, enchanting aura. Indeed, Othello's charismatic authority seems pinched and diminished in the harsh light of his forensic self-defense. It is as if in dissociating himself from magic he is admitting his changed status in regard to group function—admitting, in other words, to betraying his aim-inhibited sexual bond with the group for the sake of an exclusive, individualized sexual bond with Desdemona. He is rapidly becoming more and more "housed." Under the eyes of everyone whose charisma hunger he stimulates, and in the presence of a clearcut mission, Othello transforms himself into a creature of argument and conventional procedure. His posturing before the council contradicts what might be expected of a charismatic leader, even a bearer of situational charisma. He responds to Brabantio in rationalized, quasilegalistic terms, as if, uncharacteristically, he is relying on the traditional and bureacratic authority of Venetian law rather than on his own antinomian charismatic authority. In the space of one scene, it would seem, Othello shrinks from the revolutionary self-restraint of "Were it my cue to fight . . . " to bluff litigiousness: he even calls a witness.

The scene in the council chamber reveals a fundamental change in Othello's status as a leader, and in the health of the "joint venture" of sexual energy that Newman describes between leader and group members. That Othello should endanger his honor for the sake of his wife proves that there has been a shift in the libidinal ties that previously bound him to his charismatic followers. A new and overt sexual liaison replaces those tacit, aim-inhibited ties. As a result, Othello's group of followers becomes attentuated from him, evidenced by the Moor's abandonment of the subject of personal honor in his dealings with Brabantio and the duke.

For all his pretext of resolving the crisis, Othello never actually redresses his affronted honor. The recourse to the duke's authority, to a third-party judgment, undoubtedly would frustrate the idealized expectations of Othello's martial cohort. At this moment, therefore, Othello becomes disengaged from the charismatic symbols by which he had established his reputation, and with which his followers identify. Iago, listening to his general's special pleading, would be unable to miss the baleful evidence of change, the proof of Othello's individuation from the group ideal. In a series of suggestive rhetorical reemphases—including "Let housewives make a skillet of my helm" (1.3.272)—Othello isolates himself from the charismatic symbols that until now had sustained his group and blithely stakes his reputation on his ability to resist his wife.[14]

Clearly Othello's authority has shifted to the domestic sphere, regardless of any impressions to the contrary that he himself might have. This shift leads to the destruction of his army, or at least of his charismatic command of that army. As Freud noted in *Group Psychology and the Analysis of the Ego*:

In the great artificial groups, the Church and the army, there is no room for woman as a sexual object. The love relation between men and women remains outside these organizations. Even where groups are formed which are composed of both men and women the distinction between the sexes plays no part. There is scarcely any sense in asking whether the libido which keeps groups together is of a homosexual or of a heterosexual nature, for it is not differentiated according to the sexes, and particularly shows a complete disregard for the aims of the genital organization of the libido.

Even in a person who has in other respects become absorbed in a group, the directly sexual impulsions preserve a little of his individual activity. If they become too strong they disintegrate every group formation. (1960, 94)

As soon as Othello's "sexual impulsions," to use Strachey's phrase, no longer remain undifferentiated, as soon as his individual activity becomes strong enough to impell him to take a wife, the group organization disintegrates.

Iago is of course the pivotal figure in the disintegration. His reaction can be seen as one of punitive outrage both to libidinal rejection and to the symbolic confusion occasioned by Othello's new status. The trajectory of Iago's destructiveness, so bewildering in terms of rational power relations, makes somewhat more sense in terms of the breakdown of charismatic authority. His attempts to ruin Cassio's reputation and Othello's peace of mind, while successful enough, are mere warmups for his efforts to wreck the marriage and destroy Desdemona. Indeed, more than his undoing of Cassio or Othello, Iago's destruction of Desdemona is in his interests both as revenge for the marriage and as a means of restoring Othello to the group (although he articulates neither motive). This is not to suggest that Iago has a cogent plan to restore a group bond, nor that he even wants such a restoration—if we can speak about Iago's "wants" at all. Nevertheless his actions can be seen as an almost instinctive protest against the realignment of Othello's charismatic intensity. The dissolution of Iago's ties to Othello, manifest in his weird self-solicitousness, reflects (among other things) the breakdown of a binding group psychology. It might be seen as a form of dissent-from-the-dissenters run amok.

We might go further. Iago's determination to bring about Desdemona's destruction is arguably an acknowledgment that she has replaced him and the group members in the libidinal structure of the group. It would then be an equal retribution for Othello's abandonment of the group "for woman as a sexual object."[15] H. R. Coursen has remarked that "the marriage . . . suggests that Othello's private life, his love for Desdemona, the call of his 'body natural,' supersedes his public role, his Venetian generalship, his 'body politic'" (Coursen 1976, 172). This is an interesting comment, but we should resist over-polarizing Othello's two bodies. Because he is a charismatic, Othello's body natural is inextricably bound to his body politic, which never can be an immortal part of him, as are the bodies politic of hereditary kings. This distinction is not lost on Iago. He cannily exploits the vulnerabilities of the charismatic group dynamic—its mortality, as it were. Iago seems to recognize that Desdemona's sexual presence has altered Othello's affect, destroying forever the undifferentiated sexual and emotional ties that have simultaneously bound his followers to him and bound him to his followers. The marriage has undermined the charismatic economy, and Iago seizes on this first sign of Othello's individuation from the group. He then directs his divisive, negating energy toward exacerbating the breakdown of systemic mutuality. Soon enough the shared experience that Othello had previously represented is diffused and unavailable, while the entire social group on stage reels in a chaos of delusions about love, duty, honor, and group cohesion.

As Iago intuits, jealousy is the appropriate weapon to direct against someone whose crime is manifest as a libindinal realignment, a turning from group to individual ties. Freud observes, "Feelings of jealousy of the most extreme violence are summoned up in order to protect the choice of a sexual object from being encroached upon by a group tie" (Freud 1960, 93).[16] Such jealousy, as in Othello's case, proves that the group ties have broken down. Iago's ability to incite jealousy in his general would therefore spur him on, insofar as Othello's jealousy itself constitutes a rejection of Iago and the other followers who make up the now endangered group. The sublime aptness of jealousy as a weapon gives Iago's vengeance a Yahwistic cast, recalling the gory symmetry of "an eye for an eye," as well as perhaps explaining Shakespeare's association of Yahweh's "I am that I am" with Iago's "I am not what I am" (1.1.65). That the passion of jealousy is utterly new to Othello we know from his own assertions (3.3.180–96) as well as from Lodovico (4.1.260–64), although once we identify the group structure we can conclude without their statements that "the genital organization of the libido," like narcissism, has been absent from the successful army that Othello led in the past.

Othello eschews jealousy in act 3 ("Away at once with love or jealousy!" [3.3.196]), mistakenly thinking that he would be able to dismiss an erring Desdemona as if the libidinal realignment had never taken place, as if his sexual love for a woman had had no effect on the group ties. His delusion, or lack of intuition, is so perfect that even the blunt instrument of Iago's insinuations is enough to coax forth the passion poised, in Freud's view, "to protect the choice of a sexual object." Prior to Desdemona the distinction between the sexes played no part in the group organization. But Othello's marriage ends all that. He falls into what Nietzsche in *The Birth of Tragedy* calls a "spell of individuation" (1967, 73), paradoxically destroying himself and his bride with the very emotion (jealousy) meant to protect their sexual separation from the encroachment of group ties.

Let me conclude with a curious paradox. Despite the obvious destructive force of jealousy in the catastrophe, Othello is ultimately undone not by the irrational green-eyed monster but by his reliance on a halting, untried rationalism. Nevo notes that "Iago's subtlest stratagem is his enlisting on the devil's side the whole paraphernalia of rationality—the wisdom of the worldly Venetian world—whereby he subverts the instinctive responses Othello becomes afraid to trust" (1972, 195). Othello listens to Iago's allegations as if he were in a court of law; he asks for proof and argument in what amounts to a legalistic approach to establishing Desdemona's guilt, comparable to his own approach in establishing his dubious innocence in the matter of his marriage. But this is an absurd state of affairs—once again we might try to imagine Tamburlaine in a similar situation. If Othello were being rigorously Tamburlainian, he could never allow Iago to calumniate Desdemona in the first place. It is a measure of the already blemished state of his sense of honor that he hears any such slander without swiftly punishing the slanderer. The reason is not that he trusts Iago, but that he no longer entirely trusts himself.

Iago capitalizes on his captain's burgeoning reliance on rationalism. Indeed, he relishes it, since his safety depends on Othello's inability to apply such irrational criteria as honor and loyalty to Iago's own conduct. Moreover, Iago realizes (at least instinctively) that Othello's irrational force—the force of his previous authority, the force that had forged his reputation, initiated the libidinal ties among the group members, and eventually won Desdemona—can be diverted to the irrational triviality of jealousy, like to like. Although often ascribed to his Moorish temper, the force of Othello's jealousy actually gains its momentum from his charisma, like a powerful river turned from its course (cf. Dow 1978, 84).

If patterned to fit the symbolic group ideal, the murder of Desdemona probably would not have affected Othello's charismatic status. His violence as an unencumbered (or uncircumscribed) charismatic leader would have been mitigable, even assimilable into the extraordinary needs of his followers. But once Othello is "housed"—and once he turns to rationalism—he has separated himself from his own charismatic symbols and dissolved the bonds that gave direction to his superior power. Further, once he becomes Desdemona's husband Othello is judged as a member of her traditional milieu, even though he can never completely be assimilated into polite society. Recall, for instance, that the crucial witness to Othello's first act of violence against his wife is Lodovico, a member of her caste. Our revulsion coincides with his. On the other hand, one can imagine taking Othello's side, not justifiably, but under the sway of Othello's charisma. The Moor would of course remain a Bluebeard, and his sympathetic followers would be pirates. But the charismatic group would survive, manifesting a revolutionary flair in confrontation with the constraints of Lodovico's traditional ideals of gentility. Justifiably or no, his violence would have left his power intact if he had been able to incorporate his horrific deed into the charismatic tenor of a mission, in the way, for instance, that Tamburlaine does in murdering the virgins of Damascus. Othello's astonishment and despair when he recognizes his powerlessness to do just that makes this tragedy his rather than Desdemona's.

4

CHARISMA AS CATASTROPHE

Samson's Gift

Samson Agonistes thematizes the ebb and flood of a gift of divine grace, throwing into relief the stages of group breakdown and reformation around a charismatic figure. The drama is surprisingly intelligible as a flow chart of charisma. And the catastrophe gathers force when we recognize that Samson dies at the pinnacle of his renewed charismatic power. His death reunites the Danites. His extraordinary feat of strength reorganizes his followers around a shared experience of his Nazarite authority, reinvesting the last judge of Israel with the charismatic symbols he established before his fall from grace. The success of that same charismatic act, however, poignantly emphasizes the tragedy of Samson's loss at the supreme moment of group perfection.

Milton set for himself a significant dramatic challenge. Like Sophocles' *Oedipus at Colonus,* the play opens with an already fallen hero: "Strongest of men," laments the chorus, "To lowest pitch of abject fortune thou art fallen" (168–69). But whereas Sophocles never restores Oedipus' charismatic authority, describing no demonstrable rehabilitation of his symbolic leadership nor of his vaunted craftiness and commanding presence, Milton's play traces just such a rehabilitation. Not even Shakespeare dared write a tragedy of this kind, opening with an abject and fallen protagonist. Milton doubtlessly had ulterior motives in taking up this challenge—ulterior, that is, to strictly dramatic concerns or to poetic engagement with his Greek and Hebrew predecessors. As has often been observed, his own political predicament after the Restoration, including his being placed under house arrest, resonates in the abject Samson "Eyeless in Gaza at the Mill with

slaves" (41). And perhaps Samson's simultaneous spiritual rehabilitation and death reflect the mixture of political pessimism and supernatural one-upsmanship of the man who had already described himself

> In darkness, and with dangers compast round,
> And solitude; yet not alone, while thou
> Visit'st my slumbers Nightly, or when Morn
> Purples the East.
>
> (*Paradise Lost* 7:27–30)

Urania's nocturnal inspiration, the remedy for Milton's solitude,
might profitably be compared to Samson's charismatic infusion at the
end of the play, those "rousing motions" with which, so far as we can
tell, the blind and stubborn prisoner becomes conscious of his
renewed gift of grace. Both the blind old poet and the blinded judge
of Israel are politically abject sufferers who, through divine intervention, rebound to an exquisite and utterly personal superiority.

In Samson's inspired final action, however, we also witness a
group phenonmenon. The renewal of his personal superiority charismatically effects a rehabilitation of group cohesion, underscoring the
intersubjective value of his victory. He may not be saved in the Christian sense, but he restores himself to his tribe as the type of the messianic martyr. It is difficult to say whether, on agreeing to entertain the
Philistines, Samson seeks anything more than personal revenge. Yet,
by the time he agrees to go with the officer, his relation to the chorus
has subtly changed, as has the chorus's attitude toward Samson as a
leader. His motive may very well have been influenced by group considerations, although we can only speculate on this subject.

In any case, once Samson is dead his personal motive becomes
irrelevant, allowing Manoa instantly to mythologize that final access
of violence as *both* personal revenge and the proof of salvationistic
leadership:

> Come, come, no time for lamentation now,
> Nor much the cause: *Samson* hath quit himself
> Like *Samson*, and heroicly hath finish'd
> A life Heroic, on his Enemies
> Fully reveng'd hath left them years of mourning,
> And lamentation to the Sons of *Caphtor*
> Through all *Philistian* bounds. To *Israel*
> Honor hath left, and freedom, let but them
> Find courage to lay hold on this occasion.
>
> (1708–16)

Invoking honor (a virtue often associated with charisma), Manoa emphasizes the group value of Samson's act. He casts his son in the unwonted role of revolutionary leader and enjoins the Israelites as potential followers. In urging group formation Manoa points to the expressly charismatic basis of Samson's leadership. The revenge, the freeing of Israel, the bringing of eternal fame to his father's house (as if promising lineage charisma)—"all this," declares Manoa, "With God not parted from him, as was fear'd, / But favoring and assisting to the end" (1718–20). The continual, "not parted" presence of the Israelite god confirms Samson's gift of divine grace, and accordingly (in Manoa's new myth) establishes the charismatic authority of Samson's leadership.

John Guillory has suggested that we interpret *Samson Agonistes* in the light of Weber's *Protestant Ethic*, in particular the notion of *Beruf*, which usually means "calling" (Latin *vocatio*). He claims that Milton "openly attaches the life of Samson to the history of Protestant election or vocation" (1988, 150); and as evidence he quotes the chorus's description of Samson (addressed to the Israelite god) as a figure "such as thou hast solemnly elected, / With gifts and graces eminently adorn'd" (678–79). The word "elected" will certainly call to mind Protestant election, but we should note that it is quickly followed by "gifts and graces," literal translations of the word *charismata*. Indeed, the frequent references in the play to Samson's "gift," as well as to his Nazaritism and his unstable but salvationistic authority, make even Milton's version of Samson seem preeminently charismatic. For example, a few lines earlier in the speech quoted by Guillory the chorus speaks of Samson's "Secret refreshings, that repair his strength" (665). These secret refreshings are charismatic interventions from the deity, far more important to and characteristic of Samson's authority than an idea of calling. Guillory of course recognizes that there is more to Samson than merely falling away from his vocation, that even in regard to his Nazaritism "he was called to much *more* than obedience to vows" (1988, 153). And in this much I would agree with his interpretation: while "the history of Protestant election and vocation" may provide Milton with a Christian connection to the Israelite judge, Samson's defining authority exceeds the conventions of calling.

It also must be added that Weber himself never made the association between *Beruf* and charisma, and certainly not in the Samson tale.[1] As I will discuss in detail below, for Weber and for most twentieth-century biblical scholars, Samson is a consummately charismatic figure. Milton's Samson too is best understood in terms of his charisma, as it is manifest in his supernatural endowments *and* in his relationship to his followers. Neither of these conditions would be particularly relevant to an interpretation of Samson in terms of *Beruf*, which should give us pause. Samson's tragedy, in tandem with his triumph, emerges from the effect of his gift on his charismatic group.

At the end of the drama, however, the group experience of Samson's charisma has a puzzling status. Once Samson is gone the charismatic group bond dissolves, at least insofar as he had been the tribal ruler. Only the mythology of his renewal can sustain—indeed rehabilitate—the now leaderless Danites. Consequently both Manoa and the chorus appropriate Samson's feat for the group cause. They instinctively convert the renewed supernatural endowment in the "faithful Champion" (1751) to a proof of permanent divine accommodation for the tribe, and even for the federation of tribes. "Living or dying," declares the chorus after hearing of Samson's revenge, "thou hast fulfill'd /The work for which thou wast foretold /To *Israel*" (1661–63). By invoking the ancient prophecy, the chorus manipulates Samson's act as a charismatic symbol, a supernatural rallying point for an enduring group experience. At one stroke this new proof of charisma justifies Samson's butchery and organizes the charismatic group (in this case all Israel) around the symbolic leadership of the dead champion.

Nevertheless, there is some irony in an emphasis on the bonding force of the charismatic symbols after Samson's death, when in fact Samson's original charismatic gift had undermined group authority at the social level. As John Steadman has suggested, Samson's "special relationship with his Deity dominates all other personal ties, and all human relationships are in varying degrees compromised by his vocation as a Nazarite" (1987, 237–38).[2] Danite group dynamics are particularly puzzling in the light of Samson's Nazaritism. Steadman concludes that, because of his holiness, "Samson becomes increasingly isolated from his fellows, as the dictates of the Spirit lead him outward and onward beyond conventional relationships as son or husband or warrior, beyond the advice and consolation of friends, and beyond the guidance of the Scriptures themselves" (1987, 238). Virtually from the beginning, therefore, Samson was separated from other tribe members and from the need to manage and deploy his own charismatic symbols. In consequence, his Nazarite oath and the accompanying gift of superhuman strength, both effectively isolating him from his followers, can only become the means of group bonding if they are seen as symbols of an inclusive connection to divine legitimation and authority.

Yet Samson himself never articulates the link between his feats and the group destiny, as he freely admits. Imprisoned at Gaza and defending his actions as deliverer, he in fact blames the Israelite officials for their failure to make this important link and for missing the chance to advertise his great deeds:

> That fault I take not on me, but transfer
> On *Israel's* Governors, and Heads of Tribes,
> Who seeing those great acts which God had done
> Singly by me against their Conquerors
> Acknowledg'd not, or not at all consider'd
> Deliverance offer'd: I on th' other side
> Us'd no ambition to commend my deeds,
> The deeds themselves, though mute, spoke loud the doer.
>
> (241–48)

Samson seems to have had time to think about his leadership role, and he has concluded that the symbolic import of his deeds, specifically its organizing power, has been wasted. The Israelites missed a unique promotional opportunity, according to Samson, despite his best efforts as a deliverer. He even implies that he had already delivered Israel from bondage, if only the governors and chiefs could have represented his deeds in the correct manner.

But it is difficult to credit Samson's claims, or to exculpate him as a leader. His personal resistance to the symbolizing process, his lack of "ambition to commend [his] deeds," constitutes a signal failing of charismatic administration. Unlike such warrior chieftains as Joshua or David or even Tamburlaine, Samson refuses to manipulate his awesome symbolic value, and he utterly neglects the distribution of charismatic capital among group members. That his group survives as a group, and even maintains a consciousness of its own divine mission, has little to do with Samson's management of the group dynamic. His separateness has prevented any gathering of lieutenants or loyal aides to preserve the charismatic group into the next generation, and the nature of Samson's gift clearly prevents the passing on intact of his charisma. The postrevenge group therefore coheres and survives not through Samson's design but largely thanks to the rhetorical efforts of such mythifiers of his behavior as Manoa and the chorus (and finally Milton himself). They too have learned from Samson's experience of defeat. After having unsuccessfully capitalized on his earlier feats of strength, and after Samson himself has faulted the Israelite leaders in front of the chorus, both Manoa and the chorus deftly "commend" his final feat as a definitive symbolic event.

Samson's bringing down of the temple represents the high point of group perfection: the deliverance from Philistine servitude, the triumph of Israelite prophecy, and the symbolic apex of the tribal confederacy. His unarmed power confirms his *ruah*, or "spirit of the Lord," a plausible Hebrew equivalent of the word *charisma*. The tragedy inheres in the loss of the deliverer and nominal group leader at the moment of such profound unity. Yet, as much as Samson might encourage it, the symbolic impact of the event is not primarily of his doing—as always, for him the deeds themselves speak loud the doer. The tragic pathos, the poignancy of simultaneous triumph and loss, we owe to the chorus and Manoa. Although Samson just before his death stimulates the charisma hunger of the group, in fact it is the chorus and Manoa who articulate and deploy the newest Samson myth, when, as Guillory puts it, "his life becomes fully narratable" (1988, 152). In the final analysis the tragedy is of their making and for their ends, and it is they who transform Samson's gift into the kind of charismatic social adhesive it never seems to have been during his lifetime.

What Is a Judge of Israel?

Most twentieth-century commentators regard Samson as a charismatic figure. I would like to digress briefly in this section to consider some of this commentary, and to establish the prevalence of Weberian concepts in recent analysis of Milton's source. I conclude the section with a discussion of Judges and of Nazaritism in several sixteenth- and seventeenth-century writers. This latter discussion is not an attempt to establish sources for *Samson Agonistes* so much as to provide an alternative conceptual background for the biblical material, one that might have been familiar to Milton.

The Samson story appears in the Book of Judges, 13:1–16:31. The name of the book is a translation of the Vulgate *Liber Judicum*, which refers in turn to the Septuagint *Kritai* (Interpreter's Bible 1953). The Hebrew word for *judges* is *shofetim*, and it may be that the book got its name from 16:19, where the deliverers are called *shofetim*. But as the Interpreter's Bible notes: "the verbal root from which the term is derived occurs only twenty times in the entire book, and the participle (*shofet*, 'judge') occurs only six times."[3]

In any case, the term *judge* can be somewhat misleading in the biblical context. Neither the Greek *krites* ("decider") nor the Latin *judex* ("judge") has the full connotation of the Hebrew *shofet*, the former terms emphasizing juridical and decision-making capacities over other leadership qualities (cf. Interpreter's Bible 1953).[4] The Israelite leaders should not be confused with magistrates; they were more than judicial arbiters, according to the New Bible Dictionary (1974), and their designation as judges may be a result of the Dueteronomic editor's association of the men with Deborah, who fulfills both a military and a judicial role (cf. McKenzie 1967, 119). The term *shofet* in the Book of Judges "covers the broad concept of rulership, including the aspects of judge and champion" (Malamat 1976, 153n. 1). As Weber notes in his *Ancient Judaism*, the *shofetim* "were, in general, far from actual bearers of legal wisdom" (1952, 84). He adds that by tradition normal legal counsel lay in the hands of the *zekenim* (elders), while priests dealt with the ordeal and the trial-oracle. In contrast, the *shofetim* were "partly mere charismatic war leaders, partly, perhaps, also endowed with the charisma of judicial wisdom" (1952, 40).[5]

Judicial wisdom plays no part in the Samson story, however, despite the formulaic assertion at Judg. 16:31, "now he had iudged Israél twentie years."[6] As Tomoo Ishida has suggested, this formula—"*wayyispot* (or *saphat*) *'eth-yisrael*"—"is used as a sort of *terminus technicus* signifying the charismatic leaders who spontaneously rose up, organized tribal leagues called 'Israel,' and ruled over them until their death" (1973, 529).[7] Samson is predominantly a warrior, one of the national heroes (also called redeemers or saviors) who rose during a period of civil disorganization between the death of Joshua and the later institution of the kings. As Abraham Malamat points out, "the Samson cycle represents the clash with Philistines in the western part of the country, an enemy which by virtue of its superior technology and its military aristocracy (*seranim*) was destined to jeopardize the very existence of Israel" (1976, 153; cf. Zeitlin 1984, 150). That Samson defeats the Philistine host at Ramath-Lehi using only the jawbone of an ass no doubt is meant to underscore the impotence of mundane technology in confrontation with Yahwistic power, a didactic point emphasized as well by the redactor's mention of Shamgar, son of Anath, who slays six hundred Philistines with an ox-goad (Judg. 3:31). Indeed Shamgar and Samson, who both fight the Philistines, are the only example of the duplication of enemies in the Book of Judges; this fact highlights the relation between their charismatically endowed weapons and their well-armed military oppressors. (A Christian commentator could scarcely resist the typological link to Jesus of Nazareth and the well-equipped Romans.) Samson's final defeat of the Philistines is of course accomplished without any weapon at all, using only the roof and pillars of their own temple, "the Edifice where all were met to see him" (*SA* 1588). As a divinely selected deliverer, a bearer of *ruah*, he once again transforms something apparently innocuous (in terms of weaponry) into an instrument of extraordinary power, a conduit of Yahwistic vengeance.

There can be little doubt regarding the charismatic character of these magical transformations—and particularly of their literary representation (cf. Weisman 1977, 402). But the effect of such deeds on group function varies widely. Deliverance is an unstable form of social organization and could never furnish a succession or regime of charismatic judges (Weisman 1977, 401; Halpern 1981, 114). Rather, the period of the judges is best seen as one characterized by "sporadic leadership" (Malamat 1971, 130). Deliverance from oppression arises unpredictably after long stretches of leaderlessness and putatively sinful retrogression among the Israelites: by reducing the accounts to one example of each oppressor and each tribal leader, the Book of Judges seeks to provide a didactic paradigm of the ebb and flood of human error and divine grace, the latter repeatedly manifest in the charisma of the deliverer.

The charismatic organization of the judges' period finds various terms of expression in seventeenth-century biblical commentary, much of which Milton would have known. In its Argument to the Book of Judges, for instance, the Geneva Bible explains that the ingratitude of the Israelites "prouoked [God's] vengeance . . . to their vtter destruction," of which were provided "most euident signes by the mutabilitie of their state" (108). The vengeance entails the torment of tyrants, the loss of liberty, and slavery, "to the intent they might fele their owne miseries and so call vnto him and be delivered" (108). The Argument then explicates the social situation and the function of the *shofetim*:

> Yet to shewe that his mercies indure for euer, he raised vp from time to time suche as shulde deliuer them and assure them of his fauour and grace, if they wolde turne to him by true repentence. And these deliuerers the Scripture calleth Iudges, because they were executors of Gods iudgements, not chosen of the people nor by succession, but raised vp, as it semed best to God, for the gouernance of his people. (108)

The statement that the judges were so called "because they were executors of Gods iudgements" furnishes a unique and somewhat distorted interpretation of the problematic term *judge*. But it also reflects an important characteristic of the deliverer-god relationship, establishing in principle, as Halpern has remarked, that "the 'judge' is at once the counterpart and the agent of the god" (1981, 118). A judge or prophet is "raised up," as demonstrated in numerous call-narratives in the Hebrew Bible, when the people "call vnto" Yahweh to be delivered. Thus the deliverer's deeds not only free Israel but also glorify the god who raised up the savior.

Yet, for some early modern readers, justice remained the chief virtue of the judge, embodying both an *ethos* and a practical social responsibility. In *The Boke Named the Governour* (1531), for example, Thomas Elyot marshals the period of the judges as evidence that "the best and most sure governance is by one king or prince" (7). He explains that Moses was a single sovereign who, upon his death, "resigned it [sovereignty] to Joshua, assigned by God to be ruler after him" (8). "After the death of Joshua," Elyot continues, "by the space of 246 years succeeded from time to time one ruler among the Jews, which was chosen for his excellency in virtue and specially justice, wherefore he was called the judge, until the Israelites desired of Almighty God to let them have a king as other people had" (8). Like the Geneva Bible Argument, Elyot's remarks somewhat distort the social role of the judges, favoring a more judicial civic function than the text supports.[8] Moreover, it seems that Elyot is at pains to suppress the charismatic element of the *shofetim* (a word he would not have known). At least in this brief passage, the judge as governor or prince demonstrates no warrior ecstasy, no supernatural endowments, no feats of strength. The judge for Elyot seems to be a transitional political figure along the lines of a Florentine chancellor, "chosen for his excellency in virtue."

It is difficult to place Samson among Elyot's gubernatorial judges, not least because he was by no means chosen for his virtue. Indeed, Samson was set apart before his birth, as John Lightfoot affirms in his *Harmony of the Old Testament* (1647): "he was born supernaturally of a barren woman, and becomes the first Nazarite we have upon record" (1822, 2:161). Lightfoot describes Samson as predominantly a warrior hero, a lifelong antagonist to the Philistines. On one hand, "he killeth a lion without any weapons, findeth honey in the carcass"; on the other, after proposing a riddle to thirty Philistine gallants and being betrayed by his wife, "he pays them with their own countrymen's spoil: fires the Philistines' corn with three hundred foxes; is destroying them all his life, but destroys more at his death:—a type of Christ" (1822, 2:161). The last remark requires a fairly myopic typological eye, but it confirms the charismatic genealogy that would be so important to Christian commentators. As Christopher Hill has remarked in regard to such commentators in the seventeenth century, "part of the object of typology, whether conscious or not, was to minimize the savagery of the Old Testament; Samson was transformed from a bloodthirsty bully to a type of Christ" (1993, 75). Thus, as Lightfoot concludes, Samson "died gloriously by his own hand" (1822, 2:162). This statement suggests both an antetype of martyrdom and a warrior *ethos*, the code of the *miles gloriosus* who sacrifices himself "utterly to destroy and not to spare" the enemy (1822, 2:146).[9]

The warrior *ethos* pervades the Samson story, as it does the sagas of his predecessors. The warrior class was a prominent segment of Israelite society in the period of the judges. The *gibborim*, or "men of valor," were sons of property owners, and therefore they were not only entitled to carry arms but also able to afford to outfit themselves (Weber 1952, 16; cf. Weisman 1977, 406). Milton's Manoa, it should be recalled, calls himself the richest of his tribe (1479). With the clear exception of Jephthah (a harlot's son), the judges seem to have risen from the *gibborim*, and their charismatic military heroism is bolstered by the wealth and status of their sib (*Sippe* in Weber's terminology; also translated *clan*) (cf. Weber 1952, 475 [translators' note]).

Nazarites were a professional elite among the *gibborim*. According to Weber, these "separated ones" were "ascetically trained warrior ecstatics who—in the single certain tradition—left their hair unshorn and abstained from alcohol and originally, also, from sexual intercourse" (1952, 94–95). Samson is one of these warrior ecstatics—"a typical berserk," as Weber puts it: "When the spirit of Yahwe seized him he destroyed lions, set fire to the fields, tore down houses, and with any implement at hand slew any number of men and practiced other acts of wild battle fury. He certainly stands as representative of a type in the tradition" (1952, 94).

Yet it should be noted that, for all its charismatic ascetic attributes, Nazaritism had a wider meaning than merely warrior ecstasy, both in later Israelite tradition as well as in seventeenth-century interpretation. The locus classicus of the term in the Hebrew Bible is Numbers 6, which states the laws and prescriptions—including growing long hair and abstaining from wine—which would apply to both men and women when they "doeth separate them selues to vowe a vowe of a Nazarite to separate *him selfe* vnto the Lord" (Num. 6:2). The biblical chapter makes no mention of the *gibborim* or of a warrior ecstasy that might be associated with the vow. But the prescriptions of Numbers 6 probably represent a "later pacifistic tradition" in which "Nazariteship is transformed into an asceticism of mortification by virtue of a vow to lead a ritualistically exemplary life, above all, to abstain from uncleanness" (Weber 1952, 95).[10]

The Nazarite vow is of signal importance to Milton's Samson, as it is to seventeenth-century commentators such as Lightfoot. He places Nazaritism in the category of "absolute" as opposed to "conditional" vows:

There were, and are, vows "absolute," and without any such condition, whereby men, out of conscience of their duty, bound or bind
themselves to as strict obedience and service of God, as they can.
. . . [S]uch was the general end of the vow of the Nazarites, to set
themselves peculiarly to some service of God. . . . Nazaritism was
properly a vow of humiliation, that a man would chastise himself,
and deny himself his ordinary delight of "liberty" and neatness.
(1822, 7:161)

This last point, that Nazaritism is "properly a vow of humiliation"
entailing self-denial of liberty and neatness, provides an interesting
backgound to *Samson Agonistes*. Although forced on him, Samson's
humiliation in Gaza, manifest in filth and enslavement, might well be
a sign of the retrenchment of his Nazarite asceticism. This is an
altered asceticism from that of the ecstatic berserk, but it too is present
in Milton's hero. Weber maintained that the original purpose of
Nazarite asceticism, like the preparation for magical ecstasy, was the
preservation of full physical power (cf. 1952, 95). On the other hand,
Lightfoot speaks of "not a little care and circumspection" (1822, 7:161)
as the traits characterizing a Nazarite. Milton merges the warrior
ecstatic who regarners his charismatic strength in deprivation with
the late-tradition Nazarite, employing, I think, the Philistine humiliations as reinitiations of Samson's vow. Moreover, in clear contradiction with the Judges story (let alone the Samson saga), Milton's Samson seems gradually to acquire—and perhaps even to return to—"not
a little care and circumspection."

Self-humiliation is the key to late-tradition Nazaritism, as is seen in
Lightfoot's curious interpretation of the Nazarite's long hair.[11] The
pre-Gaza Samson, however, could hardly be described as a man under
a vow of humiliation. Not until his imprisonment, "from the top of
wondrous glory . . . To lowest pitch of abject fortune . . . fall'n" (167,
169), does Samson seem to fulfill Lightfoot's notion of the Nazarite.
The humiliations of grinding at the mill with slaves, of blindness, and
of filth and isolation, artificially furnish the ascetic conditions of a
renewed "absolute" vow. Indeed, Samson maintains that

> The base degree to which I now am fall'n,
> These rags, this grinding, is not yet so base
> As was my former servitude, ignoble,
> Unmanly, ignominious, infamous,
> True slavery, and that blindness worse than this,
> That saw not how degenerately I serv'd.
>
> (414–19)

He himself recognizes a manliness and a sort of cleanness in his new abasement, particularly in contrast to his "degenerate" servitude to Dalila. Without question, Samson's transgression, his profaning of the Nazarite vow, has caused his present predicament; he says as much himself later in the play, reminding Harapha of his divine *auctoritas* and of his personal failure too: "I was to my part from Heav'n assign'd, / And had perform'd it if my known offense / Had not disabl'd me" (1217–19). But Samson's disabling offense occurred in tandem with a less visible disability, his unresponsiveness to group needs and to the necessary relationship of mutual transferences. The transgression and subsequent imprisonment supply a foundation of abasement and humiliation from which Samson can build a circle of transference. The crescendo of his returning gift gains genuine deliverer's authority only as Samson's followers (or his choral audience) begin to see their deficient strength mirrored in Samson and to see his crisis as theirs.

Darryl Tippens refers to Samson's humiliations as a kenotic experience, an emptying or impoverishment reminiscent of the emptying out of divinity from the son of the Christian god, a "kenotic parabola of abasement and exaltation" (1986, 175, 177). Such kenotic abasements reunite Samson with the original symbols of his charismatic authority, linking his separateness to Nazarite asceticism and anticipating the reversal of fortune inherent in the kenotic parabola. The newly imposed Philistine humiliations also elicit unaccustomed care and circumspection in Samson's attitude, not to mention a new and ruthless self-reflectiveness. As his hair grows the humiliations deepen, culminating in the final disgrace of wearing Philistine livery to exhibit his deliverer's strength at a circus entertainment before the conquerors of his people. This deepest humiliation precedes Samson's highest or most resonant exaltation. But, as Tippens puts it, "to descend does not merely cause ascent; kenosis does not merely lead to exaltation—they become synonymous entities" (1986, 182). A similar qualification might be made about Samson's charisma. His Nazarite retrenchment does not in and of itself ensure a renewed charismatic status. Rather, a new synchrony of personal prowess and group formation is necessary—a circle of transference, a mutual responsiveness—so that a new coherence can be established between Samson's charismatic symbols and his followers' relationship to those symbols.

Recalcitrant Confederacy

Before that new synchrony is established at the end of *Samson Agonistes*, the Israelites and their deliverer experience little mutual responsiveness. In this respect their relationship is analogous to that of the other tribes with earlier deliverers. As both Samson and the chorus remark, the Israelite response to the sporadic leadership of the judges was chronically unreliable and at variance with the supposed Yahwistic aim. Not only do the Israelites fall into recurrent periods of sinful activity (including incest and idolatry) from which they must be rescued (equally sporadically) by a divine bestowal of grace, but they also recalcitrantly fail to respond to their deliverers. Israelite historiography (or mythography) records in a pattern of unsuccessful group ventures a debilitating attenuation of charismatic mutuality.

Milton makes this dubious group behavior a central theme of the confrontation between the chorus and Samson, thus calling attention from the start to Samson's charismatic status and to the paradigmatic rehabilitation of the interdependent relationship of authority between the Yahwistically endowed deliverer and the Israelite nation. Joan Bennett speaks of Samson's "growing superiority over the Chorus," noting that "from the beginning the Chorus, as well as Samson, is a bearer of guilt" (1989, 124). The chorus in effect shares guilt for the breakdown or failure of group response, a fact that provides Samson with a platform. In articulating his frustration with his followers, he displays an uncharacteristic interest in political analysis after a lifetime of having been an oblivious political actor. Perhaps this signals the start of his "growing superiority," which might better be understood as a shift toward a new mutuality, accompanied by Samson's newfound consciousness of his own authority and leadership responsibility. He complains peevishly about the Israelites' ingratitude to their leaders, telling how he was betrayed by his own people, "the men of *Judah*," while he hid from the Philistines at the rock Etam (Judg. 15:8):

> the men of Judah to prevent
> The harass of thir Land, beset me round;
> I willingly on some conditions came
> Into thir hands, and they as gladly yield me
> To the uncircumcis'd a welcome prey.
>
> (256–60)

Samson's contempt for the men of Judah in this situation might well reflect the commentary in the Geneva Bible. The commentators, like

Milton's Samson, blame the followers for their weakness, even though they are not of Samson's tribe: "Thus they had rather betray their brother, then vse the meanes that God had giuen for their deliuerance" (Judg. 15:13, margin).

Is this a fair criticism, coming either from Samson or from the commentators? After all, Samson makes no attempt to dissuade the men or to promise them a swift victory, despite apparently knowing that he had the strength to defeat the Philistines. To the contrary, he more or less tricks the men of Judah into thinking he will surrender without a fight. But once he arrives in Lehi, as Milton's Samson tells the story, he broke the cords with which he had been bound, flew on his enemies, "and with a trivial weapon fell'd /Thir choicest youth" (263–64). The weapon was the celebrated jawbone of an ass, "lately slaine" according to another marginal note in the Geneva Bible.[12]

Samson's bitter recollection of Ramath-Lehi ("Jawbone Heights") centers on his disappointment in his followers:

> Had *Judah* that day join'd, or one whole Tribe,
> They had by this possess'd the Towers of *Gath*,
> And lorded over them whom now they serve.
>
> (265–67)

The chorus sympathizes with Samson's complaint and a few lines later provides further examples of group breakdown:

> Thy words to my remembrance bring
> How *Succoth* and the Fort of *Penuel*
> Thir great Deliverer contemn'd,
> The matchless *Gideon* in pursuit
> Of *Madian* and her vanquisht Kings:
> And how ingrateful *Ephraim*
> Had dealt with *Jephtha*, who by argument,
> Not worse than by his shield and spear
> Defended *Israel* from the *Ammonite*.
>
> (277–85)

Underlying the dissatisfaction with followers' responses to deliverers is a critique of the Israelite tribal confederacy. As Weber pointed out, "confederate unity found expression in that a Yahwe certified war hero or war prophet regularly claimed authority also beyond the boundaries of his tribe" (1952, 83). Samson retrospectively asserts his claim to that unifying authority beyond his tribal boundaries, and, like the chorus (and the Geneva Bible commentators), indicts the confederacy for not recognizing his "Yahwe certified" status.[13]

Committed to the elusive ideal of tribal confederacy and mutual responsibility, Samson and the chorus level their most contemptuous comments not at the oppressors (Midianites, Ammonites, or Philistines) but at the Israelites themselves. Samson is said to have been betrayed by men of Judah, Gideon by those of Succoth and Penuel, Jephtha by Ephraimites. These are Hebrews against Hebrews, the confederacy of tribes crumbling from within as a result of internal disloyalty. And, significantly, the deliverers' vengeance on their so-called brothers can be as devastating as that wreaked on outsiders. As will be recalled, Gideon (an Ezrite from Manasseh) returns to Succoth and Penuel in the afternoon after defeating the Midianite kings in the morning: "he toke the Elders of the citie, and thornes of the wildnes and breers, and did teare the men of Succóth with them. Also he brake down the towre of Penuél and slewe the men of the citie" (Judg. 8:16–17). Similarly, Jephtha's Gileadites execute in cold blood forty-two thousand Ephraimites who had refused to fight the Ammonites, identifying them at the riverside "For want of well pronouncing *Shibboleth*," as Milton puts it (*SA* 289).

Yet, for all his bitterness afterward, Samson never punishes members of the confederacy during his reign as judge. The complaints he voices in *Samson Agonistes*, rather than reflecting a murderous indignation akin to Gideon's or Jephtha's, instead reveal a surprisingly sensitive understanding of the charismatic relationship. As I note in earlier chapters, the binding together of a charismatic group depends on the inner subjection of group members to the leader's charisma: "charisma manifests its revolutionary power from within, from a central *metanoia* [change] of the followers' attitudes" (Weber 1978, 2:1117). Samson (via Milton) seems aware of this need for inner subjection; he may be bitter, but he recognizes the futility of trying to force a "central *metanoia*" in groups who do not respond to his charismatic claim (such as the men of Judah)—the chorus, according to Bennett, might be included among such groups (1989, 126).[14]

Unfortunately, however, Samson does not see fit anywhere along the line to encourage followers to join his revolution—as for example Absalom does in his rebellion against David.[15] Milton's Samson instead draws a parallel between the Israelites' sporadic moral corruption and their refusal to follow their deliverer. He observes—once again with remarkable analytical detachment and political savvy—that "in Nations grown corrupt / And by thir vices brought to servitude" (268–69) ingratitude for "worthiest deeds" (276) is to be expected. Rather than seeing the value of subordinating individual will (what Freud terms "self-solicitousness") to the charisma of him "Whom God hath of his special favor rais'd / As thir Deliverer" (273–74), the tribal confederates scuttle group function and "despise, or envy, or suspect" (272) that divinely chosen figure. At the mill in Gaza Samson is both self-righteous about his deeds and at the same time resigned to the failure of the tribal confederacy to embrace his authority.

Nevertheless, while it is fascinating to hear Samson articulate the charismatic group ideal, his complaints have a false ring. His own responsibilities as a leader probably should have included the manipulation of his charismatic symbols. In some measure, of course, Samson is right to recognize the limits of his charisma. As Weber points out in an important passage, "Charisma is self-determined. . . . Its bearer seizes the task for which he is destined and demands that others obey and follow him by virtue of his mission. If those to whom he feels sent do not recognize him, his claim collapses" (1978, 2:1112–13). Weber might well be describing Samson's mission as a deliverer. The Israelites fail (or refuse) to recognize his mission, despite their obvious acknowledgment of his supernatural gift of strength, and as a result Samson's charismatic claim—that is, his claim to group leadership—collapses. But, as Smith (following Weber) has emphasized, besides the proofs of a disembodied charismatic force (magical acts, plunder, prophecy, feats of strength), "leaders must also appear to be full of conviction—as convinced of their own powers or message as they expect others to be" (1992, 167). In the case of a berserk or ecstatic warrior, a role Samson seems to fit at times, leaders "would exhibit in their own behavior such inspiring or contagious states of excitement as would compel 'unreflective imitation' on the part of their audience" (1992, 168).

For reasons never given in Milton or in Judges, Samson does not inspire "unreflective imitation" as, evidently, other charismatic judges had done in organizing and leading armies. Weber maintained that for a charismatic leader to succeed, followers would have to regard it as their *duty* to uphold the leader's claim. Needless to say, the Israelites (*vide*: the men of Judah) do not feel a duty to honor Samson's charismatic claim, nor do they recognize in crises their need for his leadership, at least not with sufficient hunger to enter into a lasting revolutionary merger with him (cf. Smith 1992, 168).

Followers' duty notwithstanding, part of the fault lies with Samson. He makes no attempt to manipulate his charismatic image, to mythify himself and thereby respond to his potential followers' psychological (as well as actual) need for an omnipotent figure. Smith speaks of the "mutual transference" of group relationships, describing what he calls the "positive feedback" that characterizes successful responsiveness in charismatic groups: "The leader demands and gets idealization. . . . In return, she produces in her followers an ever more adventurous, stimulated, and exhilirated condition that substitutes for their deficits of mirrored strength. . . . This circle of transference—the leader's exhibitionism and mirroring, the followers' voyeurism and idealization—is what constitutes the positive feedback in such extraordinary groups" (1992, 175–76). This "circle of transference" has never been a characteristic of Samson's relationship to the Israelites, nor even to his own tribal members. So far as we can determine, Samson demands nothing from his would-be followers, failing throughout his long career to create in them the idealization with which his mirrored strength—his charismatic claim—would substitute for their own deficits and encourage them to feel a duty to follow their deliverer.

Samson proves to be a disappointing leader until the end of Milton's play. As Smith notes, "dissapointments follow when incumbents of authoritative roles possess qualities of unresponsiveness that isolate them and make them unavailable to their constituents' needs for merger. They might be austere or distant, absorbed in personal gratifications, unempathetic, morally obtuse, corrupt, abusive, or despotic" (1992, 185). Samson has a dash of all these faults. His "qualities of unresponsiveness" clearly isolate him and make him unavailable to the Israelite's general need for merger against the Philistine oppression. Samson's lifelong separateness, maybe even Nazaritism itself, contradicts his belated concern for confederate unity. "Samson," according to Weber, "was held to be a purely individual hero fighting out his feuds" (1952, 85). It is exceptional that, "despite his lack of a popular following" (Malamat 1971, 130), he was called a deliverer-judge.

Milton captures the ambiguity surrounding Samson's leadership status, sowing just enough doubt in the early scenes to lay a foundation for a reversal in the form of a charismatic acclamation in the final speeches of the play, what Mary Ann Radzinowicz calls "the consensus of a chastened quieted people" (1978, 108). But at first in the play Samson offers too much special pleading, too much rationalization about his past leadership, where the sweep of internal law and group bond should have carried the day—where the circle of transference should have held firm. In contrast we might recall *Tamburlaine* and the suborning of Theridamas (who is not only of a different ethnic group but also an enemy) or the ecstatic pledges of Northumberland and Hotspur in *Richard II*. Compared to such displays of charisma hunger Samson's leadership authority leaves much to be desired. That Samson derides the Israelite tribes (and the chorus, too) for not following him may mean that he at least recognizes how his separation from the group has damaged the chances of deliverance. But he does not demonstrate genuine charismatic responsiveness until his final moments. Ironically—and perhaps tragically—Samson's postmortem authority survives in the acclamation he never hears and in the charismatic group experience he never really shares.

Public Person and Pariah People

Samson's growing hair signals his renewed charismatic claim and inextricably links his natural body to a group experience. The returning hair indicates not only a revived strength but also the restructuring of Samson's relationship both to his god and to his tribe. His bodily indignities at the mill anticipate the physical triumphs made possible by his restored gift. But it must be noted that the shared experience of Samson's bodily change, the mutual value of his charismatic strength, results from a conscious recognition and management of his extraordinary physical powers. Without this consciousness there would be no group responsiveness. Only because Samson recognizes the initiatory value of the forced humiliations at Gaza can he regain the symbolically humiliated status of a Nazarite. And only by means of this newly acquired perspective can he dissemble his aim after the rousing motions, transforming for himself and his prospective followers the final humiliations of the temple into a triumph of deliverance.[16] As the pattern of charismatic asceticism is established, as Samson embraces his abjection—"to take shame unto [himself] before God and men," in Lightfoot's phrase (1822, 7:162)—his Nazaritism paradoxically begins to reflect not a renewed apartness but a nascent group connection.

This group connection manifests itself as the tribal chorus's newfound sympathy with the blind and humiliated Samson. Milton the dramatist in this respect enhances his source, no doubt with the intent of linking the Danite transformation to Christian congregational unity. As the play progresses the chorus undergoes a metanoia, a change from the earlier Danite (and indeed Israelite) alienation from their deliverer. Although it is difficult to trace the step-by-step development of this metanoia, by the time of Harapha's departure the chorus has changed its attitude toward Samson: genuine sympathy, a prelude to group formation, replaces the distancing pity of the earlier scenes.

Samson seems to be aware of the gradual change, even to the point of signaling his interest in a group connection. In his blustery speech to Harapha he indicates that, despite the personal distractions of Manoa and Dalila, his relation to his people *as followers* continues to dominate his mind. (He is speaking to the giant, but perhaps we should assume that the chorus can overhear his speech.) The story he tells Harapha we have already heard in detail in his first complaints to the chorus regarding his tribe's desertion of their deliverer. But now Samson deliberately contrasts the private with the public role, the individual with the group leader:

> But I a private person, whom my Country
> As a league-breaker gave up bound, presum'd
> Single Rebellion and did hostile Acts.
> I was no private but a person rais'd
> With strength sufficient and command from Heav'n
> To free my Country; if their servile minds
> Me their Deliverer sent would not receive,
> But to thir Masters gave me up for nought,
> Th' unworthier they; whence to this day they serve.
>
> (1208–16)

There is a curious dichotomy in these lines, a kind of double creation: "I a private person" (1208) versus "I was no private but a person rais'd . . ." (1211). The second description is of course a revision of the first, as Samson makes it clear to Harapha that he has divine strength: "I was to do my part from Heav'n assign'd" (1217). But the two descriptions sketch a progression from (misconstrued) private person to charismatically endowed public persona. This is more than "situational charisma," more than simply a leader arising in time of distress (cf. Tucker 1968, 744). The "person rais'd . . . To free [his] Country" has messianic qualities, and his progress from private to public person reflects the ideal development of a charismatic experience, a shared *public* experience of group deliverance.

As we have seen already, Samson holds his people responsible for the failure of that shared experience of charismatic bonding. That the Israelites should have considered him a "league-breaker" only swells his contempt for their misunderstanding of his public mission, his unifying aims as a deliverer. But it may be somewhat unfair for Samson to blame his would-be followers (represented by the chorus) for past obtuseness and, likewise, for their present inability, along with that of his interlocutor Harapha, to recognize the renewal of his "strength sufficient and command from Heav'n." After all, as Anthony Low has remarked, "the nature of Samson's mission and the character of his heroism are beyond [the chorus's] initial understanding—

but that is hardly surprising. Not even Samson himself knows what to expect" (1974, 124). Yet the chorus comes to understand Samson's mission and, in doing so, or as a function of doing so, establishes a group bond unlike any that has existed during Samson's years as a judge of Israel. As I suggest above, however, Samson himself never fully experiences that group connection despite his increasing self-consciousness of himself as a Nazarite, as a leader, and as a member of a mutually interdependent group.

The basis of the chorus's understanding is an identification with the symbols of Samson's charismatic asceticism. Weber describes the Israelites as what he terms a pariah people, an ethnic community that believes in blood relationship and excludes exogamous marriage and social intercourse: "They live in a 'diaspora' strictly segregated from all personal intercourse, except that of the unavoidable sort, and their situation is legally precarious" (1946, 189). These pariah communities are, Weber suggests, "negatively privileged status groups" who attain their sense of dignity from "specific deviation":

> The sense of dignity of the negatively privileged strata naturally refers to a future lying beyond the present, whether it is of this life or of another. In other words, it must be nurtured by the belief in a providential "mission" and by a belief in a specific honor before God. The "chosen people's" dignity is nurtured by a belief either that in the beyond "the last will be first," or that in this life a Messiah will appear to bring forth into the light of the world which has cast them out the hidden honor of the pariah people (1946, 189–90).

Paradoxically the chorus's consciousness of its dignity and "specific honor before God" comes from an identification with Samson's abjectness. This identification in effect confirms, or perhaps re-forms, the pariah community with Samson as its messianic leader. No doubt Milton's Danites believe that their dignity depends on a future vindication; and it is clear that their traditionalism embodies a consciousness of their negatively privileged status. But the play allows the Danite chorus to express this belief only in its sympathetic identity with Samson's loss of dignity: the group begins to function *as a group*—and maybe this is appropriate for a pariah community—when it accepts as a charismatic symbol of future honor the forced asceticism of Samson's degradation and dishonor.

In reflecting on the chorus's response to Samson's final act, Bennett suggests that "the Chorus enters into Samson's victory as deeply as its bondage to the law permits. Its faith in their world's predictability has been restored by the literal fulfillment of the promise of Samson's birth" (1989, 137).[17] But before the chorus is aware of that literal fulfillment it has already experienced a metanoia, visibly shifting its attitude to sympathetic identity with Samson's predicament, and even to a need for a bond with Samson as a leader. After Harapha leaves, Samson addresses the chorus, reflecting on his situation in the starkest terms possible. He calculates that Harapha will not report back that Samson had challenged him to fight (because he would not want to confess that he had refused the challenge). Then, with a businesslike stoicism regarding his present affliction, Samson utters a powerful and profoundly charismatic threat:

> Much more affliction than already felt
> They cannot well impose, not I sustain;
> If they intend advantage of my labors,
> The work of many hands, which earns my keeping
> With no small profit daily to my owners.
> But come what will, my deadliest foe will prove
> My speediest friend, by death to rid me hence,
> The worst that he can give, to me the best.
> Yet so it may fall out, because thir end
> Is hate, not help to me, it may with mine
> Draw thir own ruin who attempt the deed.
>
> (1257–67)

The charisma of this speech, its force as an appeal to the group, grows out of Samson's absoluteness about life and death. This absoluteness destabilizes the relationship between the chorus and Samson, at once establishing a leader-follower dynamic and threatening to remove that dynamic. Furthermore, Samson promises to destroy his (and the pariah community's) enemy in the instant of utmost destabilization of the charismatic group. Thus, in a single gesture, Samson manages to organize the alienated membership of his tribe around an unstable social situation in the present while confirming the ultimate stability of the providentially ensured future.

Samson characterizes his own death as a both a relief and a challenge, threatening to "Draw thir own ruin" on the Philistines who attempt to kill him. The underlying force of this threat—supported by the knowledge that Samson's strength allows him to do the work of many hands—is linked indissolubly to Samson's gift: his divinely given strength accredits his threat and, coupled with the degradation and dishonor of Samson's bondage, reflects in a kind of living metaphor the precarious condition of a negatively privileged pariah community. As if emblematic of the entire Israelite nation, Samson embodies the contraries of what Weber terms "specific deviation": indignity and death serve ironically as earthly signs of hidden honor and divine blessing. Even before any act furnishes the proof, the chorus can recognize in Samson, to use Bennett's phrase, "their world's predictability." The chorus thereby identifies with the newly entrenched symbols of Samson's charismatic revolution, and, for the first time perhaps, begins to experience Samson as a group phenomenon.

Milton leaves little question that Samson's speech has a transforming effect on the chorus. The euphoric exclamation of a follower *in statu nascendi* replaces the detached choral observations of the earlier scenes:

> Oh how comely it is and how reviving
> To the Spirits of just men long opprest!
> When God into the hands of thir deliverer
> Puts invincible might
> To quell the mighty of the Earth, th'oppressor,
> The brute and boist'rous force of violent men
> Hardy and industrious to support
> Tyrannic power, but raging to pursue
> The righteous and all such as honor Truth.

(1268–77)

Suddenly the chorus recognizes Samson as the deliverer Samson himself has claimed to be all his life. A metanoia has clearly—and somewhat unaccountably—taken place in the Danites. In contrast to its earlier standoffishness, the chorus now reveals a charisma hunger and, at the same time, acclaims Samson the leader who will satisfy that hunger. We recall that Smith describes certain charismatic leaders as demonstrating a "risk-taking exhibitionism supported by conviction and grandiosity" (1992, 175). Samson's challenge to Harapha and his speech on Philistine ruin fit this description; moreover, the "risk-taking exhibitionism" that he demonstrates seems simultaneously to awaken the chorus's need for a leader and to supply the idealized symbols of omnipotence necessary to the formation of a charismatic bond between leader and followers.

It is difficult to know why Samson has not heretofore inspired the same kind of awe—that is, the kind of awe that is manifest in what Heinz Kohut called "selfobject transferences"—why indeed he has not before now quickened the Danite appetite for charismatic leadership. It may be, as Steadman notes, that his Nazarite separateness has always alienated his prospective followers. His warrior ecstasies, rather than fulfilling the extraordinary needs of a group, instead seem to have had an isolating effect on Samson. Recall Manoa's description when he first sees his son at the mill:

> That invincible *Samson*, far renown'd,
> The dread of *Israel's* foes, who with a strength
> Equivalent to Angels' walk'd thir streets,
> None offering fight; who single combatant
> Duell'd thir Armies rank't in proud array,
> Himself an Army.
>
> (341–46)

With strength equivalent to that of angels, a single combatant against armies, Samson, as he once was, embodied the charismatic superiority of a consecrated and ascetically separated superman. Manoa defines his son in terms of his charisma, or *ruah*, the recipient of "gifts desirable . . . giv'n with a solemn hand / As Graces" (358, 359–60). Milton's Pauline language—"gifts desirable . . . As Graces," or *charismata*—retroactively merges Samson's endowments with the Christian struggle. Samson's nurture, in Manoa's words, was "Ordain'd" holy, and Samson himself "Select, Sacred, Glorious for a while, / The miracle of men" (362, 363–64).

Conspicuously absent from Manoa's description of his son, however, is any characterization of Samson as a ruler or a leader—or, for that matter, as a judge. The transformation of Samson into a genuine leader occurs only after his humiliations at Gaza, what I have referred to as the forced asceticism of his degradation, and particularly after this asceticism is recognized by the chorus. It is signally important to the interpretation of the tragedy to note that the chorus undergoes its metanoia and begins to experience Samson as a charismatic *group* phenomenon before Samson feels the rousing motions. This is important because it makes Samson's decision to dress in livery and go to the temple more than merely a personal act (regardless of his motive): the decision affects group stability. It reveals for the first time the interdependence of Samson and the Danites, along with the systemic mutuality at work in Samson's newly constituted charismatic group. The force of the tragedy inheres in this systemic mutuality, or more exactly in its shattering, in the devastating loss of Samson, now a leader, at the pinnacle of group interdependence and group success.

Girt with Friends

Between the chorus's sudden identification with Samson—"Oh how comely it is and how reviving"—and Samson's rousing motions is interposed the first exchange with the officer. Samson responds indignantly to the officer's message, refusing to cooperate with the Philistines who he says wish to "make a game of [his] calamaties" (1331). Samson's "stoutness" (1346), as the officer terms it, is not surprising; it seems a predictable continuation of the obduracy we witnessed in his exchange with Harapha. On the other hand, there is a subtle difference in the relationship between the chorus and Samson, a clear, if nuanced, indication of a new dynamic. More than at any other time in the play the chorus regards Samson with what might be termed vested sympathy, as though his actions might affect more than merely himself—as though, finally, a group ideal exists among the Danites. Further, and most significantly, Samson acts like a leader for the first time in his career, taking into consideration the dependency of his followers on his actions. The charismatic corpus agens at last—and in anticipation of the catastrophe—includes both the individual leader and the group.

Samson demonstrates a rare consciousness of his charismatic authority in the dialogue with the chorus that Milton sandwiches between the officer's departure and Samson's farewell. We should particularly note his ability to sway the chorus in these brief passages, proof positive of a leadership capacity he never before has demonstrated. This is the true judge of Israel, heir to the authority of Deborah, Gideon, and the other great leaders. When Samson pointedly rejects the officer's message, adding a cryptic threat for good measure—"Perhaps thou shalt have cause to sorrow indeed" (1347)—the chorus quails, worrying that such defiance will only bring harsher treatment. But Samson, all of a sudden concerned with symbolic behavior, upbraids the chorus:

> Shall I abuse this Consecrated gift
> Of strength, again returning with my hair
> After my great transgression, so requite
> Favor renew'd, and add a greater sin
> By prostituting holy things to Idols;
> A *Nazarite* in place abominable
> Vaunting my strength in honor to their *Dagon*?
> Besides, how vile, contemptible, ridiculous,
> What act more execrably unclean, profane?
>
>   (1354–62)

In these lines Samson transforms himself from the disgruntled (and failed) deliverer of the first exchange with the chorus. Here he has become part teacher and part leader. His reference to his "Consecrated gift" establishes his divine auspices, while his half-scolding questions forcefully (and uniquely for Samson) testify to his newfound will to manipulate the symbolic value of his gift. At this moment in the drama Samson becomes a genuine group leader: the group aim and the charismatic symbols are synchronized, and Samson's manipulations of his own symbolic import crafts a group experience from his personal resistance.

But the chorus must be led to understand the symbolism. At first there is a reasonable choral objection to Samson's refusal to go with the officer: "Yet with this strength thou serv'st the *Philistines,* / Idolatrous, uncircumcis'd, unclean" (1364–65), the chorus argues, recalling Manoa's earlier bafflement about why Samson would rather labor at the mill than "sit idle on the household hearth" (566) ("Wilt thou then serve the *Philistines* with that gift / Which was expressly giv'n thee to annoy them?" [577–78]). Whereas with Manoa Samson exhibits little consciousness of the symbolic value of his charismatic gift, responding in effect that he considers it undignified and embarrassing to languish idly, for the chorus Samson has a moral, strategically informed lesson. He begins by pointing out that he has so far used his gift "Not in thir Idol-Worship, but by labor / Honest and lawful to derserve my food" (1365–66). The chorus counters that Samson might as well perform at the temple entertainment if he does so without believing in it: "Where the heart joins not, outward acts defile not" (1368). But Samson, with theological subtlety worthy of a scholastic, explains the difference between will and coercion to the attentive chorus:

> Where outward force constrains, the sentence holds;
> But who constrains me to the Temple of *Dagon,*
> Not dragging? the *Philistian* Lords command.
> Commands are not constraints.

$$(1369-72)$$

On the surface this statement simply distinguishes between obedience and the free will to resist. But it also contains a powerful hint of strength in reserve, of the physical capacity to resist an entire military society (in fact Samson a few lines later muses on how many Philistines might die if they were to try dragging him).

This hint of strength is all Samson needs at this juncture to demonstrate his generalship, manipulating his own charismatic symbolic value in order to organize the Danites around his self-idealization. "If I obey them," he says of the Philistines, "I do it freely":

> venturing to displease
> God for the fear of Man, and Man prefer,
> Set God behind: which in his jealousy
> Shall never, unrepented, find forgiveness.
> Yet that he may dispense with me or thee
> Present in Temples at Idolatrous Rites
> For some important cause, thou needst not doubt.

(1373–79)

There is no firmer proof of Samson's manipulations than this passage. He begins his speech by rejecting the chorus's suggestion that he go to the temple and ends by offering his own quasitheological justification for being "Present in Temples." The effect of this somewhat manipulative rhetoric is to destabilize the chorus's expectations, to keep the chorus in a dependent attitude toward Samson's next act. When, a moment later, Samson begins to feel "Some rousing motions in me which dispose / To something extraordinary my thoughts" (1382–83), the chorus is balanced on a threshhold of fulfillment, wavering between ruinous detachment (brought on by fear) and a merger with or a surrender to Samson as a shared charismatic experience.

It matters less, in terms of the group response, whether the rousing motions are providential or instinctive than that Samson uses what John Rogers calls his "agential ambiguity" (1996, 126) to organize and manipulate the chorus's charisma hunger. Samson clinches the group's dependence on him with a remarkable reversal, irresistibly destabilizing the Danites' expectations. He announces:

> I with this Messenger will go along,
> Nothing to do, to be sure, that may dishonor
> Our Law, or stain the vow of *Nazarite*.

(1384–86)

The stunning reversal is reminiscent of Othello's comparable reversal, at the moment of his greatest generalship in the play, when he agrees to accompany Brabantio to the Council chamber. And just as, with sudden acquiescence, Othello destabilizes the expectations of his followers Iago and Cassio, primed as they are for extraordinary violence from their chief, so Samson also destabilizes the expectations of the chorus. In Smith's terms, Samson fosters a dynamic that leads in a far-from-equilibrium direction, creating in the chorus a sudden dependency and, moreover, a centralization of authority (cf. Smith 1992, 198). His action undermines the chorus's autonomy, erasing both his own Nazarite separateness (at least in terms of group needs) and also the choral (or Danite) detachment that is evident earlier in the play. The result of Samson's manipulations, somewhat counterintuitively, is a stronger group bond, a more pronounced dependence of Danite followers on their leader.

There is in Samson's "I am content to go" (1403), which he says to the officer, a wealth of hidden meaning. His contentment is the product of what Lightfoot calls "care and circumspection" (1822, 7:161), unwonted qualties which now have led Samson to a renewed secrecy, a renewal of his Nazarite vow. But the reason he agrees to perform in livery does not represent only a renewed Nazarite separateness. It also reflects his resurgent social status as a deliverer. He has had secrets in the past, and has before concealed his strength from both friend and foes (as when he allowed himself to be bound by the men of Judah). But this is the first occasion (to our knowledge) on which Samson has, with expert dissembling, concealed his intent from his enemies while all but confiding in his followers. First, just before the officer's second appearance, he thrillingly asserts,

If there be aught of presage in the mind,
This day will be remarkable in my life
By some great act, or of my days the last.

(1387–89)

These lines seem to promise an extraordinary act, offering an insight (and perhaps a glimpse of divine prophecy) in just the way Samson refused to divulge his intentions when taken at Etam. The chorus, reeling from Samson's surprise decision to go with the messenger, suddenly finds itself included in Samson's divine deliberations. There could be no better demonstration of the symbolic mutuality of charisma: as a result of this timely inclusion, this assertion of group identity, the chorus (and by extension all Israelites) will suffer and overcome *through* Samson.

Thus, in his farewell speech, Samson addresses genuine followers for the first (and tragically the last) time in the play, reinforcing the symbolic promise of his choice to go, to dress in livery, and to humiliate himself. Unlike the earlier humiliations forced on him by the Philistines, this new humiliation is chosen freely; the distinction, lost on the officer and the Philistine hierarchy, should now be amply clear to the chorus. It is this distinction, this shared secret of Samson's will, that confirms the group bond. "Brethren, farewell," Samson says,

> your company along
> I will not wish, lest it perhaps offend them
> To see me girt with Friends; and how the sight
> Of mee as of a common Enemy,
> So dreaded once, may now exasperate them
> I know not.
>
> (1413–18)

Whether Samson is worrying about his own or his followers' safety is less important than his acknowledgment of their shared identity. He imagines that the Philistines will see them as a unified people, and the image of Samson "girt with Friends" provides the chorus with an idealization of shared experience. After the reversals of the prior speeches this idealized image of group identity fulfills the need for heroic selfobject transference, satisfying the chorus's charisma hunger while at the same time clarifying the inescapable interdependence of Samson and his followers.

The chorus responds to Samson's farewell speech with a hymn to his charisma:

> Go, and the Holy One
> Of *Israel* be thy guide
> To what may serve his glory best, and spread his name
> Great among the Heathen round:
> Send thee the Angel of thy Birth, to stand
> Fast by thy side, who from thy Father's field
> Rode up in flames after his message told
> Of thy conception, and be now a shield
> Of fire; that Spirit that first rusht on thee
> In the camp of *Dan*
> Be efficacious in thee now at need.
>
> (1427–37)

The invocation of "that Spirit" and the call for it to be "efficacious" has an odd force in the mouth of the chorus. In speaking of Samson "now in need" the chorus also reveals its own extraordinary need, and in so doing links its fate to that of Samson. The play at this moment provides an excellent anatomy of charismatic group dynamic: both the leader's magical ability to satisfy extraordinary needs and the group's survival depend on the efficaciousness of supernatural intervention. If any component of the charismatic dynamic—supernatural auspices, leader's manipulation of the gift, or followers' emotional dependency—were absent, the final deliverance would fail. But because the divinely inspired Samson is "girt with Friends," and therefore the leader of a charismatic movement, his feat of strength at long last results in deliverance.

Again, the tragic circumstance of *Samson Agonistes* is that at the supreme moment of group cohesion, Samson dies. We witness in Milton's play an unusual coincidence of catastrophe at the pinnacle of charismatic success, a rendering of charisma as catastrophe. The coincidence amplifies the tragedy of Samson's death. At the end of the play we (along with the Danites) are left with a leaderless charismatic movement and an uninheritable set of charismatic symbols. If the Israelites are now free, then they are also bound to a rigid set of symbolic ideals that identify their revolutionary success. Such symbolism, born of personal charisma, rarely retains its original meaning and its pertinent force after the early stages of a movement or following the death of the charismatic founding figure. As the Willners have pointed out, and as we have seen with Tamburlaine particularly, charismatic symbols soon imprison the charismatic leader. Once the charismatic movement changes, the original charismatic ideal becomes ossified and impractical.

But this imprisonment never occurs in Samson's story. He passes from the scene before his charismatic symbols become disengaged from his revolutionary movement. His death forestalls routinization, saving him from imprisonment in his own constraining symbolic authority. The hidden irony of Milton's tragedy is that, *mutatis mutandis*, the charismatic symbols of Samson's revolution would only have replaced the Philistine chains. In this respect Samson's death is a fortunate fall, sparing him the symbolic enslavement, or the enslavement to symbols, that will plague the Israelite kings.

5

EROTIC CHARISMA

The Tragedies of Cleopatra

This final chapter, on erotic charisma in early modern tragedies of Cleopatra, by necessity will be more speculative than earlier chapters. There is no sociological literature on erotic charisma per se, and to imagine an ideal type of erotic-charismatic authority it has been necessary to combine disparate sources on eroticism, sexuality, and social psychology. Moreover, in applying this ideal type to Cleopatra I have not confined myself to one representation of the Egyptian queen but have considered the Antony and Cleopatra tragedies by Samuel Daniel, Shakespeare, Charles Sedley, Thomas May, and John Dryden. Throughout the chapter I shift from one Cleopatra to another, comparing the figuration of erotic charisma across dramas. While this is probably not a justifiable practice in literary-critical terms, here I am most concerned with identifying Cleopatra's erotic charisma and tracing its connection to her tragedy.

Weber mentioned the possibility of erotic charisma but never developed the idea, although he wrote perceptively on the tension betwen eroticism and rationality in religion and in what he termed the religious rejections of the world. As we have already noted, all group psychology contains an erotic component. Freud maintained that group cohesion depended on aim-inhibited libidinal ties, and that the bond between leader and followers contained an erotic charge, albeit a suppressed or sublimated one. Recent social theorists have linked Freudian group psychology and charisma. For instance, as noted in Chapter 3, Ruth Newman has remarked that "the charismatic leader heavily taps sexual energy," stipulating that "the sexual flow of energy comes from the group to the leader as well as from the leader to the group" (1983, 206). Similarly, Donald McIntosh speaks of the "heavily libidinized" relationship of followers to a prophetic leader (1970, 905); and Ralph Hummel, specifically comparing Weber and Freud, observes that the charismatic experience exists for a follower when, among other phenomena, there is complete personal devotion to a leader, or "love projection" (1975, 760). As Arthur Schweitzer suggests regarding Hitler's charisma: "It was quite natural for many followers to turn in their fraternal or erotic love to glorifying and worshiping the leader in the form of various cults and rituals. Love turned into glorification and natural charisma was linked with personality cult" (1984, 89). Schweizter sees a "twofold symbiotic relationship" between what he calls "natural" charisma and personality cult, a concept that will be interesting to apply to Cleopatra's curious mixture of personal magnetism and cultic status. The force of erotic love, or libidinal ties, is undeniable in group formation, and the particular urgency of charismatic groups tends to amplify the erotic component.

But to establish the importance of erotic love in charismatic group function is not yet to identify and describe erotic charisma. Erotic charisma is difficult to define—though we seem to know it when we see it—and particularly difficult to discuss in terms of group action. Puzzling questions arise: Is there routinization of erotic charisma? Is there a circle of transference or group interdependence where eroticism supplies the charismatic organizing force? Is there, in fact, such a thing as an erotic group? The most difficult question to answer refers to the Freudian model of group psychology. If aim-inhibited libidinal ties are the criteria of group cohesion, then how can a group be formed and cohere when the libidinal aim is no longer inhibited— when, in fact, the ties between group members are overtly manifest in eroticism and libidinal satisfaction?

Eroticism and charisma have analogous properties in terms of their social reception. Both represent a resistance to rationality, although we should not forget that eroticism is itself a rationalization of sexual life. Weber remarks that "the extraordinary quality of eroticism has consisted precisely in a gradual turning away from the naive naturalism of sex" (1946, 344). Yet, despite its sophistication of putative naturalism, eroticism nonetheless is identified with the deepest animal instincts: "Eroticism was raised into the sphere of conscious enjoyment (in the most sublime sense of the term). Nevertheless, indeed because of this elevation, eroticism appeared to be like a gate into the most irrational and thereby real kernel of life, as compared with the mechanisms of rationalization" (Weber 1946, 344–45). The erotic, as Weber suggests, comes into being through a conscious effort to give symbolic value to sexual life, to sophisticate natural or animal sex. Georges Bataille too, as Suzanne Guerlac points out, defines eroticism as "the *conscious* activity of the sexual animal"; the erotic object gives meaning (1990, 91–92).[1] We find an elaboration of this idea in Bataille's *L'Histoire de l'erotisme*: "The attraction of femininity for men—and of masculinity for women—represents in eroticism an essential form of animal sexuality, but profoundly modified. What directly excites animals . . . affects men through symbolic figures."[2] Paradoxically—though not surprisingly—the symbolic value created by this conscious effort idealizes the erotic as the only real or natural or irrational possibility in a social structure replete with constraining rationalizations.

This paradox underscores the most important component of eroticism for this study, its symbolic structure. Symbolic representation indicates the existence of an audience (however small), recasting the subjective inner experience, even when that experience depends on spontaneous physical excitation, as a shared ideal. In this respect the erotic symbols are comparable to the charismatic symbols so often discussed in earlier chapters. Erotic symbols bear a significant resemblance to the symbolic idealization of a charismatic leader at the (usually disruptive) beginning of a movement. Just as a charismatic movement, to maintain some stability, requires the symbolic idealization of its revolutionary, innovative force, so eroticism manifests itself as a profoundly shared experience in a symbolic idealization of desire, objects of desire, transgression, and taboo. Eroticism, and in particular erotic ecstasy, displaces individual identity with an ineffable union with another (or an Other) body and spirit. Weber describes the union in terms of love: "the erotic relation seems to offer the unsurpassable peak of the fulfilment of the request for love in the direct fusion of the souls of one to the other. This boundless giving of oneself is as radical as possible in its opposition to all functionality, rationality, and generality" (1946, 347). It is difficult not to recall, in connection with Weber's notion of "boundless giving," the stunning radicalism of Juliet's vow of love to Romeo: "My bounty is as boundless as the sea, /My love as deep; the more I give to thee, /The more I have, for both are infinite" (2.2.133–35). The tenor of this speech, its perfection of desire and fulfillment in the paradoxical "the more I give . . . The more I have," reflects what Weber regards as "the unique meaning which one creature in his [or her] irrationality has for another, and only for this specific other" (1946, 347).

The comprehension of that "unique meaning," mirroring the perfection of desire, is mediated by interpretation: "from the point of view of eroticism, this meaning, and with it the value-content of the relation itself, rests upon the possibility of a communion which is felt as a complete unification, as a fading of the 'thou.' It is so overpowering that it is interpreted 'symbolically': as a sacrament" (Weber 1946, 347). The erotic sacrament is the illusion of the fading of the other, the "thou." But that illusion of complete unification—or perfect intersubjectivity—cannot be experienced without a conscious interpretation of "the possibility of communion." And that conscious interpretation takes a symbolic form, stabilizing an ideal of pure communion in animal sexuality. This symbolic ideal is the embodiment of "boundless giving of oneself," in radical opposition "to all functionality, rationality, and generality." The lover, therefore, would know himself or herself "to be freed from the cold skeleton hands of rational orders, just as completely as from the banality of everyday routine" (Weber 1946, 347).

The words "everyday routine" are familiar from earlier discussions of Weber's notion of the opposition between the disruptive force of charisma and everyday routine, *Alltag*. Like charisma, eroticism is disruptive, both in terms of inner experience and as a social phenomenon. Bataille conceived eroticism as a disturbance of order (1987, 13), even a fatal disturbance. He maintained that the business of eroticism is "to destroy the self-contained character of the participators as they are in their normal lives" (1987, 17). If this is a valid (though typically extreme) statement, then eroticism might be seen as a valuable tool in charismatic organization. By fostering what Smith calls far-from-equilibrium conditions it would furnish an ideal agent of the kinds of dissipative structures in which charismatic groups flourish. As Bataille remarked, "it is certain that the erotic life cannot be *regulated*."[3] But that unruly component is precisely the factor to be managed and manipulated by the bearer of erotic chrisma. Unruliness and disruptiveness frame the dissipative structure of erotic-charismatic interaction.[4]

Isis and the Erotic Sacrament

If we can accept that erotic and charismatic symbols are formed by means of a similar, and similarly paradoxical, compromise between conscious rationalization and the revolutionary breaking of everyday rational constraints, then I think that we might begin to see how eroticism can serve as an organizing principle in charismatic group psychology. The paradoxical character of erotic symbolism is comparable to the paradox of charismatic symbolism: the most powerful symbolic idealizations of a charismatic movement, such as the Christian cross or the Franciscan rope belt, are invariably the product of a later normative stage of the movement, a time far removed from the advent of the extraordinary (even supernatural) virtues suggested by the symbols. Indeed, as is clear in late stages of lineage and office charisma, the farther a group extends itself from the original charisma the more important the symbols of that charisma become (as in *Richard II*). Perhaps a similar pattern is evident in erotic symbolism. The farther society separates itself from animality—and the more its members see themselves as prisoners of rationality—the more vital to sexual life (or to the illusion of life itself) become the symbols that idealize animal sexuality.

The symbolic idealization of animal sexuality in effect de-animalizes sex, raising erotic experience to a symbolic, sacramental plane. Cleopatra inhabits, indeed epitomizes, this sacramental plane, mystifying with cultish symbolism the complete communion of lovers. Her eroticism claims sacred auspices, transforming animal sexuality and consciously revaluing it as a symbol of utter intersubjectivity.[5] Cleopatra presents herself as a devotee of Isis, imbued with the supernatural erotic power of a divine figure. This self-presentation is ubiquitous in the plays of the sixteenth and seventeenth centuries. In Daniel's *The Tragedie of Cleopatra*, for example, Cleopatra asks "Am I the woman, whose inuentiue pride, / (Adorn'd like *Isis*,) scornd mortalitie?" (35–36, continuous numbering). The lines are ambiguous: is it the woman or her "inuentuie pride" that is "Adorn'd like *Isis*"? But the ambiguity is telling. It is almost a dramatic necessity to mingle the symbol with the woman, to merge the charismatic eroticism of Isis with Cleopatra's human attributes of inventiveness and pride. Even in this condensed description there is evidence of Cleopatra's manipulation of a symbolic ideal of eroticism. Her own charisma is both derivative and creative, both sexual and consummately symbolic of sex.

In *Antony and Cleopatra* the religious symbolism is a constant element. Cleopatra dresses in "the habiliments of the goddess Isis" (3.6.17), Antony refers to her (despairingly) as "our terrene moon" (3.13.153) or earthly Isis, goddess of the moon, and on the Cydnus she is got up as as the goddess of love: "O'erpicturing that Venus where we see / The fancy outwork nature" (2.2 206–7). Eroticism and divinity commingle to form the basis of her authority;[6] they are interchangeable and indistinguishable. John Alvis has suggested that Antony and Cleopatra "strive to make a religion of erotic passion while failing to grasp the regenerative sacramental potency offered by the sort of personal love which trains the soul in selflessness" (1978, 185–86). Although, as both Weber and Bataille indicate, personal love has a more complicated relationship to "selflessness" than

Alvis acknowledges, the notions of a "religion of erotic passion" and
of the "regenerative sacramental potency" of love aptly categorize
the ubiquitous erotic symbols surrounding Cleopatra, and to some
extent Antony as well, in all the tragedies.

In Charles Sedley's *Antony and Cleopatra* (1677), for instance, Caesar remarks of the pair,

> The names of Emperor and Queen they scorn,
> And like immortal Gods themselves adorn.
> He does for *Bacchus*, she for *Isis* pass,
> And in their shapes, the wondr'ing Crowd amaze.
>
> (17)[7]

Much might be made of the "wondr'ing Crowd." To wonder is to
reject Horace's stoical dictum, "Nil admirari," which presumably
offends Caesar's ideal of how a crowd should react and by extension
how rulers should conduct themselves before their followers.[8] Wonder is also, however, the aim and constant recourse of ancient philosophy, a suprarational response to phenomena. Such a response
would perhaps be reserved for the passing of two gods. But most
important to our analysis is the manner in which Antony and Cleopatra, in the guise of Bacchus and Isis, organize a unified response from
the crowd. This may not be active group function, but it seems evident that Caesar is describing a charismatic experience—and that,
ruefully, he recognizes the charismatic force of the divine "shapes."
(We might compare Richard II's description of the charismatic Bolingbroke in the "supple knee" passage.) In her answer to her brother,
Octavia attempts to deflate the charisma of the pair, scoffing at the
possibility of divine presence in human affairs: "To Gods of their own
honour leave the Care, /Since they both Jealous and Almighty are"
(17). Octavia deliberately minimizes the religion of passion, proving
herself a truer stoic than her brother in respect to wonderment. "I fear
so high you'l my concernments press," she complains, "You'l break
on that you never can redress" (17). Her "concernments" require a
resistance to charismatic symbols, and she would like her brother to
ignore Bacchus and Isis as mere masquerades, and to replace wonder
with rationality. She in effect rejects the religious symbolism, attempting to separate Cleopatra from the source of her erotic charisma.

But Sedley's Octavia is a rare skeptic in this regard. In contrast to
her, most characters in the tragedies are incapable of separating Cleopatra from her erotic-charismatic symbols. Moreover, Cleopatra's
identification with the religious symbols seems real enough, as does

Antony's, in both dramatic and emotional terms. This is notably evident in Dryden's *All for Love* (1678), a tragedy which opens in the temple of Isis with a conversation between two priests. Antony himself "here in Isis' temple lives retired" (1.60); he has withdrawn to the temple after Actium, "his heart a prey to black despair" (1.61). Although under the circumstances his despair is not suprising, his choice to withdraw to the temple of Isis nonetheless seems to confirm his discipleship in, and his emotional need for, the "religion of erotic passion."

Perhaps it is worth recalling at this juncture Weber's stipulation that "the erotic frenzy stands in unison only with the orgiastic and charismatic form of religiosity" (1946, 349). Cleopatra's religiosity simultaneously promises and celebrates erotic frenzy. She at once creates a cultic religious bond and—through the meaning of the bond itself—rejects the cultic group for the "complete unification" with her lover. This doubleness is inseparable from erotic charisma, and it places Cleopatra in the powerful position of one who can foster a group crisis by enacting the symbolism of the group itself. Conversely, she can resolve the group crisis by reasserting her *charismatic* identity with the symbolism of erotic frenzy—in effect she replaces a transgressive act with a taboo. In this manner Cleopatra can manipulate the dissipative conditions endemic to a cultic (and charismatic) experience of eroticism.

But she is also vulnerable to group breakdown when her manipulations and her administration of the charismatic symbols falter along the way. Erotic sacrament and erotic sacrilege clash, which, as Eisenstadt notes, is probably to be expected: "The charismatic fervor is rooted in an attempt to come into contact with the very essence of being, to go to the very roots of existence, of cosmic, social and cultural order, to what is seen as sacred and fundamental" (1968, xix). So far, so good. Applied to Cleopatra the notion of charismatic fervor seeking the roots of "what is seen as sacred and fundamental" is consistent with the ideal of an erotic sacrament, which is itself "an attempt to come into contact with the very essence of being"—the symbolic truth of complete communion with another being. "But," as Eisenstadt continues, "this attempt may also contain a strong disposition to sacrilege: to the denial of the validity of the sacred, and of what is accepted in any given society as sacred" (1968, xix). From the Roman point of view Cleopatra in all her various representations is a walking sacrilege, an Isis-worshiper who tempts Pompey, Julius Caesar, and Marc Antony into adultery. Her sexuality is a frank affront to the institution of marriage, and her religion of passion offends stoicism, *romanitas*, and protoimperial reserve. To classical Roman writers, as Geoffrey Bullough points out, she was always "the enemy of *gravitas*" (1964, 5:218). Perhaps this sacriligeous character fuels Cleopatra's charisma where Antony is concerned; perhaps, as in other kinds of charisma, Cleopatra's erotic magnetism is enhanced by her rejection of what Antony holds to be sacred institutions.

It should be borne in mind, however, that eroticism, once it becomes more than an inner experience, is itself a symbolic attenuation of the putative "fading of the 'thou.'" Erotic-charismatic authority depends on that symbolic attenuation to organize itself as a group phenomenon. But in doing so something of its original force is compromised. As Eisenstadt concludes, "the very attempt to reestablish direct contact with these roots of cosmic and of sociopolitical order may breed both opposition to more attenuated and formalized forms of this order, as well as fear of, and hence opposition to, the sacred itself" (1968, xix). Cleopatra's authority is continually threatened by precisely this duality. Her eroticism gains its charismatic force by its fervor to come into contact with the root of the cosmic, social, and cultural order. Her charisma is therefore associated with the sacred, and, in Weber's terms, with a "boundless giving of oneself," which, again, is seen in radical opposition "to all functionality, rationality, and generality." But to establish a rulership, or to foster leadership conditions, as Cleopatra does, calling for the symbolic idealization of this charismatic fervor is in effect to attenuate and formalize the erotic sacrament. As a result, built into Cleopatra's erotic charisma is an inevitable resistance to the formalized symbols of her authority. This is of course a common feature of charismatic authority. As we have discussed in earlier chapters, charisma and traditional authority, which begin as polar opposites, generally formulate some kind of compromise, inevitably diluting the original charisma and attentuating or formalizing the charismatic symbols.[9]

Erotic charisma is no different in principle, although the evidence of the compromise may be more difficult to discern. We have often had recourse to recall what I termed (in the Introduction) the central paradox of charismatic group function: precisely, that the emphasis on a group ideal tends to destroy the individuality of the human being at the group's center, and that, conversely, the emphasis on the autonomy of an individual charismatic leader destroys the group ideal. This paradox, while resonant in an analysis of erotic charisma, does not perfectly explain the erotic-charismatic leader's dilemma. Such a leader, like Cleopatra, might well be threatened by a weighty emphasis on the group ideal over her own erotic centrality. But her sense of individual autonomy, though destructive to the group ideal, contains a prerequisite myth of mutuality (as opposed to absolute autonomy): simply put, her sacredness supposedly comes into being in tandem with a radical communion with an Other. This originary mutuality is at the heart of the erotic sacrament, which can seem confusing. When we compare erotic charisma to other pure types, there seems to be a skewing of the symmetrical relation between group ideal and individual autonomy.[10]

In any case, for all the hyperbole addressed to her uniqueness, Cleopatra, like other charismatic leaders, must compromise with other forms of authority, both charismatic and traditional. Nevertheless it is valuable to remember that her erotic charisma is in direct opposition to her own institutionalized charismatic authority, which officially threatens the Roman hegemony (but not for the same reason as does Antony's giving of new kingdoms to Cleopatra). In all the tragedies Cleopatra is the only genuine dynastic ruler, a legitimate holder of lineage charisma. Her rulership represents a form of political stability unfamiliar to the Rome of Julius Caesar, Antony, or Octavius, none of whom inherited his rulership (a crucial fact underscored by the scene on the young Pompey's galley in Shakespeare). Ironically, in plays obsessed with genealogical legitimation, only Cleopatra, descendant of the Ptolemies, has bona fide credentials.

Yet it is difficult to measure the importance of Cleopatra's dynastic authority to herself or to Antony. Cleopatra does not identify herself, nor does Antony identify her, as primarily a ruler, despite frequent references to her generically as "Egypt." Indeed, in all the plays, only Octavius displays a noticeable level of political detachment from Cleopatra's personal charismatic claim. His need to conquer Egypt, and even to display Cleopatra as a trophy of war, are anomalously impersonal, setting him off from the other principal characters' attitudes toward the Egyptian monarch. But Octavius clearly has ulterior motives for his supposed detachment. As his sister says bitterly of him in Sedley's tragedy:

> your Pride and endles Thirst of sway,
> To gain my friends, my Quarrel you pretend,
> But universal Empire is your end.

(34)

Among the other characters Cleopatra is far less emblematic than she apparently is to Octavius of a stable regime or of a national entity worth conquering. To the others she represents almost exclusively a disruptive force. And in this regard too Octavius is an anomaly: he only regards Cleopatra as a disruptive force for strategic reasons (which is his sister's point with "my Quarrel you pretend"); his overall ambition is to subsume not the disruptive force of Cleopatran charisma but the permanent Egypt—not the body natural, but rather the body politic. He will make proximate tactical use of Cleopatra's disruptive natural body to justify his actions, but genuine conquest requires the utter annihilation of the immortal body politic.

Neither Antony nor even Cleopatra has much concern with the Egyptian body politic.[11] Cleopatra's erotic-charismatic claim is manifest in direct opposition to her lineage authority and in conflict with an immortal component to her authority (Cleopatra's "immortal longings," it will be recalled, in fact invoke death, without the least thought given to the immortal body politic of Egypt).[12] Her disruptiveness coincides with her erotic power over Antony, a form of pure charisma antagonistic to traditional or legal-bureaucratic authority— although it must be said that we find little of what might be termed bureaucracy either in Rome or in Egypt in any of the tragedies. Once again Sedley's Octavia is apropos: she indicts her brother for circumventing the Roman bureaucracy:

> *Rome*'s once great *Senate* now is but a name;
> While some with fear, and some with Bribes you tame.
> Men learn at Court what they must there repeat,
> And for Concurrence, not for Council meet.
>
> (34)

Under Octavius, according to his sister, corruption has destroyed the legal-bureaucratic process. Of course this political evasion of Roman "Council" cannot be construed as a charismatic resistance to a hidebound form of authority. It reflects instead—at least in Octavia's view—a meanness in the character of her brother's authority.

In Egypt we find nothing comparable to the Roman senate, no figure powerful enough to bribe. Yet there are indications in the tragedies that Cleopatra's conduct is deliberately disruptive of well-established Egyptian law and custom. In the fourth act of Daniel's *The Tragedie of Cleopatra*, for example, the Egyptian chorus reflects censoriously on the state of the state:

> Misterious Egipt, wonder breeder,
>   strict religions strange obseruer,
> State-ordering Zeale, the best rule-keeper,
>   fostring still in temprate feruor:
> O how cam'st thou to lose so wholy
>   all religion, law and order?

And thus become the most vnholy
of all lands that Nylus border?
How could confus'd Disorder enter
where sterne Law sate so seuerely?
How durst weake lust and ryot venter
th'eye of Iustice looking neerely?
Could not those means that made thee great,
Be still the meanes to keepe thy state?

(1190–1204)

Following a soliloquy by Cleopatra, this choral interlude is addressed specifically to the breakdown of governance in Egypt, the failure or neglect of royal authority. The chorus complains of the loss of religion, law, and order in Egypt, where once "temprate feruor" energized "State-ordering Zeal, the best rule-keeper." Now "weake lust and ryot" have disturbed the state and disorder has entered "where sterne Law sate so seuerely."

It is important to recognize the parallel between erotic charisma and the very forms of disorder which the chorus itemize as destructive to the Egyptian polity. These forms of disorder, lust and riot, are in fact the means by which Cleopatra holds Antony ("When rioting in Alexandria," complains Shakespeare's Octavius, "you / Did pocket up my letters" [2.2.72–73]). Lust and riot constitute frank transgressions against stable social order, and against communal morality as well. But when combined with Cleopatra's personal magnetism these transgressions become symbols of a supersocial charismatic license. I do not want to force the connection between charisma and disorder in Daniel's play, nor would it be appropriate to assert that all disorder is charismatic. Yet the social rift brought on by Cleopatra's excesses, what she herself terms her "lusts" in Daniel's tragedy, is clearly linked to symbolically charged eroticism, a charismatic alternative to those strict rules of state religion and the temperate fervor that had kept Egyptian excess in check. Temperate fervor, a suggestive oxymoron in the context of lust and riot, is displaced by the violence of social disorder, which in turn is idealized by Cleopatra as an alternative to state religion. Lust and riot initiate the erotic sacrament and by symbolic extension are transformed into the pomp of Isis worship.

Yet Cleopatra's disruptiveness is not in itself sufficient to preserve her personal charisma.[13] Signs abound of her failure to retain the original force of her own erotic-charismatic authority. In all the tragedies—except Daniel's, which begins with a maternal theme—

Cleopatra gradually abandons erotic or sexual symbols in favor of martial and Roman symbols. Critics have often echoed Shakespeare's Octavius's contention that Antony "is not more manlike / Than Cleopatra; nor the queen of Ptolemy / More womanly than he" (1.4.5–7). For instance, as T. McAlindon puts it, "Cleopatra's aggressive triumph in love emasculates Antony, consigns him, as an eloquent stage direction indicates, to her band of fanning eunuchs" (1991, 234) (the stage direction is at 1.1.9). But is Antony actually "consigned" to the band of eunuchs? Has he lost his identity among them and become, as Octavius maintains, as womanly as Cleopatra? I would argue against such oversimplified interpretations. As McAlindon in fact notes, Cleopatra's aggressivity "unbinds the richly feminine element of [Antony's] nature" (1991, 234). Such unbinding, we might add, has a mutual resonance, enacting what Weber speaks of as the "overpowering" communion of the erotic sacrament.

With mutuality in mind it is interesting to review a notorious symbol in *Antony and Cleopatra* of Antony's putative emasculation, Cleopatra's recollection of one night's revelries:

> that night
> I laugh'd him into patience, and next morn,
> Ere the ninth hour, I drunk him to his bed;
> Then put my tires and mantles on him, whilst
> I wore his sword Philippan.
>
> (2.5.19–23)

This playful transvestism reverberates in the Roman, particularly Octavian, opinion of Antony's lapsed masculinity (as well as of Cleopatra's distorted femininity). As Janet Adelman points out, "the exchange of clothing . . . inevitably suggests a disastrous exchange of sexual authority and consequently a violation of the proper hierarchical relation between man and woman" (1973, 91). Given this interpretation it is difficult not to see the recollected scene as proleptic of Actium, or of some imaginary eclipse of Mars by Venus, or even of the castration of Osiris. But these are not the only possibilities, as Adelman notes. Cleopatra in Antony's military garb calls to mind the traditional image of the *Venus armata*, or the Bellona of Sedley's Cleopatra. Their exchange of clothing implies a more profound exchange of sexual roles, what Adelman terms "the cosmic and natural harmonies signified by divine transexuality" (1973, 94–95).[14] This transexuality is characterized by "boundary dissolution" and a simultaneous desire to merge and to remain intact, psychological states of mind that might well describe the threshhold of the erotic communion.[15]

Thus, Cleopatra's recollections of wearing the "sword Phillipan," while ominous if we read as Romans, might on the other hand reflect a unique mutual exchange. And this exchange might be seen as the basis of the erotic-charismatic bond.

But how does one read the scene as an Egyptian—or, more accurately, as a Cleopatran? Critics do not ask this question, ignoring the possibility that the exchange of costumes might have negative implications for Cleopatra's authority. It is worth asking, therefore: How would the exchange of sexual roles affect Cleopatra's erotic symbols? What would be the implications for her charismatic authority? After all, not only Antony's authority is threatened by this exchange. Although Cleopatra's transvestism is always thought (especially by the dramatis personae) to be an insult to Antony, we should recognize that in the charismatic dialectic of the play it may also signal the decline of Cleopatra's personal erotic charisma. There would be a characteristic Shakespearean irony in such a signal of decline: while at her most playfully erotic, reversing sexual roles and donning the symbol of both phallic power and terrible justice, the symbols of her own eroticism begin to fade.

This is not so far-fetched a possibility. Dressed in Antony's sword, Cleopatra enacts not only an erotic mutuality but also, less mutually, her own need as a ruler to match Antony's institutionalized charisma: his Roman generalship, his triumvir status (in Dryden he is called "Emperor"), and his martial myth. It is noteworthy that as the play progresses Cleopatra becomes more Roman whereas Antony, as far as I can tell, has no recurrence of his masquerade in "tires and mantles." Cleopatra dresses and attempts to fight as Bellona—of course she fails because she is only a symbolic figure, desperately adducing formalized versions of authority to her weakening, diluted erotic fervor (cf. Adelman 1973, 93)—and she kills herself in the tradition of a Roman martyr (though not in the bloody Roman manner). As Barroll puts it: "Antony has dwindled to nothingness, she must seek other analogies. Once we heard of her trading clothes with him; we saw her trying to be his kind of soldier at Actium; now she tries to be another part of him: magnanimous Antony" (1984, 174). It is true that she dresses for her suicide in her erotically symbolic robes (in *All for Love* she calls them her "dear relics /Of [her] immortal Love" [5.466–67]). But this is the final, mordant irony. She has been stripped of all her eroticism, all possibility of mutuality or complete sexual unification. Her death may be a tactical coup, but because it is a suicide it is the antithesis of mutual exchange or overpowering communion. To the contrary, Cleopatra dies imitating Antony's magnanimity and simultaneously reducing her own exalted charismatic eroticism to a rationality in concert with Octavian tactics and, as I will discuss below, with rule-keeping Egyptian religion.

The Dialectic of Charisma

In the Antony and Cleopatra tragedies (again, Daniel's excepted) we encounter a dialectic of charisma that affects both principal characters. Antony's charismatic generalship contends with his own charisma hunger and with Cleopatra's erotic-charismatic authority. At the same time, Cleopatra's charisma is in constant dialectical contention with both Roman institutional charismatic authority and with Antony's personal charisma. The gradual—and reluctant—Romanization of Cleopatra neutralizes the irrational force of her own original charisma. This is one dimension of her tragedy, amplified by her loss (and destruction) of Antony. It is indeed difficult to locate any positive results of what Adelman terms "cosmic and natural harmonies"; the "divine transexuality" manifest in the exchange of clothing scarcely contributes to enduring symbiosis or communion of subject and other, since the charismatic dialectic inexorably divides the two lovers. For similar reasons, it is not easy to accept McAlindon's view that there is a natural cycle to the defeat of the "grizzled" Antony in Shakespeare's play, and that the lovers' sad ending implies renewal and regeneration (1991, 223). These seem to me abstract and optimistic readings—"abstract" in the sense I mention in the Introduction. Tragedy, I note there, tends to cast protagonists down into the rational, order-driven realities of society from the heights of such powerful abstractions as genealogical superiority or semidivine bodily status. Antony and Cleopatra, whose charisma is in dialectical conflict, fail at the very forms of mutuality that might preserve them in their semidivine superiority. Like all tragic figures, they fall from the heights of their abstractions into social life and consciously come to recognize their loss of symbolic superiority. If the tragic experience to some degree involves thinking, then Antony and Cleopatra are consummate tragic figures, for they acknowledge and recoil from their own loss of divine status.

Their charismatic dialectic never really resolves itself in any of the plays, and it is therefore mistaken, I think, to speak of cosmic harmonies or natural regeneration. Conflict retains its sovereignty until the end of each tragic version of the story, playful transexuality and regenerative myths notwithstanding. The younger generation, it should be remembered, takes over by force, and the older generation commits suicide. The shattering of the erotic bond emphasizes this

untimely truncation, the constraints of rationalization and resacral-
ization replacing the charismatic disorder of Cleopatra's symbolic
reign (and, less visibly, of Antony's charismatic generalship). I am
inclined to agree with John Alvis when he suggests that the "regenerative sacramental potency" is missing from Antony's and Cleopatra's
religion of passion. The couple, he maintains, share a "mutual narcissism" that eventually leads to "physical dissolution, the natural outcome of the insulary logic that has characterized their relationship all
along" (1978, 191, 193–94). In Alvis's view only utter selflessness—as
opposed to mutual narcissism—would free the lovers: "sacramental
love requires a dying of the self, but through this act of selflessness
lovers free themselves to lead a new life in this world. . . . The sexual
bond opens the lovers to other forms of love so that spreading from
its sexual basis their largesse extends to other people and to other
activities" (1978, 196).

But Alvis is speaking of love, not eroticism. His ideal of the sexual
bond reflects the notion of a generative force, akin perhaps to McAlindon's observation regarding Cleopatra's symbolic value that in Plutarch "Venus and Isis were one and the same generative deity" (1991,
231). The missing component in both of these versions of sacred sexuality—or sacramental regenerative force—is violence. It is violence
that distinguishes eroticism from love, not necessarily overt violence
but the symbolically sublimated expression of violence. As Habermas
observes, paraphrasing Bataille on the subject, "for Bataille happiness
and power are indissolubly fused in the heterogeneous: In the erotic
and the sacred Bataille celebrates an 'elemental violence'" (1984, 87).
We need not "celebrate" this notion of elemental violence, but if we
ignore it we will fail to appreciate the cannibalizing frenzy of the
erotic sacrament. The presence of such a frenzy is evident even in the
contrast of Alvis's notion of the "dying of the self" in lovers' relations
to the opposite idea in Weber that the erotic involves the "fading of
the 'thou.'" In the former we find self-abnegation or self-effacement,
in the latter, utter consumption of the Other. The difference is striking
when we consider the elemental violence of Cleopatran eroticism, let
alone the cannibalized and consumed Antonine will.

Consider in this context Shakespeare's Antony, "unqualitied with
shame" (3.11.44), as he pitiably explains his strange conduct at
Actium:

> Egypt, thou knew'st too well,
> My heart was to thy rudder tied by the strings,
> And thou shouldst tow me after. O'er my spirit
> Thy full supremacy thou knew'st, and that

Thy beck might from the bidding of the gods
Command me.

(3.11.57–61)

Antony is referring to his flight from the sea battle. He ordered his
own ships to follow Cleopatra's as they abandoned the fight, an unaccountably cowardly act for Antony and a disastrous tactical blunder.
But the interest for our analysis is not so much the tactical error as
Antony's explanation. He blames Cleopatra ("Egypt") for his behavior, which seems unmanly of him. He complains that Cleopatra knew
too well that Antony's "heart was to thy rudder tied by strings," and
that he would be unable to resist following wherever Egypt strayed.
There is in his complaint the sense that Cleopatra is a known quantity,
a shared experience, "almost as if," according to Summers, "the flight
of her ships were intended as a public demonstration of her mastery
over him rather than merely the result of her fear in battle" (1984,
124). Antony's language makes sense only if we recognize, as Antony
apparently does, a relationship of follower to leader, and, further, if
we acknowledge the fundamental violence of Cleopatra's erotic-
charismatic authority over Antony's will. In the context of Antony's
flight, Agrippa's impromptu eulogy for him, uttered much later in
the play, is ironic indeed: "A rarer spirit," he says, "never / Did steer
humanity" (5.1.31–32).

The appearance of the word *spirit* in both passages is significant,
perhaps more so than the overt connection with steering. Antony
laments Cleopatra's "full supremacy" over his "spirit," and the word
points to an inner experience as well as to an experience superior to a
bodily one, an ecstasy. Adelman sees the entire subject of Actium in
terms of spiritual and bodily ecstasy. She suggests that the water
("Cleopatra's terrain . . . as a generative goddess") "leads us to
Actium and Antony's desertion of himself," a prerequisite of his
erotic experience: "The emotional and imagistic nexus of the play lies
in the sexual process itself, where one must lose oneself to form a new
union. The Roman horror of that loss and the ecstatic union which the
lovers feel as they die are two elements in the same process: for the
dissolution of personal boundaries is both our greatest fear and our
highest desire" (1973, 148–49). Once again the notion of boundary
dissolution has strong resonance with Weber's "fading of the 'thou,'"
but here too Adelman romanticizes the erotic bond. The supposed
"ecstatic union which the lovers feel when they die" is more delusion
than reality, proof, ironically, of the dissolution of the erotic bond
rather than of the dissolution of personal boundaries. With Antony's
death the thralldom of erotic charisma is meaningless, and Cleopatra's

charismatic symbols become ossified "relics" (Dryden's word for her robes) of a disruptiveness and an authority that no longer have a social manifestation. This separation from the charismatic authority of her eroticism brings Cleopatra's tragedy into sharp relief. She dies alone clinging to obsolete symbols, her charismatic claim languishing. To see her death as a triumph of love, as many critics have done, is to neglect both the consuming drive of the erotic sacrament and the vanity of objectless desire.

Antony and Cleopatra are perhaps better analyzed, especially at Actium, in terms of what Ruth Newman has characterized as "piper's charisma" (after the Pied Piper of Hamelin). Newman recognizes the "suprasexual" element of the charismatic bond, in which "the kind of sexual energy aroused is such that the desire is to lose all boundaries." Moreover, she continues, "it is not as in intercourse, where boundaries disappear or become blurred momentarily and are reclaimed afterwards. With charismatic enticement the sexuality is closer to what the late Dr. Pierre Turquet, in a lecture, called *oceanic submersion*. The goal is to be part of and never reemerge: to transcend one's own boundaries, to become lost within a greater whole" (1983, 206; Newman's emphasis). This is very close to Adelman's analysis, with a felicitous "oceanic" connection. But charismatic submersion implies a symbiotic interdependency somewhat more *socially* problematic than the dream of complete union. The "freedom from choice" that accompanies charismatic enthrallment carries with it profound, but irrational, responsibility: "There are times when the symbiosis between leader and led is so strong that the follower is held responsible for the pains and aches and bad feelings of the leader, who is claimed to be so at one with his followers that their very thought forms can cause great distress and even danger to his life" (Newman 1983, 206). The twists and turns of Cleopatra's moods, always in tandem with Antony's real or supposed emotional changes, reflect exactly this kind of supernatural symbiosis. But, as Newman points out, there is a "Faustian bargain" to be kept: "the leader must take over the responsibility for the consequences of all the followers' acts so long as they are part of the group, *and they need never be blamed* (1983, 206; my emphasis). This bargain provides followers with the freedom from choice necessary to Weber's notion of the metanoia or internal change that shifts group support to a charismatic leader.

In Antony's case his charismatic (or "oceanic") submersion mitigates his own culpability at Actium, at least during the battle: "O, whither have thou led me, Egypt?" (3.11.51) he moans helplessly afterward. That he recognizes his charismatic self-abnegation, his abrogation of responsibility, signals the beginning of his catastrophe. In self-disgust he now separates himself as soldier and leader from himself as follower—indeed, he says before Cleopatra arrives, "I have fled myself" (3.11.7), which is ambiguous under the circumstances since he has both fled *from* himself and fled *to* himself. In any case, he deliberately detaches himself from Cleopatra's charismatic leadership, and in doing so opens a breach of self-solicitousness that utterly isolates him from the erotic sacrament. He may rally back with Bacchanalian gusto—"Some wine within there, and our viands!" (3.11.73)—but his heartstrings no longer suffer a symbiotic connection with Cleopatra's rudder. It is doubtful that he ever regains his honor. He dies, deceived, in isolation.

If Cleopatra is Antony's piper, his charmer, then his detachment from her erotic-charismatic domination elicits her destruction as well. She is a prisoner of her own gifts just as much as Antony (cf. Newman 1983, 203): without him her erotic charisma does not exist. The tragic moment hinges on this binding mutuality. The transgressive, antinomian character of Cleopatra's charismatic eroticism sweeps Antony along, producing the phenomenon of "Egypt" as a shared, utterly consuming experience. But that same transgressiveness and antinomianism fosters a set of internal taboos to protect the intersubjective bond—one is reminded of Paul's taboo on dissent from the dissenters. Only Antony's willful obedience of Cleopatran transgressive strictures protects them both from disaster, averting the threat of intersubjective dissolution of the erotic bond.

Is this the vaunted triumph of love? Such a volatile social structure seems to contain too much of Bataille's "elemental violence" to satsify the amorous ideal. And let us recall in this context Smith's notion that far-from-equilibrium systems operate by means of "entropy production and the scavenging of entropy" (1992, 189), thriving in dissipative structures. The seeming "love" of Antony and Cleopatra thrives— when it thrives—in just such a dissipative structure. It is a love that only survives by creating and managing the threat of its own extinction, an entropy-scavenger, *a fortiori* self-dissipating. Such eroticism is a far cry from cosmic harmonies. Perhaps the traitor Photinus's epithet in Sedley sums it up best: he speaks of the love of Antony and Cleopatra as their "mutual flame" (52), a description that conflates their shared passion with the violent consumption inseparable from their eroticism.[16]

Only the ongoing dialectic of charisma in the tragedies sustains Antony's relative autonomy, highlighting the fluctuations between his inability to resist being steered (with heartstrings tied to Cleopatra's rudder) and his ability to "steer humanity" himself, as Agrippa puts it.[17] The alternation between Antony's personal charisma and his charisma hunger anatomizes both the rivalry and the threat of consuming violence—or violent consumption—that is inherent in the erotic bond. The plays proceed through stages of competing mutualities and mutually exclusive shared experiences. The union of the two lovers, itself an experience of charismatic eroticism, is brought about by the evasion and even the annihilation of other charismatic claims, chiefly Antony's generalship, but also, more implicitly, Cleopatra's dynastic rulership. It would seem that on the early modern stage the mutual flame can only be fueled by violent rejections of competing mutualities.

We can trace the pattern of these rejections in the ebb and flood of Antony's personal charisma. As a triumvir, as a superior soldier, as the avenger of Julius Caesar, Antony displayed and, in flashes, continues to display extraordinary abilities and personal magnetism, raising his prestige among both Romans and Egyptians.[18] Antony repeatedly acts to confirm his prestige in a concerted effort to match Cleopatra's magic (or, perhaps, to outjuggle the "gypsy" juggler). His giving away of kingdoms, for instance, is a consummately charismatic gesture, a means of refocusing attention on his personal claim, a means of dialectically contending with Cleopatran eroticism. Such "wonderful liberality" (North 1880, 157) should remind us of the irrational economic distribution of booty, a hallmark of charismatic organization. But we should also note that this particular charismatic attribute had been a part of Antony's repertoire from the beginning. According to Plutarch, "that which most procured [Antony's] rising and advancement, was his liberality, who gave all to the soldiers and kept nothing for himself: and when he was grown to great credit, then was his authority and power also very great, the which notwithstanding himself did overthrow by a thousand other faults he had" (North 1880, 156–57).

As earlier recipients of Antony's bounty, the soldiers are no doubt envious of their general's generosity to Cleopatra, which at least in part explains why the Romans under Antony do not share his doting attitude toward Cleopatra. This difference of opinion (if "opinion" describes it) is obvious from the first lines of Shakespeare's play when Philo complains that "this dotage of our general's /O'erflows the measure" (1.1.1–2). In the same vein, Sedley's Canidius (Antony's general), explaining why the Roman troops refused to follow Antony, remarks, "Their general Discontent at her [Cleopatra] was lowd: /But Souldiers are a rude uncivil Crowd" (11). In *All for Love* the soldierly resistance to Cleopatra is even more pronounced. Ventidius remains antagonistic toward the Egyptian queen throughout the play and

seems to speak for Antony's army as well. In act 1, for example, when
Antony asks why the soldiers refused to march, Ventidius has his
unwelcome answer ready:

> They said they would not fight for Cleopatra.
> Why should they fight, indeed, to make her conquer,
> And make you more a slave? to gain you kingdoms,
> Which, for a kiss at your next midnight feast,
> You'll sell to her? Then she new-names her jewels,
> And calls this diamond such or such a tax;
> Each pendant in her ear shall be a province.

(1.359–65)

The Roman resistance to Cleopatra could hardly be made clearer. But
we should note that the soldiers (and Ventidius) misinterpret the
character of Antony's relationship to Cleopatra. Indeed, they refuse
to equate his generosity to her with his "wonderful liberality" to
them, key to his advancement. Antony may be enthralled but he is
not precisely a slave. His experience of Cleopatra's erotic charisma
bears little resemblance to the transactional relationship imagined by
Ventidius in which Antony "sells" kingdoms to Cleopatra for sexual
favors. In truth, such a rational economic arrangement would be in
conflict with a genuinely charismatic relationship.

Of course that conflict is the point of the soldiers' objections. For
selfish reasons—to protect their inner experience of Antony—they
rationalize the charismatic relationship of Antony and Cleopatra,
attempting to reduce it to transactional terms. While they seem to dis-
parage Antony's behavior as irrational, in fact it is not rationality they
crave but a redirected irrational economy, a display of bounty favoring them instead of Cleopatra. But the soldiers cannot objectively
conceive their own charisma hunger, and therefore, especially in *All
for Love*, they remain blind to the parallel between their relationship
to Antony and Antony's relationship to Cleopatra. It would be sense-
less to argue that the Roman legions followed Antony, that they stood
like mute iron statues in his presence, as a result of a rational economic arrangement. And it is similarly absurd to think that Antony
showers kingdoms on Cleopatra as part of a rational transaction, or
for that matter that she receives his gifts as payment. In fact, Sedley's
Cleopatra articulates a distinction along these very lines. Explaining
the disaster at Actium, she claims that it is traitorous soldiers, such as
the ones who refused to follow Antony and her, who rely on such economically rational arrangements: "Base Mercenary Souls that fight
for Pay," she says, "To morrow Kill, whom they defend to day" (26).

She contrasts this base mercenary behavior with that of princes—"But Princes Minds on Springs of Honour move, / And what can they not do, wound up by Love?" (26)—invoking charismatic attributes of honor and love as cures for the disease of mean economic rationality. The call of honor and love, the duty to identify with these irrational symbols of ideal character, not only raises princes above the "uncivil crowd" but also links honor and love (perhaps erotic love) as extraordinary rulership qualities manifest in times of social distress.

It is with just such attributes in mind that Antony liberally gives away kingdoms. He does not seem concerned, as does Shakespeare's Octavius, with the political ramifications of having given Cleopatra "the stablishment of Egypt, made her / Of Lower Syria, Cyprus, Lydia, / Absolute queen" (3.6.9–11). His concern, or more properly his impulse, drives him to establish *himself* as a charismatic force in Egypt. It is ironic that Antony demonstrates his authority in dialectical opposition to Cleopatra's, despite his beneficence to her. He at once "establishes" her as an "Absolute queen" and resists or opposes her charismatic enthrallment. Shortlived though it may be, Antony's prestige confronts Cleopatra's erotic charisma in a lucid demonstration of the dialectic of charisma at work.

Indeed, at times there is enough dialectical tension between their personal charismas to make Antony seem nearly autonomous, notwithstanding his outbreaks of acute emotional dependence (and his military alliance with Egypt). But this is a dialectic without synthetic resolution, and, in consequence, a cloud of ambiguity surrounds Antony's motives. When he gives kingdoms, for example, it is difficult to determine whether he does so charismatically, with recourse to personal prestige, or whether he does so in the manner of a follower confirming his *duty* to Cleopatra's charismatic claim. If the latter is the case, then his repeated insistence that no recompense is commensurate with Cleopatra's value might well be taken at face value, as when Dryden's Antony exalts, "She deserves / More worlds than I can lose" (1.368–69). In either case, it is clear that to the Romans, including Antony's soldiers, the motive force behind Antony's wild liberality is irrelevant. They discern no difference between the possibility that Antony's acts might be driven by personal charisma or that they are solicited by charismatic enthrallment.

In Thomas May's *The Tragoedy of Cleopatra, Queene of Aegypt* (acted 1626; first edition 1639), there is an intriguing twist on the common theme of Antony's excessive generosity to Cleopatra. Antony gives the crowns of Cyprus, Coelosyria, and Phoenecia to the Egyptian queen, to the predictable accompaniment of grumbling from his lieutenants. But in response to the grumbling Antony takes the high ground, invoking a superb *romanitas*: "Admire not frends," he says, "the goddlike power of Rome /Is more declar'd by what it gives away /Then what it holds" (1.2.95–97). May's marginal note beside this passage cites Plutarch, but the use of the phrase "Admire not" clearly refers to Horace's "Nil admirari." Antony is challenging his possessive lieutenants with ideal Roman conduct, not in this case sto-ical *apatheia* but rather a conqueror's *magnanimitas*. Antony's defense of his behavior is followed by a supportive speech from Canidius, a speech remarkable for its legitimation of the erotic religious symbol-ism associated with Cleopatra:

> I cannot chuse but thinke how fitt a state
> For *Cleopatra* Cyprus kingdome is.
> And shall beleeve that it was ominous
> That noble *Julius Caesar* after all
> Those fower rich triumphs which hee held at Rome
> When hee resolv'd with like magnificence
> To build a temple to the Goddesse *Venus*,
> From whome his house derive theire pedegree,
> Within his stately temple, to expresse
> The image of that Goddesse, hee sett upp
> Faire *Cleopatraes* figure in the place,
> Supposing her to bee the Queene of love.
>
> (1.2.99–109)

How different from Sedley's Octavia May's Canidius appears in this passage. Not only does he acknowledge Cleopatra's identity with the goddess of love, but he also provides a pedigree for this identity, claiming that no one less than Julius Caesar had seen Cleopatra as Venus and had, a generation earlier, erected her image in Rome. We can draw several genealogical implications from the passage: that Caesar's earlier setting up of "*Cleopatraes* figure" in the temple legiti-mates Antony's presenting her with a crown; that Caesar (who also loved her) participated in the religion of passion; even that Cleopatra, as queen of love, somehow provided Caesar with his genealogical legitimacy, since the pedigree of his house derived from Venus. But most significant in this passage is May's interpolation of Cleopatra's eroticism as a stable religious myth complete with its own set of sym-bols and historical precedence.

The merging of Antony's liberality with Cleopatra's eroticism sug-gests an ideal intermingling of personal charismatic claims. It is a delusory ideal, however, insofar as Antony increasingly loses the charismatic management of his actual followers. His liberal gestures may be old tricks, versions of his earlier *praestigiae*, but in reality they have become simulacra. Like so many other charismatic figures I have discussed, the Egyptian Antony has become separated from his own charismatic symbols: his liberality, symbol of the shared experience of his generalship, has lost its immediacy for his followers, dividing the charismatic group from one of the original signs of its incorporation. In terms of the group's daily function, as Philo's complaint probably indicates, the more Antony becomes submerged in Cleopatran erotic charisma and the more he seeks to satisfy his own charisma hunger, the less able he is to act as the center of a charismatic experience for his followers.

We trivialize Antony's tragedy if we ignore the enormous power of his original charismatic claim—the height of martial myth from which he topples. Moreover, we should recognize that, throughout the tragedies, all the Romans regard Antony with expectancy, anticipating a resurgence at any moment of his gift for bringing well-being to his faithful followers (cf. Weber 1978, 2:1114). For Antony has clearly been in his career a bearer of salvationistic charisma, a heroic figure in times of social and military distress. In Shakespeare's tragedy it is indeed the loss of this salvationistic strain that Octavius laments. He calls for Antony to "Leave thy lascivious wassails" (1.4.56), recalling his quondam charismatic leadership as the height from which he has fallen to his present erotic enthrallment. Octavius's description of Antony's army in retreat from Modena is one of the few glimpses we have of the source of Antony's personal charisma:

> When thou once
> Was beaten from Modena, where thou slew'st
> Hirtius and Pansa, consuls, at thy heel
> Did famine follow, whom thou fought'st against,
> Though daintily brought up, with patience more
> Than savages could suffer. Thou didst drink
> The stale of horses, and the gilded puddle
> Which beasts would cough at: thy palate then did deign
> The roughest berry, on the rudest hedge;
> Yea, like the stag, when snow the pasture sheets,
> The barks of trees thou browsed. On the Alps
> It is reported thou didst eat strange flesh,
> Which some did die to look on: and all this—
> It wounds thine honour that I speak it now—
> Was borne so like a soldier, that thy cheek
> So much as lank'd not.
>
> (1.4.56–71)

Antony's exceptional asceticism in the mountains establishes his personal charismatic claim. His ability to survive in a manner impossible for ordinary mortals—he drank the "gilded puddle" and he ate "strange flesh,/Which some did die to look on"—confirms his heroism, just as the marvel that his cheek "So much as lank'd not" suggests a supernatural, or superhuman, physical endurance. As Weber repeatedly maintains, the charismatic hero "gains and retains [authority] solely by proving his powers in practice" (1978, 2:1114), and the Alps adventure served precisely this purpose. Octavius's point is that no such proof of charismatic powers will be forthcoming as long as Antony remains enthralled by Cleopatran eroticism.

The point is well taken, but Octavius's (or Shakespeare's) choice of examples is worth exploring further. Why, for instance, choose to demonstrate Antony's prowess by showing him in retreat? Why not mention his numerous victories, not least at Philippi? It is as though actual martial superiority is not in Octavius's interest to praise. According to Vivian Thomas, Octavius's speech "focuses on the image of the *ideal Roman*" (1989, 125; emphasis in original). Similarly, Theodora Jankowski maintains that Antony's Alpine survival demonstrates how his "soldier's reason managed to keep his body so under control that he maintained his 'mean' and did not seem to suffer the excess that one would expect of someone on a starvation march" (1989, 99–100). But I am not sure that Octavius intends to praise Antony's "reason" or his putative "mean," let alone his *romanitas*. Rather, it seems to me that Octavius praises a kind of extremism or ascetic excess. And not so coincidentally it is also excess—bodily and antiascetic—which he condemns in Antony, his Egyptian wassails. Shakespeare has subtly rendered a comparison of like qualities cast as opposites. The contrast of the wintry Alps and sultry Egypt translates into an inversion of Antony's appetites: extreme hunger and gross surfeit alternate in his conduct. In terms of charismatic power, we might observe that in the Alps Antony satisfies charisma hunger, while in Egypt he manifests a charisma hunger of his own.

Missing from both versions of Antony's appetites is any hint of moderation. Octavius in effect condemns Antony by the praise of Alpine asceticism, for rational restraint characterizes the Roman ideal of rulership. The excesses of Antonine will, charismatic or merely luxurious, represent to Octavius and to the rest of us who know the imperial story a last vestige of the republican fervor for personally heroic individuals. In *Antony and Cleopatra* moderation and control characterize the incipient Pax Romana, stigmatizing Antony's princely excesses, like Cleopatra's erotic symbolism in the final scenes, as obsolete and irrelevant to the newly routinized charisma of the Caesarean succession.

Curiously—and ominously—only Cleopatra imagines a quality of moderation in Antony, and this only when he is apart from her. When Alexas returns to Alexandria, bearing the "treasure of an oyster" (1.5.44) from Antony, now in Rome, Cleopatra asks, "What, was he sad, or merry?" (1.5.50). Alexas answers safely, choosing neither: "Like to the time o' the year between the extremes / Of hot and cold, he was nor sad nor merry" (1.5.51–52). Cleopatra's interpretation of this obviously calculated observation betrays a suspect exuberance:

> O well-divided disposition! Note him,
> Note him, good Charmian, 'tis the man; but note him.
> He was not sad, for he would shine on those
> That make their looks by his; he was not merry,
> Which seem'd to tell them, his remembrance lay
> In Egypt with his joy; but between both.
> O heavenly mingle! Be'st thou sad, or merry,
> The violence of either thee becomes,
> So does it no man else.
>
> (1.5.53–61)

The speech contains a glaring contradiction. Cleopatra praises Antony's "well-divided disposition" and the "heavenly mingle" of joy and sadness in him, reminding us perhaps of the phrase "temprate feruor" used to describe the Egyptian state religion, "the best rule-keeper" in Daniel's tragedy. At first glance Cleopatra seems to condone Antony's version of temperate fervor, describing a moderation between extremes (of hot and cold, as Alexas puts it). But at the same time she declares that the "violence" of either extreme becomes Antony. This implausible contradiction probably describes Cleopatra's confused emotions better than it describes Antony's disposition.

We should note, however, that Cleopatra is well aware of the threat of Antony's personal charisma, his status as a Roman leader. Even amid a flurry of contradictory exclamations, she admits that "he would shine on those / That make their looks by his." A clearer description of what we have called the mirroring of selfobject tranference could not be found than "those / That make their looks by his": Cleopatra acknowledges Antony's charismatic appeal as the opposite of his charisma hunger, an antithetical social force to her erotic-charismatic claim. She cannot counter this threat while Antony is away from her, except in the fantasy that he is not prey to the violence of extremes while in Rome. Yet moderation would neutralize the erotic sacrament they share. So in the end Cleopatra's exuberance regarding Antony's "well-divided disposition" is insincere, not merely because he is off in Rome but also because a well-divided disposition would not accommodate charisma hunger.

In *All for Love* we find a striking contrast to the "well-divided disposition." Dryden's Antony openly displays the violence of extremes, revealing the impotence of his personal charisma in contention with his charisma hunger. We observe Antony among his troops through the eyes of Charmian, herself a follower of a charismatic dynast, whose narration blends a Cleopatran chaos of incredulity, disappointment, and triumph. "I found him, then," she begins,

> Incompassed round, I think, with iron statues,
> So mute, so motionless his soldiers stood
> While awfully he cast his eyes about,
> And every leader's hopes or fears surveyed.

> (2.47–51)

This is an image of Plutarch's Antony, the charismatic general holding his troops in thrall, but also of the fantastical Cleopatran Antony who shines on those "who make their looks by his." Along with Charmian we observe and feel the force of an irrational, charismatic relationship in which the soldiers share a profoundly intersubjective experience, their motionlessness expressing their duty to Antony's charismatic claim. Yet the emphasis of the scene is on movement, not motionlessness, on divisive distraction rather than undivided attention. Dryden engineers the charismatic military tableau so that the soldiers' enthrallment might be seen as parallel to, and feebler than, Antony's enthrallment to Cleopatra. In fact Antony breaks the spell over his men when Charmian delivers her message from Cleopatra, requesting one last farewell. Charmian reports that Antony "fetched an inward groan," and, worse, "He seemed not now that awful Antony / Who shook an armed assembly with his nod" (2.62, 65–66). Before our eyes Antony is himself transformed into a follower—of love, of the erotic sacrament, of Cleopatran charisma—and his self-object transference to Cleopatra is as complete as that of his own followers who find their deficit strength mirrored in him.

But what deficit strength does Antony see mirrored in Cleopatra? And in what manner exactly does she satisfy his charisma hunger? The answer to these questions, I think, lies in the balance between Cleopatra's transgressive appeal and in the taboos with which she conserves and even enhances that appeal. But, before we explore transgression and taboo, it must be acknowledged that Cleopatra's implementation of her transgressive appeal has a charismatic basis. It is both heterogeneous and self-determining. As Enobarbus remarks, "she makes hungry, / Where most she satisfies" (2.2.243–44), a characterization that makes perfect sense when the hunger at issue is charisma hunger. The more a leader satisfies the charisma hunger of a follower, the more hunger that follower feels. There is no such thing as a surfeit of charisma: no one can have or experience too much. The shared experience of a charismatic bond continually renews itself for as long as the central figure continues to "prove" his or her extraordinary claim: literally, then, charisma "makes hungry where it most satisfies."

Transgression and Taboo

I would like to conclude this chapter with a brief consideration of Cleopatra's ability to mirror Antony's deficit strength through her skillful manipulation of transgressive behavior and taboos. All the tragedies contain evidence of this mirroring. All the Cleopatras at one time or another demonstrate what we might term a will to transgress and to commit sacrilege. Antony, on the other hand, lacks the will to transgress. The Egyptian queen creates a charismatic dynamic by satisfying Antony's hunger for that same deficit will in himself.

Describing Antony's conduct at Actium, Plutarch, in North's version, makes the observation that "he was not his own man (proving that true which an old man spake in mirth, that the soul of a lover lived in another body, and not in his own)" (1880: 212). The Antony who lives in another body when he flees—according to Plutarch showing "he had not only lost the courage and heart of an emperor, but also of a valiant man" (North 1880, 212)—is the same Antony who sees his deficit strength mirrored in Cleopatra. He follows her from the sea battle for the same reason that he defies Rome earlier in the story. This may seem contradictory, but in fact the same impulse that allows him to say "Let Rome in Tiber melt" (1.1.33) inspires him to follow Cleopatra. Sedley's Antony speaks of a "secret Sympathy in Love" (25), but the sympathy between Antony and Cleopatra contains more of self-object transference, more of the mirroring of deficit strength, than of a symmetrical exchange of sympathetic feeling. Cleopatra in her manner and indeed in her very existence represents a defiance of Roman tradition. But, more than that, she exhibits an implacable will to transgress against and overturn all constraints on her subjective autonomy—Roman, religious, Egyptian, or dynastic. This extraordinary willfulness she expresses erotically, creating a set of charismatic symbols in which Antony sees his own lack of transgressive will reflected. He accepts the erotic sacrament, responding to the breaking of constraints in Cleopatra's charismatic claim, and through an inner experience of metanoia is transformed into a follower. It should come as no surprise, therefore, when in *All for Love* Antony remarks to Cleopatra "we have loved each other / Into our mutual ruin" (2.244–45). The systemic mutuality of their charismatic interdependence made a "mutual ruin" inevitable.

Earlier I noted that Cleopatra is in the powerful position of manipulating the inherent doubleness of erotic charisma, that she simultaneously creates a cultic religious bond (through Isis symbolism) and rejects the cultic bond for what Weber terms "complete unification with her lover." Moreover, as Daniel's chorus complains, Cleopatra rejects traditional Egyptian morality, disrupting the law and order of the community. For as long as she remains in a rebellious posture toward traditional authority—represented by law, social order, and the old, rule-keeping state religion—Cleopatra continues to nurture a charismatic claim despite her lineage constraints. She survives *charismatically* by establishing a compromise between her cultic persona and her individual erotic autonomy (complete unification with Antony). But, like all personal charismas, Cleopatra's is shortlived. Before Antony's death, even before the decisive Roman victories, Cleopatra begins to lose her grasp on the doubleness of erotic charisma. She fails to maintain the necessary balance between transgressive act and taboo, between, in other words, her individual desire for Antony and the abstraction of that desire in the religious symbolism (replete with taboos) that serves as the basis of the shared experience of her charisma.

Cleopatra's concession to ritual sacrifice in Daniel's tragedy is testimony to her failure. She embraces sacrifice as a symbolic form, suggesting that she has lost the will to transgress as well as the ability (or maybe "will" again) to balance transgression and taboo. Sacrifice is a form of taboo. As Walter Burkert notes, "through solidarity and cooperative organization, and by establishing an inviolable order, the sacrificial ritual gave society its form" (1983, 35). Similarly, according to René Girard, "the purpose of the sacrifice is to restore harmony to the community, to reinforce the social fabric" (1977, 8). When Cleopatra performs a ritual sacrifice over Antony's tomb in Daniel's tragedy she may well be seeking such harmony, such reinforcement. She seems to be making reparations for her sacriligious conduct and, indeed, to be reestablishing herself within the protective limits of rule-keeping religion. Her ritual, in Burkert's terms, "creates and affirms social interaction" (1983, 23; cf. 34), as is evident in her soliloquy:

> I must goe take my leaue
> And last farewell of my dead *Anthony*:
> Whose deerely honour'd Tombe must heere receaue
> This sacrifice, the last before I dye.
>   O sacred euer-memorable Stone,
> That hast without my teares, within my flame,
> Receiue th'oblation of the wofull'st mone
> That euer yet from sad affliction came.
> And you deere reliques of my Lord and Loue,
> (The sweetest parcells of the faithfull'st liuer,)
> O let no impious hand dare to remoue
> You out from hence, but rest you heere for euer.
> Let Egypt now giue peace vnto you dead,
> That lyuing, gaue you trouble and turmoyle.
>
>   (1087–1100)

Certainly the prayer to the stone solicits communal cooperation: "let no impious hand"—"Let Egypt." But is there also a hint of Cleopatra's remorse for the damage done to the community by her transgressions? More to the point, how should we interpret her actions apart from her speech? What does it mean to perform a ritual (animal?) sacrifice on the tomb of one's recently departed lover?

In this context we should remember that the word *sacrifice* means "making sacred" (cf. Girard 1987, 226), and that, for Burkert, it is "the basic experience of the sacred" (1983, 3; cf. Shuger 1994, 153). Moreover, as Bataille points out, sacrifice confirms prohibition and taboo, distancing the community from transgression (cf. 1987, 83–85).[19] For Cleopatra, religious sacrifice is a capitulation to the old mysteries ("Misterious Egipt," as the chorus says). It may be that "sacrifice itself releases erotic energies" (Shuger 1994, 164), but those energies are controlled by a ritual framework in direct conflict with the dissipative energies of Cleopatra's erotic charisma. Her oblations are meant to resacralize both herself and Antony, who presumably transgressed by sharing the erotic sacrament. Yet this resacralizing gesture inexorably diminishes the transgressive and sacriligious character of her eroticism.

The sacred element established by complete unification with Antony dissipates in the presence of communal mediation. Debora Shuger has suggested that "sacrifice violates the contours demarcating the autonomous individual" (1994, 193), and to the extent that Cleopatra's erotic charisma is autonomous (in confrontation with Egyptian society) we might see her sacrifice in these terms. Associating sacrifice and eroticism, Shuger adds: "The erotic longings for total union with the beloved, the collapse of the individual into the *conjunctio*, the violent inner divisions of the chimerical self either erode the boundary separating self and other or disintegrate the self into warring factions. The individual dissolves into the group, the desired object, or the personae of the *automachia*" (1994, 193–94). Ironically, for Cleopatra the sacrifice that dissolves her individuality into the group also conflicts with her erotic *conjunctio*. The erotic-charismatic sacrament is neutralized by the restoration of traditional rites.[20] Even if Cleopatra is sacrificing to Isis, her practice shifts emphasis from her own transgressive (erotic) sacredness to the rationalized sacredness of ritualistic state religion.

The final irony in Daniel's play is that Cleopatra sacrifices herself, metaphorically reintegrating her erotic otherness into the communal rites (although the actual restoration of the social fabric is blocked by the Roman intervention in Egyptian affairs). The death scene is reported by a Nuntius who finds Cleopatra

> Glittering in all her pompous ritch array . . .
> Euen as shee was when on thy cristall streames,
> O CYDNOS shee did shew what earth could shew.
> When Asia all amaz'd in wonder, deemes
> VENUS from heauen was come on earth below.
>
> (1463, 1466–68)

All Cleopatra's symbolic power is on display as she prepares for death, her wonder-inspiring eroticism and her likeness to Venus recalling May's description of the temple statue. But in Daniel's tragedy we have the real body of Cleopatra, animality and symbol combined with the pomp of a sacrificial victim on the altar. The Nuntius reports her invocation of death:

> And therefore to, the rather vnto thee
> In zeale I make the offring of my blood,
> Calamitie confirming now in mee
> A sure beliefe that pietie makes good.
> Which happy men neglect, or hold ambiguous,
> And onely the afflicted are religious.
>
> (1535–40)

Cleopatra here articulates her capitulation to traditional belief, claiming that calamity has transformed her transgressive impulse to piety. And then, with newfound religious "zeale," she offers a sacred sacrifice of her own blood:

> And heere I sacrifize these armes to Death,
> That Lust late dedicated to Delights:
> Offring vp for my last, this last of breath,
> The complement of my loues deerest rites.

> (1541–44)

The exchange of lust for sacred piety is embodied in "these armes," once used to embrace Antony, now offered to the asp. The offering she makes of her body and of her life constitutes a restoration of religious taboos and a displacement of the transgressive delights of lust. Her last breath signals the end of "loues deerest rites," the conclusion of the erotic sacrament. In its place we now find the sacrifice. Marveling, the chorus asks in the last couplet: "Doth Order order so / Disorders ouer-thro?" (1761–62).

Although we might reasonably expect an anticlimax in the tragedies after Antony's death, the catastrophes are not complete until Cleopatra fully relinquishes her charismatic claim. The sham pretence of her robes, her imitation of Venus or Isis, is merely a parody of erotic worship in the absence of her worshiper. It provides the last bitter proof, if proof is needed, that the unraveling of the charismatic balance completes the catastrophe. Reabsorbed into traditional Egyptian mystery, her transgressive autonomy expunged, her charisma compromised, the solitary and suicidal Cleopatra perfects the tragic tableau.

EPILOGUE

In preceding chapters I explored the tragic reverberations accompanying several different kinds of charisma. Pure charisma and its
routinization, lineage charisma, office charisma, and erotic charisma
have each contributed to the analysis of group function on the early
modern stage. Yet there remain charismatic figures who do not neatly
fit Weberian, revisionist, or hybrid categories of charismatic authority. Not all of these figures appear in tragedies—Henry V, for instance,
who has obvious charismatic qualities—nor does group dissolution
always affect the catastrophes of plays as powerfully as in the works I
chose to discuss. Still, it is worth meditating briefly on two charismatics I left out, George Chapman's Duke of Byron and Shakespeare's
Coriolanus, both of whom have palpable charismatic credentials but
fail to sustain a group response.

Coriolanus manifests what might be called *anticharisma*. He is a
martial hero (and sometime leader) who confounds charisma hunger.
His salvationistic charisma at the gates of Corioli cannot be denied,
although, as will be recalled, in the early part of the battle the Romans
refuse to follow him. He excoriates the soldiers for cowardice—"you
shames of Rome!" (1.4.31)—and, as the Volscians open the gates to let
out their army, he demands that the Romans rise up from the trenches
behind him:

> So, now the gates are ope. Now prove good seconds!
> 'Tis for the followers Fortune widens them,
> Not for the fliers. Mark me, and do the like!

> (1.4.43–45)

But, tellingly, the soldiers refuse to follow him and Coriolanus (whose name of course is still plain Martius) is locked in the city alone. Presumed slain, he astonishes the Romans gathered outside the walls by prevailing in isolated combat against the Volscians. His extraordinary courage inspires others to join him: "Oh, 'tis Martius!" cries a general, "Let's fetch him off, or remain alike" (1.4.62–63). To "remain alike" here means to fight alongside Coriolanus and share his fate (cf. Shakespeare 1976, 131n), but the language resonates with an implication of mirrored deficit strength. In martial action Coriolanus exhibits remarkable charisma, not only alleviating distress but also, through sheer bravery, causing a metanoia in followers' responses.

This martial charisma clings to Coriolanus, transforming his customary affect from antisocial to socially magnetic. For example, after taking the city of Corioli he rushes out to Cominius who, about a mile from the city, is engaged in battle with Aufidius and the Antiates. The news of the victory at the city has not yet reached Cominius, and of course his soldiers have not seen Coriolanus's astonishing feat of courage inside the gates. Nevertheless, when Coriolanus arrives covered in blood and flushed with his recent victory he singlehandedly turns the tide of this battle too. It is significant that he accomplishes this victory not by isolating himself but by consciously becoming a leader. With a hortatory speech he instantaneously establishes a bond with a group of Cominius's soldiers, expressly mirroring their deficit strength in his own valor. "If any such be here," he begins,

> As it were sin to doubt—that love this painting
> Wherein you see me smear'd; if any fear
> Lesser this person than an ill report;
> If any think brave death outweighs bad life,
> And that this country's dearer than himself;
> Let him alone, or so many so minded,
> Wave thus to express his disposition,
> And follow Martius.
>
> (1.6.67–75)

The soldiers reply in unison: "O me alone! Make you a sword of me!" And, according to the stage direction, *They take him up in their arms, and cast up their caps.* The response, and the subsequent victory, reflect Coriolanus's force as a bearer of pure, salvationistic charisma. He even promises booty to the soldiers, presumably replacing their conventional forms of payment with an irrational economic relationship: "March on, my fellows," he exhorts, "Make good this ostentation, and you shall / Divide in all with us" (1.6.84–86). Brockbank notes that Coriolanus may be offering to share the honor rather than the spoils. But honor is a charismatic value, bolstering the irrational organization of troops under Coriolanus in contrast to conventional military discipline. One is irresistibly reminded of Tamburlaine.

Yet, unlike Tamburlaine, Coriolanus resists his own charismatic idealization and refuses to acknowledge the mutuality of his extraordinary conduct. It is not that his modesty prevents his leadership. His reluctance to take any reward—"cannot make my heart consent to take / A bribe to pay my sword" (1.9.37–38)—might well be construed as a charismatic gesture, an unexpected asceticism that would only increase his authority. And indeed in reputation his charismatic appeal fulfills all the superficial critieria. As Brutus points out, all of Rome turns out to see his return, "All tongues speak of him" (2.1.203), and the common people in particular press to see him in a great "pother":

> As if that whatsoever god who leads him
> Were slily crept into his human powers,
> And gave him graceful posture.
>
> (2.1.216–19)

Coriolanus is seen as a god entering Rome, his "human powers" invested with a god's grace. We are unlikely to find a more definitive description of charismatic manifestation in daily life, and the sentiment is echoed later in the play (also by a hostile witness) who describes Coriolanus at the head of the army against Rome after his banishment:

> He is their god. He leads them like a thing
> Made by some other deity than nature,
> That shapes men better; and they follow him.
>
> (4.6.91–93)

This speech too describes a force superior to human limits, a martial figure endowed with supernatural attributes. Once again we recognize the foundation for an exceptional charismatic claim.

But between these two descriptions of Coriolanus as a god there is his disastrous attempt at politics, proof of his absolute rejection of an interdependent relationship off the battlefield. His refusal to show his wounds to the citizens is emblematic of a more profound refusal to share his natural body: he in effect denies prospective followers the *kleros* of a charismatic experience. Menenius, who early in the play introduces the metaphor of the body politic (drawn from

Plutarch but analogous to the Pauline version), later tries to defend Coriolanus's allegedly traitorous conduct with an extension of the same metaphor: "Oh, he's a limb that has but a disease: /Mortal, to cut it off; to cure it, easy" (3.1.293–94). This defense is rejected by one of the tribunes: "The service of the foot," says Sicinius, "Being once gangren'd, is not then respected /For what it was" (3.1.303–5). And indeed the Romans cut off the gangrened foot, banishing Coriolanus. This action raises an interesting problem. If Coriolanus were a member of a charismatic body politic similar to that described in 1 Corinthians, then, as Paul admonishes, the dismemberment of the erring "foot" would destroy the "one body." Despite his supernatural posture, however, Coriolanus has never become the focus of a shared charismatic experience. His banishment, while dangerous for Rome because of his martial skills, does not by any means precipitate the collapse of a political body.

The absence of such a collapse further isolates Coriolanus, further determines the singularity of his experience—again, despite myriad conditions that presuppose a potential group relationship. It almost seems as if Shakespeare set himself a deliberate task in *Coriolanus* to explore the limitations and tragic absurdity of a charismatic hero without a charismatic following. In the last analysis I would not say that Coriolanus's tragedy results directly from his charismatic failure, nor that the play's catastrophe depends on a breakdown of group cohesion. But perhaps the term *anticharisma* might still be used to describe the sublime isolation of a figure who, while endowed so magnificently with charismatic qualities, nonetheless lacks the skills necessary to administer (or even to recognize) his own charismatic symbols.

I would not describe Chapman's Duke of Byron in quite the same way, although Byron too exhibits charismatic endowments while lacking a group of followers. The first description of him in the play underscores his extraordinary qualities:

> for he is a man
> Of matchless valour and was ever happy
> In all encounters, which were still made good
> With an unwearied sense of any toil,
> Having continued fourteen days together
> Upon his horse; his blood is not voluptuous
> Nor much inclined to women; his desires
> Are higher than his state and his deserts
> Not much short of the most he can desire,
> If they be weighed with what France feels by them.
>
> (I.1.1.61–70)

The mixture of asceticism and physical strength might remind us of Shakespeare's Antony in retreat from Modena, although the two men are fundamentally different: Byron, after all, is not "much inclined to women." Chapman paints a portrait of a courtier both charismatic and ambitious, destined, it would seem, to become the conscious center of a movement:

> Ambition also cheek by cheek doth march
> With that excess of glory, both sustained
> With an unlimited fancy that the king,
> Nor France itself, without him can subsist.
>
> (I.1.1.79–82)

The notion of excess, which I discussed in the last chapter in regard to Antony's asceticism (and his appetites), here is applied to both Byron's glory and his ambition. His exaggerated sense of his own worth contributes to his potential value as a charismatic leader, giving credence to a later description of his "loyalty, /Which is more than hereditary" and his "valour, which is more than human" (I.2.1.59–61).

But despite Byron's charismatic potentialities, he never achieves the leadership status we might expect. His frustrations with the king's treatment of him mirror a frustrated deployment of his extraordinary qualities. Notably, he sees himself as a dismembered body part. When he complains of his frustration, specifically of being removed from leadership, he characterizes his removal in terms of its effect on the coherence of the army:

> When I left leading, all his army reeled,
> One fell on other foul, and as the Cyclop
> That, having lost his eye, struck every way,
> His blows directed to no certain scope;
> Or as the soul departed from the body,
> The body wants coherence in his parts,
> Cannot consist, but sever and dissolve;
> So, I removed once, all his armies shook,
> Panted and fainted and were ever flying,
> Like wandering pulses spersed through bodies dying.
>
> (I.3.2.96–105)

Echoes of the Pauline or the Plutarchan metaphor of the body can be heard in Chapman's passage. Byron casts his erstwhile leadership in familiar terms, expressly emphasizing the catastrophic consequences of dismemberment (with the added intensity of severing the soul from the body). This articulate lament for a lost charismatic relationship characterizes Byron's plight throughout the two parts of the play. Although Chapman does not structure the play around group dissolution, the isolation of Byron, of which his dismemberment from the army's body is emblematic, resonates in and indeed amplifies our experience of his tragedy.

We could probably multiply such examples. Even Chapman's *Bussy D'Ambois* has some of these same characteristics, as do numerous secondary characters like Hotspur and the young Pompey. Other kinds of charismatic authority also appear in early modern drama, from Antony's rhetorical charisma in *Julius Caesar* to the charismatic dignity of the imprisoned king in Marlowe's *Edward II*. But I will leave further exploration to other critics. It may be, as Thomas Mann said, that only the exhaustive can be truly interesting. Yet the idea of exhaustiveness in literary criticism, if it could exist at all, might not be altogether desirable.

Exhaustiveness has not been my aim, though I hope this study has remained interesting nonetheless. While literary analysis has governed my approach, I have also tried to examine the sociology of charisma and to establish the plausibility of linking charisma to tragic representation. Early modern drama offers a unique arena in which to explore the effects of charismatic authority on, among other things, subjectivity, the body politic, dynastic rule, eroticism, genealogy, and group membership. I would like to think that the preceding chapters provide a beginning to such an exploration, and that future scholars will find in them the rudiments of a critical language with which to discuss charisma, its transformations, and its instabilities.

It is difficult at the end of a book to see the work as a sum of its parts. To the author—at least to this author—such coherence can seem as illusory as Mann's exhaustiveness. And the layers of arguments, purportedly massing under a general thesis, can seem a peculiarly intellectual manifestation of Frank O'Hara's complaint that "there is too much lime in the world and not enough gin." But the final analysis is not mine to make. The sensible thing is merely to look forward to new ideas about charismatic group function and to encourage new applications of sociological research to literary criticism. Needless to add, I would be particularly pleased if group formation and group dissolution, so crucial in understanding leadership, came to be seen as integral to our experience of tragedy. There is still much to be done on this topic. Let me conclude, therefore, with the dual hope that this book will serve as a catalyst for the further study of charisma and tragedy and that it will soon be superseded.

ENDNOTES

Introduction: From Charisma to Tragedy

1. The most extensive discussions of charisma and cultural formations in recent years are C. Stephen Jaeger's *The Envy of Angels: Cathedral Schools and Social Ideals in Medieval Europe, 950–1200* (1994, see esp. 4–9) and also his recent article, "Charismatic Body—Charismatic Text" (1997). Both studies suggest a conflict between what the author terms charismatic and intellectual cultures, but in neither study is Jaeger concerned with group function per se. His notion of the preservation of charisma in art (1997, 121) as well as his discussion of "enfabulation" (1997, 132) are interesting to consider in connection with the separation of a charismatic leader from the symbols of his or her charismatic movement. On the other hand, the polarization of charismatic and intellectual culture leads Jaeger to doubtful assumptions regarding the transition from one form of authority to another; and I think that he unnecessarily aestheticizes charisma in his view of the human body as a work of art in charismatic culture.

2. The original of "diuersities of gifts" is *"diaireseis de charismaton"*; the Vulgate version is *"divisiones gratiarum"* (*Novum Testamentum, Graece et Latine*). The Greek *diairesis* tends to mean a dividing up, as of money in Herodotus or spoils in Xenophon; similarly the Latin *divisio* suggests both dividing and distribution of available material. This sense is lost somewhat in the word "diuersities," insofar as the notion of *difference* occludes the connotation of distribution (of spoil or anything else). The Englishing effaces a clear commodification of grace, emphasizing the mosaic of gifts in the congregation rather than the possession and apportionment of a divine product. One wonders whether this slight change in connotation was inadvertant or deliberate. In any case, the hermenuetic intervention of the sixteenth-century translators clearly suggests an even distribution of the gifts, an ideal of egalitarianism not likely to be found in the dividing of money or spoils.

3. See 1 Cor. 12:28 for Paul's graded hierarchy of those "ordeined in the Church": "*as* first, Apostles, secondly Prophetes, thirdly teachers, then them that do miracles: after that, the giftes of healing, helpers, gouernours, diuersitie of tongues."

4. The *Dictionary of Biblical Theology* notes that "charisms are not exceptional things even though some of them, like the power to work miracles, are outside the common run. The whole life of Christians and the whole functioning of Church institutions depend entirely on them. It is through them that the Spirit of God governs the new people on whom He has been poured in abundance. To some He gives power and grace to fulfill their functions, to others He gives power and grace to respond to their vocation and to be useful to the community so that the body of Christ might be built up" (70).

5. Colet 1985, 254–55: "Deus temperavit corpus, ei cui deerat abundantioriem honorem tribuendo, ut non sit scisma in corpore. Ita in ecclesia repensa sunt omnia quadam paritate, ut non sit in ea nisi unitas ex caritate et ex unitate charitas. Similtudo enim et equalitas mater est charitatis."

6. A seminal twentieth-century text on *sōma* and *sarx*, and one that has caused much debate, is J. A. T. Robinson, *The Body: A Study in Pauline Theology* (1952).

7. Victor Turner (1974, 281) quotes a poem describing an Indian temple as a body, suggesting that the metaphor draws on a universal opposition of *Sthavara* (*stasis*) and *Jangama* (*dynamis*): "My legs are pillars,/the body a shrine,/the head a cupola/of gold." It is interesting to consider Paul's metaphor of the human church as a function of the same opposition between stasis and dynamis. In this context the "one body" can be seen as a logical prelude to the management of secular charisma through metaphors and stabilizing symbols. Compare Beckwith (1993, 26), who characterizes a medieval friar's use of the body-as-church metaphor as a "static image . . . [that] draws upon an immobile, hierarchized image of the body."

8. For instance, the single Hebrew word *basar* is thought to be the source for both *sōma* and *sarx* in the Septuagint (Robinson 1952, 12). But see Gundry (1976, 16–23, 230) for discussion of the Hebrew meanings and their translation into the Septuagint. One provocative meaning of *sōma* is "slaves."

9. On Sohm, see Haley 1980, esp. 192; Tucker 1968, 732. See also Weber's criticism of Sohm's narrow application of charisma:

> It is to Rudolf Sohm's credit that he worked out the sociological character of this kind of domination (*Gewaltstruktur*); however, since he developed this category with regard to one historically important case—the rise of the ecclesiastical authority of the early Christian Church—his treatment was bound to be one-sided from the viewpoint of historical diversity. In principle, these phenomena are universal, even though they are often most evident in the religious realm. (1978, 2:1112)

10. I have not altered the translators' use of the generic masculine pronoun in *Economy and Society* and other Weberian texts.

11. Weber was well aware of the limitations of his "ideal types" and he acknowledges that they are not to be found "in historical cases in 'pure' form." But, he adds, this fact

> is naturally not a valid objection to attempting their conceptual formulation in the sharpest possible form. . . . Analysis in terms of sociological types has, after all, as compared with purely empirical historical investigation, certain advantages which should not be minimized. That is, it can in the particular case of a concrete form of authority determine what conforms to or approximates such types as "charisma," "hereditary charisma," "the charisma of office," "patriarchy," "bureaucracy," the authority of status groups, and in doing so it can work with relatively unambiguous concepts. But the idea that the whole of concrete historical reality can be exhausted in the conceptual scheme about to be developed is as far from the author's thoughts as anything could be. (1978, 1:216)

12. We might compare the notion of upholding standards to Ann Ruth Willner's related idea that "the leader who becomes charismatic is the one who can inadvertently or deliberately tap the reservoir of relevant myths" (1984, 62; cf. also Willner and Willner 1965, 82–84; Willner 1968, 73).

13. Queen Elizabeth was of course a dynastic ruler, a bearer of what Weber would term lineage charisma; yet her personal charisma is undeniable. While I cannot go into the nuances of the Elizabethan reign here, it should be noted that, despite the enormous magnetism of Elizabeth Tudor, any monarch's charisma is never pure but always dependent to an extent on the caché of the noble house (see Weber 1978, 2:1123–24, 1135–39).

14. See, *inter alia*, Greenblatt 1980, 1988, esp. 21–65; Helgerson 1992.

15. Dow claims that in his later vocational essays Weber attempted, in a utopian vision, to integrate charisma and conventional responsibility: "the hope that passion in the service of an ethic of responsibility might yet rescue man from the immaturity and inhumanity of both unexamined routine and irresponsible release" (1978, 91; cf. Gerth and Mills 1946, 77–156).

16. The term *dissipative structures* comes from the physicist Ilya Prigogine, who uses it to describe unstable conditions in the thermodynamics of nonequilibrium systems. Smith conflates the term (and the idea) with Kohut's notions of the nuclear self.

17. According to the OED, the words *charism* and *charismata* came into use at approximately the same time as *individual*, if with less frequency.

18. Nietzsche was attacked immediately for his philology by Ulrich von Wilamowitz-Moellendorff (See Kaufmann's introduction, 1968, 4–9), and Nietzsche himself came to regard *The Birth of Tragedy* as an "impossible book" (see Vickers 1973, 34). Still, objections continued in this century, though not necessarily to the philological aspects of the *The Birth of Tragedy*. See, for example, Pickard-Cambridge 1927; Snell 1953, esp. 119–21, 132; Else 1965; Vickers 1973, esp. 33–43. But see now Winkler and

Zeitlin 1989; and Williams 1993, esp. chapters 1 and 2, in which Williams attacks Snell as a representative of what he terms "progressivists."

One: Revolution to Routinization

1. As Guenther Roth explains in his introduction to Weber's *Economy and Society*, an "ideal type" is "a relatively homogeneous historical configuration . . . such as the spirit of capitalism." (1978, 1:xxxvi; see also xxxvii–xxxix).

2. When Saint Paul first mentions the charisms in 1 Corinthians 12, he refers to them as *diaireseis de charismaton* ("diuersities of gifts," in the Geneva Bible). It is worth recalling, in connection with Tamburlaine's economic practice, that the Greek word *diairesis* tends to mean a dividing up, as of money in Herodotus or spoils in Xenophon. See Introduction, n. 2.

3. There is an interesting passage on plunder in Perondinus, another possible source of Tamburlaine: "when necessity required cruelty, he was exceedingly brutal in curbing brigandage and punishing the license of the soldiery, with the result that men had learned through fear of penalty to keep their eyes, not to speak of hands, away from the plundering of all gold and treasure, while he, though but one man, appropriated virtually everything to himself" (Marlowe 1981: 327). Marlowe's Tamburlaine does not exhibit this quality. It is provocative to wonder why, if he knew this passage, Marlowe omitted it from his characterization. It is somewhat unflattering, reminiscent of the bits of Plutarch that Shakespeare omits, such as the fact that Antony had a habit of philandering with the wives of his captains.

4. Freud is discussing the church and the army in this passage. He terms both *artificial groups*, those in which "an external force is employed to prevent them from disintegrating and to check alterations in their structure" (32). He says that in artificial groups "as a rule a person is not consulted, or is given no choice as to whether he wants to enter such a group; any attempt at leaving it is usually met with persecution or with severe punishment, or has quite definite conditions attached to it" (32–33). Charismatic groups are different in this respect, since the element of choice is pivotal in the formulation of a charismatic band insofar as charisma represents a revolutionary force. Nevertheless, once the charismatic band is formed, attempts to leave it no doubt bring on persecution and punishment. And, in any case, without the mandatory element (such as conscription or national religion) the ties to the group leader—whether or not we call them libidinal—would seem to be even more important, especially for recruitment. Certainly Theridamas's recruitment depends on an irrational, emotional element as well as on a choice, rather than on anything mandatory.

5. As is well known, the Frankfurt School critics strongly supported the use of individual depth psychology for understanding mass behavior: "Whatever social associations, of whatever kind, they may enter into, human beings are individuals, and even where they throw off their usual

individual traits, and behave after a fashion allegedly characteristic of masses, they still act, insofar as their action is psychologically determined, according to the psychological causations of their specific individuality" (Frankfurt Institute 1972, 10).

6. According to Hummel, the psychology of charismatic group formation might be analyzed in terms of Freudian projection theory:

> In every case where leaders are raised to charismatic status, followers have gone through the trauma of losing a beloved object, have unconsciously projected their love onto their leader, and are consciously experiencing that love as emanating from the leader. It is from this experience that the strange characteristics of charisma derive: the total devotion of followers to the leader, the desperate intensity of that devotion, the sense of the uncanny or extraordinary when it comes to identifying the source of the leader's power. (1975, 759)

7. Compare Arthur Schweizter: "charismatic disposition and emotional attachments of followers to a leader cannot be satisfactorily analysed by an individualizing psychology" (1984, 56). This is probably true to a degree, and in fact I have found Freud's *Group Psychology and the Analysis of the Ego* more helpful that his earlier writing in terms of charismatic group formation. But insofar as Freud and Kohut problematize the coherence of individual identity they offer valuable starting places for what Schweitzer calls "charismatic disposition."

8. The pronouns *she* and *her* are in the original; Smith alternates masculine and feminine throughout his book. *Positive feedback* is a technical term central to Smith's theory of "nonequilibrium functionalism": "Homeostasis is achieved through a mix of positive and negative feedback, and complex interaction systems and social organizations are stabilized or destabilized by the forms and levels of feedback running through them" (1992, 14).

9. The idea of administering a nonequilibrium system comes from Smith (1992, 14), who suggestes that homeostasis in complex social interaction often results from mixing destabilizing elements with stabilizing ones.

10. He resembles a more typical warlord when he disposes of the Turkish kings' concubines in Part 2. : "bring those Turkish harlots to my tent,/And I'll dispose them as it likes me best" (II.4.1.165–66). He mischievously offers to "prefer" them but then gives them away as sexual prizes to his soldiers: "Take them, divide them and their jewels too,/And let them equally serve all your turns" (II.4.3.70–73). Although Tamburlaine has degraded women before (Zabina, for instance), the death of Zenocrate seems to plunge him into a gross misogyny.

11. This scene also recalls *Antony and Cleopatra*. At 3.13 the desperate Antony challenges Caesar to single combat. Enobarbus remarks scornfully (aside), "Yes, like enough: high battled Caesar will/Unstate his happiness and be stag'd to th' show/Against a sworder!" (3.13.29–31). Tamburlaine's military situation is different, but Orcanes's attitude has the same pragmatic scorn as Enobarbus's.

Two: Charismas in Conflict

1. All references are to Peter Ure's Arden edition.

2. From this perspective, Bolingbroke's status, more than Richard's, supplies a ready comparison to Elizabeth. She too made a controversial birthright claim and promised a moral revolution aimed at restoring the old status quo. The comparison probably ends there, since she produced no offspring and ended her own charismatic/dynastic claim without trying to transform it into a permanent lineage. But during Elizabeth's life her success, not unlike Bolingbroke's, depended on a sustained compromise between her personal charismatic leadership and the authority of the traditional ideals she felt compelled to embrace. This too was an Elizabethan settlement, but one of more obscure norms.

3. The anonymous play called *Woodstock* also contains a kinship pun in its opening scene. An incredulous Duke of York exclaims, "God for thy mercy! Would our cousin king/so cozen us, to poison us in our meat?" (1.1.8–9). By equating "cousin" with "cozen," the passage frankly associates cheating and betrayal with kinship. Indeed, both words are spelled "cussen" in the manuscript of the play, as seen in Wilhelmina Frijlinck's transcript of Egerton MS. 1994 (Malone Society, 1929). A. P. Rossiter modernized the spelling in his edition.

4. But it should be noted that dueling and personal combat among aristocrats or courtiers were discouraged in Elizabethan England, and therefore (although anachronistically) Bolingbroke's dissociation of the throne from personal combat would have had some legitimate justification (cf. Prosser 1967, 13–17). Satisfaction through personal combat was a vexed ethical issue that Shakespeare often exploited for dramatic purposes. But Bolingbroke's nod to the impropriety of associating the throne with violence seems rather perfunctory. The stronger implication of his statement is that he simply cannot get satisfaction or justice from the incumbent of the royal seat.

5. On genealogy in England, see Stone 1965, 23–25; Wagner 1975, 45; and also my *Conceived Presences* 1994, 6–8.

6. The *OED* confirms that both senses of the word "counterfeit" were used in the sixteenth century.

7. Kantorowicz depends heavily on this passage, but it should be noted that not everyone agrees with the importance of the "two bodies" concept in England. For example, Richard F. Hardin has objected that Kantorowicz's thesis "bears more directly on Continental than English history" and that we should be skeptical about its application to Elizabethan drama (1992, 24). In an earlier study Marie Axton had noted that in Elizabethan England "'The king's two bodies' was never a *fact*, nor did it ever attain the status of orthodoxy; it remained a controversial idea" (1977, x). She adds that this controversial idea came to prominence in the sixteenth century especially among lawyers and chiefly in response to the succession crisis. The notion of a natural body distinct from the body politic was substantially a forensic point, part of a larger argument used to oppose Elizabeth. (In addition to his *Reports*, Plowden also wrote an influential manuscript treatise supporting the right to the English throne

of Mary, Queen of Scots [cf. Axton 1977, 19]). Hardin acknowledges Axton's documentation of the "two bodies" concept in the period, but disagrees with her interpretation of the evidence (see 1992, 210n. 25). Hardin's skepticism is salutary. Moreover, there is the question of whether Kantorowicz's model is too indebted to medieval sources. But, despite the uncertainties, I am still inclined to accept Axton's general conclusion that the notion of the king's or queen's two bodies was sufficiently in circulation to have been fair game for Inns of Court dramatists as well as for Shakespeare and other professionals.

8. It is surprising that Kantorowicz does not consider charisma, since his celebrated first book, *Frederick the Second*, is a study of one of Europe's most charismatic rulers.

9. H. R. Coursen notes that "the historical Richard—more than had monarchs before him—insisted on anointment as the sacramental action that confirmed his absolute right to rule" (1982, 35). Holinshed's extensive treatment of Richard's coronation seems to bear out this idea (cf. 1807, 2:713–15).

10. We might compare Louis Marin's concept of the image or portrait of a king as his "sacramental body": "The king has only one body left, but his sole body, in truth, unifies three, a physical historical body, a juridico-political body, and a semiotic sacramental body, the sacramental body, the 'portrait,' operating the exchange *without remainder* (or attempting to eliminate all remainder) between the historical and political bodies" (1988, 14).

11. On the concept of the *rex inutilis*, see Peters 1970.

12. Richard's attitude in this regard resembles that of Marlowe's Edward II, although Shakespeare manages to give his monarch a larger degree of detachment. See *Edward II*, 5.1.40–124.

13. Identifying the form of "you" can be confusing. Richard uses "you" when observing dismally that "I live with bread like you." But this is the plural form of the pronoun, not, as in his address to Bolingbroke (as well as Bolingbroke's response), an example of the polite singular form. (Cf. Nevo 1972, 78).

14. I am grateful to Anthony Low for this observation.

15. In Daniel's version Bolingbroke brings the charges himself: "And all these faults, which *Lancaster* now brings/Against a King, must be his owne, when hee,/By vrging others sinnes, a King shall be" (bk 2, st. 98).

16. Bolingbroke mentions Henry III because his reign began the unbroken accession to the throne of first sons, until Richard, who is a grandson: Henry III, 1216–72; Edward I, 1272–1307; Edward II, 1307–1326; Edward III, 1326–77.

Three: Individuation as Disintegration

1. All references are to Harold Jenkins's Arden edition.

2. Goddard emphasizes that Hamlet cannot articulate this ambivalence or its causes: "If [Hamlet] was indeed trying to repudiate the morals

of his herd, it is absurd to suppose that he opposed to them a clear-cut moral theory of his own" (1:346).

3. Sexual taboo and sexual propriety also contribute to Hamlet's social constraint and probably motivate some of his actions, but they are not necessarily of charismatic origin.

4. All references are to M. R. Ridley's Arden edition.

5. See Elliott (1988, 55): "'Polite' is probably the aptest meaning here, with its association of Latin *politia* ('citizenship') and *politus* ('polished, refined'). . . . This genteel meaning makes *gentle* more prominent. Desdemona lives in a condition of civil, indeed metropolitan, life; and into that condition Othello himself must transfer. It is not only because he loves that he comes inside the laws of civil life; it is also because the woman of his choice happens to reside within those laws as a member of the *polis*."

6. In connecting sex and what he terms "the scene of emergency," Stanley Cavell (1987, 131) compares Othello's reappearance from the bridal chamber in Venice "to stop a brawl with his single presence" with the brawl between Cassio and Roderigo on Cyprus. While the scenes are very similar in their renderings of interrupted sexual union, they differ sharply in regard to Othello's conduct. It is true that in both scenes he stops the violence with his "single presence." But in Venice he accomplishes this feat through his passivity, his instinct for the charismatic gesture. To the contrary, in Cyprus, after threatening violence, he resorts to military discipline.

7. Apposite of the lack of development, Carol Thomas Neely remarks that at the end of the play "most of the characters remain where they started—or return there" (1985, 134). See also Susan Snyder (1972), who observes that the paradigms of comedy are contained in the first act.

8. I am taking "my demerits/May speak unbonneted" to mean, as Ridley suggests, the opposite of what it appears to mean.

9. It is true that, on landing in Cyprus, Othello says "our wars are done, the Turks are drown'd" (2.1.202), which to a slight extent may mitigate the gravity of Cassio's offense. But I am not sure Othello's statement should be taken as official sanction, nor am I clear how he would know that there were no more Turks to follow the drowned ones. Moreover, the pep talk he gives Cassio when charging him with the watch (2.3) implies that the general still sees fit to remain vigilant; and, further, the next morning he and several gentlemen inspect the fortifications (3.2.5).

10. Warburton long ago tied Othello's speech to his strength. Discussing his preference for Qq *set* over F *soft* in line 82, he noted that Othello wished to emphasize "the art and method of masculine eloquence." See *New Variorum Shakespeare: Othello* (50).

11. In his introduction to a collection of essays on Iago, Harold Bloom discusses Othello as a deity, specifically the god of war, and Iago as his ambivalent worshipper: "Even [Iago's] destruction of Othello the man remains a negative celebration of Othello the captain, a negative affirmation of the reality of the God of War" (1992, 2). Bloom's distinction between "Othello the man" and "Othello the captain" who incarnates a supernatural power echoes the separation of the body natural and the immortal body politic, a separation which in the end Othello cannot

effectively accomplish. Bloom seems to see Iago as an acolyte whose religion is war and whose god is Othello, but who is Gnostic enough to want to degrade his god (3). My view, on the other hand, is that Iago, in the twisted depths of his intuition, realizes that Othello is not a god in the immortal sense but a charismatic whose gifts of grace are waning.

12. In a well-known essay W. H. Auden refuted the notion that Iago ever replaced Cassio as Othello's lieutenant: "the use of the word *lieutenant* [in 3.3.485–86] . . . refers, surely, not to a public military rank, but to a private and illegal delegation of authority—the job delegated to Iago is the murder of Cassio" (1968, 249). I am not convinced by Auden's reasoning, nor do I see that it matters much whether Iago's role is official. At least it does not matter to Iago, so far as I can tell, since for practical purposes he becomes Othello's close aide.

13. But see T. McAlindon (1991, 145): "The way in which Othello threatens to 'come forth' with his sword of Spain against all impediments and stops, only to withdraw the threat as 'vain boast' (lines 255–68), is another important step towards final recovery. Indeed with its subtle blend of heroic assertion and ironic humility it prepares for the great valedictory speech." The notion of a recovery is persuasive, though I differ slightly with McAlindon's compelling discussion: rather than "heroic assertion" and "ironic humility" I am inclined to see humiliation and despair. Othello certainly displays a surge of his old force in his suicide, but, since he never regains his group bond and remains utterly alone in the end, I find it difficult to speak of his recovery.

14. Janet Adelman makes a similar point in connection with Othello's assertion that he fell in love with Desdemona because "she did pity" the dangers he had passed in his youth. "Making himself susceptible to Desdemona's pity," Adelman observes, "Othello unmakes the basis for his martial identity, exchanging it for one dependent on her. And in the exchange, the self-sufficiency and isolation that had been the mark of his masculine identity . . . give way before his new need for her love" (1992, 65). I would add simply that Othello's prior self-sufficiency is dependent on a complicated libidinal relation to the members of his band.

15. I disagree with G. R. Elliot that "the killing of Desdemona is quite unnecessary," even embarrasing to Iago, and that "the villain has overshot his mark" (1992, 28). To my mind the villain is right on target.

16. Given Freud's interest in Shakespeare, it is tempting to think that he might have had *Othello* in mind when writing this passage.

Four: Charisma as Catastrophe

1. In a private conversation, Wolfgang Mommsen suggested to me that the *Protestant Ethic* might be seen as a prelude to Weber's development of a theory of charisma. Research on the possible affinities between a charismatic mission and a *vocatio* would be welcome, especially in regard to the question of group function.

2. I have already noted the difficulty in assessing Samson only in terms of vocation, although it is clear that Steadman is not referring to

Protestant election. As Baruch Halpern points out, we should avoid adducing the notion of vocation to too wide an array of Israelite leaders. For his skeptical appreciation of the "call-narrative" in the Hebrew Bible, see Halpern 1981, 120–21. A discussion of the Nazarite vow and Nazaritism appears later in this chapter.

3. Nowhere is a single one of the personalities referred to in the book specifically called a *shofet*. The Lord is so called in 11:27. However, Othniel (3:10), Deborah (4:4), Tola (10:2), Jair (10:3), Jephthah (12:7), Ibzan (12:8–9), Elon (12:11), Abdon (12:13–14), and Samson (15:20; 16:31) are said to have exercised the function of a *shofet* in Israel (cf. Ishida 1973, 514). This may seem a distinction without a difference, to have exercised the function of *shofet* without being referred to as *shofet*, but the distinction is important in recognizing the role of these Israelite leaders.

4. In Mari documents (18th century B.C.E.) the term *spt*, which is related to the Hebrew words *saphat*, *sophet*, and *mispat*, "has no judicial meaning as its primary connotation, but rather it is to be translated 'to give orders, to rule, to govern, to administer'" (Ishida 1973, 518).

5. I begin with Weber's *Ancient Judaism* because it is the logical starting point for a discussion of the *shofetim* as charismatic figures. Weber's views on ancient Hebrew social structure, and in particular on charismatic leadership during the premonarchic period, have received considerable attention since they began appearing between 1917 and 1919 (in article form). The work was collected after his death as *Das Antike Judentum* (1921), volume three of his *Gesammelte Aufsätze zur Religions-soziologie*. There have been important objections to Weber's method, as for example when Baruch Halpern complains that Weber "proceeds from a superficial view of biblical testimony," neglecting to take into account literary, historiographic, or ideological underpinnings of the narrative (1981, 328–29). Like other similar objections, this one seems plausible, especially in terms of the literary interpretation of biblical narrative. As Irving Zeitlin has noted, advances in biblical and Near Eastern scholarship require that many of Weber's conclusions be "updated or corrected" (1984, xiii). But nevertheless—as Zeitlin and others acknowledge—Weber's conjectures regarding the charismatic status of the judges remain convincing, so long as one always bears in mind that he speaks in terms of ideal sociological types (cf. Weisman 1977, 407n. 39; Malamat 1976, 157–58).

6. As in earlier chapters, biblical quotations are drawn from the Geneva Bible. Milton primarily used this English version, in conjunction no doubt with the Septuagint, the Greek New Testament, the Vulgate (sparingly), and the Hebrew Bible, although it remains difficult to determine how skilled a Hebraist he actually was.

7. These charismatic tribal leaders are often distinguished as "major" judges, as opposed to the "minor" ones, who did not exhibit the same charismatic rulership. But the theory of major and minor judges is the subject of much debate. Minor judges would include such figures as Tola son of Puah and Jair the Gileadite, who, in Weisman's view, "assumed both judicial and executive responsibilities on a territorial basis" (1977, 409). As Malamat suggests, however, it may be that the difference between the judges stems merely from a difference in the literary sources

drawn upon (1971, 131). For a brief survey of the critical literature, see Ishida 1973, 514–15.

8. But see the Geneva Bible marginal note at Judg. 2:16. Beside the passage "the Lord raised vp Judges" appears the alternative translation "Or, Magistrates."

9. According to Lightfoot, in fact, the type and the antetype can exist simultaneously. In his comment on Judg. 2:1–11, the passage in which "an angel of the lord" comes to chastise the Israelites for making peace with the Canaanites, Lightfoot declares: "For this, Christ, himself, cometh up from Judah's camp, at Gilgal, to the people, assembled at some solemnity, at Shiloh, or Beth-el, and telleth them plainly, that he will no more conquer for them" (1822, 2:147). The sudden appearance of Christ among the Judites comes as quite a shock, not only emphasizing the simultaneity of divine temporality but also, given the harshness of the message, revealing a vein of ruthlessness and destructive intolerance in Lightfoot's messiah. Although the burden of the angel's message in Judg. 2:1–3 is that the Israelites should eschew the idolatry of the Canaanites, break down their altars, and "dispossess" them, Lightfoot's interpretation of this obligation is even harsher. "The several tribes," he notes with regard to Judg. 1:28–36, "are working themselves into settlement in their several possessions, but are not careful to root out the Canaanites, but suffer them to live amongst them, and so hazard themselves to be corrupted by them; and forget the command of God, which had engaged them utterly to destroy and not to spare them" (1822, 2:146). Therefore "Christ" must come and break the convenant, because (in Lightfoot's extreme view) the Israelites had spared the outsiders and had failed "utterly to destroy" them. The absolutism of this interpretation resonates, I think, in Lightfoot's later association of Samson as "a type of Christ," justifying Samson's murderousness and perhaps hinting at the fulfillment of an ongoing directive.

10. Weber adds in this context that in its original form Nazariteship could not have been dedicated to abstention from uncleanness because "Samson of the saga touches the carcass (of the lion) but was held to be a Nazarite" (1952, 95). As noted, Samson also touches the jawbone of a recently slain ass.

11. After noting that the Nazarite—whom he deems to have been male despite the inclusion of women in Numbers—"denied himself of the common 'neatness' and comeliness," Lightfoot explains the meaning and the purpose of not cutting the hair:

> For however long hair among us be accounted a bravery, and men be grown effeminate like women; yet, among the Jewish nation, it was accounted clean contrary, a sluttery, nastiness, and deformity. And they are mightily mistaken, that think that Absalom wore his hair so long, because he was proud of it: he wore it long, because he had vowed Nazaritism, and by way of humiliation, and denied himself that neatness, that he used before. For that which the apostle saith, "Doth not nature itself teach, that if a man have long hair, it is a shame to him?"—the Jewish nation consented to with all their hearts. And, therefore, they looked upon Nazarites, with their long

hair, as men under humiliation,—and that wore it so, to take shame unto themselves before God and men. And so they took up their vow, as whereby to tie themselves to a more strict way of religiousness and humiliation. (1822, 7:161–62)

Lightfoot uses the passage to condemn the corruption of his contemporaries, and at the same time he calls attention to precisely the kind of reversed expectations that accompany charismatic asceticism. Compare *Biathanatos*, in which John Donne points out that long hair should be given different moral weight when associated with different biblical figures: "*disorderly long hayre, which was pride and wantonesse in Absolon, and squallor, and horridnesse in Nabuchodonozor, was vertue, and strength in Samson, and Sanctification in Samuel* (1984, 33; emphasis in original).

12. That Samson touches the jawbone, which probably would have been deemed unclean, raises several questions about his status as a consecrated warrior and about the historical development of the Nazarite code.

13. This indictment has historical weight. As Albrecht Alt suggested, the Israelite charismatic leaders "had a following which extended beyond their own tribe; for they came on behalf of Yahweh, who was not the God of a single tribe but of the whole federation of tribes, and, therefore, their appearance brought into being an authority binding not only within the narrow confines of their home life, but beyond" (1967, 234). Alt notes, however, that no charismatic leader, including Samson, "ever succeeded in achieving an alliance between all twelve tribes, and this kind of leadership, because of its purely personal emphasis, was incapable of becoming a permanent institution." Samson's heroic actions are "at best pinpricks without any lasting effect" (1967, 234, 235), a view which, given the last section of *Samson Agonistes*, Milton probably did not share.

14. In contrast see Low (1974, 124), who argues persuasively that those in the chorus "are among the few faithful members of Israel, they remain Samson's friends in spite of adversity and possible penalty, and they deeply desire their nation's freedom, as their praise of Samson's victories and their paean to national liberators clearly reveal."

15. Although Absalom is obviously an unsympathetic figure, his suborning of the men of Israel is instructive, particularly inasmuch as he uses judging as a prelude to charismatic revolution. Note too Absalom's (or the redactor's) attention to the treatment of different tribal members of the confederacy:

Sometime afterward, Absalom provided himself with a chariot, horses, and fifty outrunners. Absalom used to rise early and stand by the road to the city gates; and whenever a man had a case that was to come before the king for judgment, Absalom would call out to him, "What town are you from?" And when he answered, "Your servant is from such and such a tribe in Israel," Absalom would say to him, "It is clear that your claim is right and just, but there is no one assigned to you by the king to hear it." And Absalom went on, "If only I were appointed judge in the land and everyone with a

legal dispute came before me, I would see that he got his rights."
And if a man approached to bow to him, [Absalom] would extend
his hand and take hold of him and kiss him. Absalom did this to
every Israelite who came to the king for judgment. Thus Absalom
won away the hearts of the men of Israel. (2 Samuel 15:1–6)

(The translation, in contemprary English, comes from the new Jewish
Publication Society version of the *Tanakh*.)

16. Samson's dissimulation might be seen as a kind of *occultatio*, disguise or masking, one of the most prominent features of the Christian kenosis. (Unaccountably, Tippens does not mention the Philistine livery in his discussion [1986, 179–81]).

17. It is confusing to find both a singular and a plural possessive pronoun referring to the chorus in the same sentence, but maybe Bennett wants to make a distinction between the chorus as a character in the play and the Danites as a group.

Five: Erotic Charisma

1. Guerlac notes that for Bataille "the erotic object must be not only a woman, but a woman as object, or, in other words, a prostitute" (1990, 92). This absolute restriction clearly does not apply to Weber's view of the erotic, nor is it important to our analysis of Cleopatra except insofar as she might be seen as a glorified sexual object serially prostituting herself to Roman generals. The interesting connection between Bataille and Weber is that they both recognize a consciousness in eroticism, a meaning-giving quality to the erotic object, and the sophistication of animal sex.

2. Bataille 1976, 8:128: "L'attrait de le féminité pour les hommes—celui de la masculinité pour les femmes—représent dans l'érotisme une forme essentielle de la sexualité animale, mais en la modifiant profondément. Ce qui excite directement l'organisme des animaux . . . atteint les hommes à travers des figures symboliques." (Cf. Guerlac 1996, 9). Compare John Winkler 1990, 17–23, esp. 17: "Sex is not, except in a trivial and uninteresting sense, a natural fact." (Cf. Shuger 1994, 176).

3. "Il est certain que la vie érotique ne peut être *réglée*" (1976, 8:41). This quotation comes from Bataille's *L'Histoire de l'erotisme* (1950–51), the abandoned early version of his *L'Erotisme* (1957). The text of the former is found in volume 8 of Bataille's *Oeuvres Completes*; for the latter, I quote from the 1962 translation by Mary Dalwood (reprinted in 1987).

4. In my discussion of erotic charisma and its symbolic manifestations I have not attempted to address the historical etiology of eroticism itself. This topic has attracted a great deal of attention in recent criticism, stemming in large measure from Michel Foucault's *The History of Sexuality*. In literary studies many critics support the claim that, as Susan Zimmerman puts it, there are "strong indications that early modern eroticism was fundamentally different from that of today," and moreover that "a profound shift in sexual sensibility took place after the seventeenth century" (1992, 7). Debora Shuger echoes this statement, suggesting a "major shift in the

cultural history of the body, occurring sometime during the late seventeenth century" (1994, 177). According to Shuger "the discovery of genital sexuality" occurred during this period, so that "the identification of the erotic with sexuality . . . emerged sometime after 1650" (1994, 177, 178). This is not the place to pursue such a large topic except to note that the "identification of the erotic with sexuality" is a somewhat different concept from the symbolic representation of animal sexuality in idealized erotic symbols. Cleopatra is more affected by the latter concept than by the former. As I noted above, her eroticism—in concert with eroticism generally—involves a simultaneous detachment from *and* identification with genital or animal sexuality.

5. Although there may be affinities between the erotic sacrament as I see it in regard to charismatic authority and Debora Shuger's notion of "sacred eroticism," the latter for the most part has a very different emphasis. See Shuger 1994, esp. 170–81.

6. I use the word *authority* advisedly to refer to the power Cleopatra has over Antony. I am aware that Weber resisted use of the term in cases simply of influence "which is derived from some kind of superiority, as by virtue of erotic attractiveness, skill in sport or in discussion" (1978, 1:214). He justifies calling an entity an authority only when there is a probability that its commands will be obeyed, although he recognizes that "here as everywhere the transitions are gradual. . . . Even the position of a 'salon' can come very close to the borderline of authoritarian domination and yet not constitute an 'authority'" (1978, 1:214). I would not call Cleopatra's erotic charisma "authoritarian" so much as "authoritative," and it is precisely because she (and her courtly salon) seem poised on a threshhold of domination that we can speak of the unstable charismatic organization of her eroticism.

7. The page number appears in parentheses since this facsimile edition does not include line numbers. It should be noted that earlier in Sedley's play Cleopatra, speaking of an upcoming battle, says of herself and Antony, "We'l in the midst of *Caesar*'s Army meet,/And like *Bellona* I my *Mars* will greet" (10). Bellona replaces the usual love-goddess, Isis or Venus. Antony's response not unexpectedly calls attention to Cleopatra's protean capabilities: "Wou'd Goddesses themselves to me endear,/In *Cleopatra*'s shape they must appear" (10).

8. See Horace's celebrated Epistle 1.6. 1–16:

Nil admirari prope res est una, Numici,
solaque quae possit facere et servare beatum.
hunc solem et stellas et decedentia certis
tempora momentis sunt qui formidine nulla
imbuti spectent: quid censes munera terrae,
quid maris extremos Arabas ditantis et Indos,
ludicra quid, plausus et amici dona Quiritis,
quo spectanda modo, quo sensu credis et ore?
    Qui timet his adversa, fere miratur eodem
quo cupiens pacto: pavor est utrobique molestus,
improvisa simul species exterret utrumque.

gaudeat an doleat cupiat metuatne, quid ad rem,
si, quicquid vidit melius peiusve sua spe,
defixis oculis animoque et corpore torpet?
insani sapiens nomen ferat, aequus iniqui,
ultra quam satis est Virtutem si petat ipsam.

["Marvel at nothing"—that is perhaps the one and only thing, Numicius, that can make a man happy and keep him so. Yon sun, the stars and seasons that pass in fixed courses—some can gaze upon these with no strain of fear: what think you of the gifts of earth, or what of the sea's, which makes rich far distant Arabs and Indians—what of the shows, the plaudits and the favours of the friendly Roman—in what wise, with what feelings and eyes think you they should be viewed?

And he who fears their opposites "marvels" in much the same way as the man who desires: in either case 'tis the excitement that annoys, the moment some unexpected appearance startles either. Whether a man feel joy or grief, desire or fear, what matters it if, when he has seen aught better or worse than he expected, his eyes are fast riveted, and mind and body are benumbed? Let the wise man bear the name of madman, the just of unjust, should he pursue Virtue herself beyond due bounds.] (Fairclough translation).

9. The perils to the charismatic leader of this process of attenuation are familiar from the analysis of *Tamburlaine*, Part 2, as well as of the conflict of charismas seen in the principal characters of *Richard II*. Othello too, albeit obliviously, suffers from a dilution of his exotic charismatic force when his marriage aligns him with more traditional authority.

10. It may be that the centrality of actual bodily mutuality to the ongoing existence of pure or genuine erotic charisma complicates even the earliest stages of symbolic idealization, and continually recomplicates that symbolism as the bodily experience is repeated. I have not worked out this knot, except to recognize that there is a difference between fulfilling one's charismatic claim through, say, an extraordinary martial performance in a period of social distress and through sexual union. The latter case seems to require simultaneous agency and idealization: animal sexuality must be eroticized *in statu nascendi* for its radical opposition to rational and social order to be recognized as a shared experience. Other forms of extraordinary behavior may operate on a less rigorous symbolic timetable. Consequently there may be, for group members, a less symbolically dependent period during which the recognition of a charisma is possible. In contrast, the mutuality of the erotic experience is a prerequisite for the establishment of an erotic-charismatic claim. This differentiates erotic charisma from other genuine charismas, redefining mutuality in structural terms. Throughout this study I have considered mutuality to be an *effect* of systemic development, but where erotic charisma is concerned it may serve both as initiator of the system and as a necessary effect. This problematic duality is less in evidence, so far as I can tell, in other kinds of charismatic organization.

11. Theodora Jankowski has remarked that "since [Cleopatra] has given her heart to Antony, she has, essentially, given away her body natural and removed it from service to her body politic" (1989, 105). I find this statement somewhat too schematic in regard to Cleopatra's "heart" as well as to the relationship of the body natural to the body politic. But there is no question about Cleopatra's neglect of her body politic. Elsewhere in her article Jankowski suggests that "Cleopatra can be seen as a reflection upon the problems Elizabeth faced in trying to rule successfully in patriarchal Renaissance England" (1989, 96; cf. also 105–7). But the association of Elizabeth and Cleopatra is strained and unconvincing, while Jankowski's reliance on exiguous New Historicist correspondences contributes little to the question of Cleopatra's body politic.

12. It is significant in the context of the Egyptian body politic that Cleopatra's children are threats not as possible Egyptian rulers but as future pretenders to the dynastically wobbly Roman crown. There is also the implication in Shakespeare and Daniel especially that both Caesarion and Antony's sons would seek to avenge their mother's and father's deaths. This threat of vengeance of course carries with it the threat of usurpation, a repetition of the accession to power of Antony and Octavius.

13. In a discussion of *Antony and Cleopatra*, Leeds Barroll notes that Cleopatra's "crossing" Antony is a failure (1984, 137); perhaps the futile crossing is symptomatic of the weakening effectiveness of her disruptive behavior—a possibility that would bode ill for Cleopatra's charismatic ability to create and to manage disorder.

14. But see Joseph Summers (1984, 122): "I do not believe the play ever suggests an androgynous ideal or even serious use of the tradition of Venus Armata. Cleopatra and Britomart have little in common: when Cleopatra actually tries to use military arms, she flees." This last point reflects my own view. Regarding androgyny it is more difficult to say: the suggestion of androgyny has erotic value and Cleopatra gathers up all such value. But Summers is right in that nowhere in *Antony and Cleopatra* is an androgynous ideal celebrated in and of itself.

15. Adelman cites Philip Slater (1968, 88) as the source of the term "boundary dissolution" (Adelman 1973, 225–26).

16. There is an interesting comparison to a passage from Robert Garnier's *The Tragedie of Antonie*, translated by Mary Sidney. A jealous Antonie complains:

Yet nought afflicts me, nothing killes me so.
As that I so my *Cleopatra* see
Practise with *Caesar*, and to him transport
My flame, her love, more deare then life to me.

(3.879–82)

The portability of the flame mocks its mutuality.

17. Linda Bamber, speaking of what she sees as a dialectic with "Nature," has noted that Antony and Cleopatra "struggle individually, and they often appear to be struggling against each other" (1982, 59).

Bamber, however, concludes that "it is the resolution to this dialectic that resolves the play" (1982, 59). The dialectical struggle with "Nature" is utterly different from the dialect of personal charismas. But I am nonetheless skeptical about any resolution of dialectical struggle in the Antony and Cleopatra tragedies: the tragic force of the plays emerges from truncation, irresolution, and reinstituted prohibitions, not from resolved conflicts.

18. Weber associates prestige with charisma and with power (cf. 1978, 1:910–12). On the other hand, Bataille associates prestige with eroticism, according to Guerlac, who defines *praestigium* as "seductive allure," citing the Robert dictionary (1990, 100). Similarly, René Girard claims that *praestigia* are "spells and phantasmagoria" (cf. Girard 1987, 295). But I am unable to confirm either of these etymologies. Lewis and Short defines *praestigium* as "a delusion, illusion, trick." There is no mention of spells or phantasmagoria. And, so far as I can determine, the word *prestige* derives from *praestigiae*, meaning "juggler's tricks."

19. Girard somewhat grudgingly quotes Bataille on this point: "on occasion Bataille is able to transcend the decadent estheticism he has so fervently espoused, and explain quite simply that 'the prohibition eliminates violence, and our violent impulses (including those resulting from the sexual drives) destroy our inner calm, without which human consciousness cannot exist'" (1977, 222).

20. Shuger contrasts group membership and the autonomous individual without giving sufficient consideration to the possibility of competing groups. Further, she concludes that sacrifice involves "defiance of social norms" (1994, 194), which is only half true. The defiance of social norms under strictly controlled and highly rationalized ritual conditions in fact confirms traditional prohibitions, restoring or securing social stability (cf. Burkert 1983, 23, 35).

BIBLIOGRAPHY

Adamson, Jane. 1980. *"Othello" as Tragedy: Some Problems of Judgment and Feeling.* Cambridge: Cambridge University Press.

Adelman, Janet. 1973. *The Common Liar: An Essay on "Antony and Cleopatra."* New Haven: Yale University Press.

—————. 1992. *Suffocating Mothers: Fantasies of Maternal Origin in Shakespeare's Plays, "Hamlet" to the "Tempest."* New York and London: Routledge.

Alexander, Peter. 1955. *Hamlet Father and Son.* Oxford: Clarendon Press.

Alt, Albrecht. 1967. *Essays on Old Testament History and Religion.* Translated by R. A. Wilson. Garden City, N.Y.: Doubleday and Co.

Alvis, John. 1978. "The Religion of Eros: A Re-interpretation of *Antony and Cleopatra.*" *Renascence* 30: 185–98.

—————, and Thomas G. West, eds. 1981. *Shakespeare as a Political Thinker.* Durham, N.C.: Carolina Academic Press.

Auden, W. H. 1968. *The Dyer's Hand and Other Essays.* New York: Vintage Books.

Austin, Norman. 1990. *Meaning and Being in Myth.* University Park, Pa.: Pennsylvania State University Press.

Axton, Marie. 1977. *The Queen's Two Bodies: Drama and the Elizabethan Succession.* London: Royal Historical Society.

Bamber, Linda. 1982. *Comic Women, Tragic Men: A Study of Gender and Genre in Shakespeare.* Stanford, Calif.: Stanford University Press.

Barber, C. L. 1988. *Creating Elizabethan Tragedy: The Theater of Marlowe and Kyd.* Edited by Richard P. Wheeler. Chicago: University of Chicago Press.

Barroll, J. Leeds. 1984. *Shakespearean Tragedy: Genre, Tradition, and Change in "Antony and Cleopatra."* Washington, D.C.: Folger Books.

Bartels, Emily C. 1992. "The Double Vision of the East: Imperialist Self-Construction in Marlowe's *Tamburlaine, Part One.*" *Renaissance Drama* 23: 3–24.

Bataille, Georges. 1976. *Oeuvres completes*. Paris: Gallimard.

———. 1987. *Eroticism*. Translated by Mary Dalwood. London: Marion Boyars.

Battenhouse, Roy. 1964. *Marlowe's "Tamburlaine": A Study in Renaissance Moral Philosophy*. Nashville: Vanderbilt University Press.

Beckwith, Sarah. 1993. *Christ's Body: Identity, Culture, and Society in Late Medieval Writings*. London: Routledge.

Belsey, Catherine. 1985. *The Subject of Tragedy: Identity and Difference in Renaissance Drama*. London: Methuen.

Bendix, Reinhard. 1977. *Max Weber: An Intellectual Portrait*. 1960. Reprint, Berkeley: University of California Press.

Bennett, Joan S. 1989. *Reviving Liberty: Radical Christian Humanism in Milton's Great Poems*. Cambridge, Mass.: Harvard University Press.

Berger, Peter L. 1963. "Charisma and Religious Innovation: The Social Location of Israelite Prophecy." *American Sociological Review* 28: 940–50.

Bloom, Harold, ed. 1986. *Christopher Marlowe*. New York: Chelsea House.

———, ed. 1990. *Hamlet*. New York: Chelsea House.

———, ed. 1992. *Iago*. New York: Chelsea House.

Bradbury, Malcolm. 1976. *The History Man*. Boston: Houghton Mifflin.

Bradley, A. C. 1991. *Shakespearean Tragedy*. 1904. Reprint, New York: Fawcett Premier.

Brooke, Nicholas. 1968. *Shakespeare's Early Tragedies*. London: Methuen.

Brown, Peter. 1988. *The Body and Society: Men, Women and Sexual Renunciation in Early Christianity*. New York: Columbia University Press.

Bullough, Geoffrey. 1964. *Narrative and Dramatic Sources of Shakespeare*. Volume 5. London: Routledge and Kegan Paul; New York: Columbia University Press.

Burkert, Walter. 1983. *Homo Necans: The Anthropology of Ancient Greek Sacrificial Ritual and Myth*. Translated by Peter Bing. Berkeley: University of California Press.

Calderwood, James. 1983. *To Be and Not to Be: Negation and MetaDrama in "Hamlet."* New York: Columbia University Press.

Camic, Charles. 1980. "Charisma: Its Varieties, Preconditions, and Consequences." *Sociological Inquiry* 50: 5–23.

Cassirer, Ernst. 1979. *Symbol, Myth, and Culture*. Edited by Donald Phillip Verene. New Haven: Yale University Press.

Cavell, Stanley. 1987. *Disowning Knowledge in Six Plays of Shakespeare*. Cambridge, Mass.: Harvard University Press.

Chadwick, Henry. 1967. *The Early Church*. London: Penguin Books.

Champion, Larry S. 1990. *"The Noise of Threatening Drum": Dramatic Strategy and Political Ideology in Shakespeare and the English Chronicle Plays*. Newark: University of Delaware Press.

Chapman, George. 1988. *The Conspiracy and Tragedy of Charles Duke of Byron*. 1625. Edited by John Margeson. Manchester: Manchester University Press.

Colet, John. 1985. *Commentary on First Corinthians*. Edited by Bernard O'Kelly and Catherine A. L. Jarrott. 1513. Reprinted, Binghamton, N.Y.: Medieval and Renaissance Texts and Studies.

Coursen, H. R. 1976. *Christian Ritual and the World of Shakespeare's Tragedies*. Lewisburg, Pa.: Bucknell University Press.

———. 1982. *The Leasing Out of England: Shakespeare's Second Henriad*. Washington, D.C.: University Press of America.

Cowan, Louise. 1981. "God Will Save the King: Shakespeare's *Richard II*." In Alvis and West, *Shakespeare as a Political Thinker*, 63–81.

Cross, F. M., W. E. Lemke, and P. D. Miller, eds. 1976. *Magnalia Dei—the Mighty Acts of God: Essays on the Bible and Archaeology in Memory of G. Ernest Wright*. New York: Doubleday.

Crutwell, Patrick. 1963. "The Morality of *Hamlet*— 'Sweet Prince' or 'Arrant Knave'?" In Jump, *"Hamlet": A Casebook*, 174–95.

Daniel, Samuel. 1963. *The Complete Works*. 5 vols. Edited by Alexander Grosart. *Civile Wars* is vol. 2. 1599. Reprinted, New York: Russell and Russell.

———. 1990. *The Tragedie of Cleopatra*. 1594. Reprinted in Shakespeare, *A New Variorum Edition of "Antony and Cleopatra*," 531–79.

Dictionary of Biblical Theology. 1973. Edited under the direction of Xavier Léon-Dufour. Translated under the direction of P. Joseph Cahill. New York: Seabury Press.

Dollimore, Jonathan. 1984. *Radical Tragedy: Religion, Ideology and Power in the Drama of Shakespeare and His Contemporaries*. Chicago: University of Chicago Press.

Donne, John. 1984. *Biathanatos*. Edited by Ernest W. Sullivan II. Newark: University of Delaware Press.

Dow, Thomas E., Jr. 1978. "An Analysis of Weber's Work on Charisma." *British Journal of Sociology* 29: 83–93.

Dryden, John. 1972. *All for Love*. 1678. Edited David M. Veith. Reprint, Lincoln: University of Nebraska Press.

Edwards, Philip. 1972 for 1970. "Person and Office in Shakespeare's Plays." *Proceedings of the British Academy* 56: 93–109.

Eisenstadt, S. N. 1968. *Max Weber: On Charisma and Institution Building*. Chicago: University of Chicago Press.

Elliot, G. R. 1992. In Bloom, *Iago*, 27–28.

Elliott, Martin. 1988. *Shakespeare's Invention of Othello: A Study in Early Modern English*. New York: St. Martin's Press.

Ellis-Fermor, Una. 1967. *Christopher Marlowe*. 1927. Reprint, Hamden, Conn.: Archon Books.

Else, Gerald. 1965. *The Origin and Form of Early Greek Tragedy*. Cambridge, Mass.: Harvard University Press.

Elyot, Thomas. 1962. *The Book Named the Governor*. 1531. Edited by S. E. Lehmberg. London: Dent.

Erikson, Erik H. 1958. *Young Man Luther*. New York: Norton.

Everett, Barbara. 1989. *Young Hamlet: Essays on Shakespeare's Tragedies*. Oxford: Clarendon Press.

Falco, Raphael. 1994. *Conceived Presences: Literary Genealogy in Renaissance England*. Amherst: University of Massachusetts Press.

Ferguson, Margaret W., Maureen Quilligan, and Nancy J. Vickers, eds. 1986. *Rewriting the Renaissance: The Discourses of Sexual Difference in Early Modern Europe*. Chicago: University of Chicago Press.

Forset, Edward. 1606. *A Comparative Discourse of the Bodies Natural and Politique.* London.

Foucault, Michel. 1976–1984. *Histoire de la sexualité.* 3 vols. Paris: Gallimard.

———. 1978–1986. *The History of Sexuality.* 3 vols. Translated by Robert Hurley. New York: Pantheon Books.

Frankfurt Institute for Social Research. 1972. *Aspects of Sociology.* Translated by John Viertel. Boston: Beacon Press.

Freud, Sigmund. 1960. *Group Psychology and the Analysis of the Ego.* Translated by James Strachey. 1921. Reprint, New York: Bantam.

Fromm, E. 1941. *Escape from Freedom.* New York: Farrar and Rinehart.

Frontain, Raymond-Jean, and Jan Wojcik, eds. 1980. *The David Myth in Western Literature.* West Lafayette, Ind.: Purdue University Press.

Gardner, Helen. 1974. "The Second Part of *Tamburlaine the Great.*" 1942. Reprinted in Ribner, ed., *Tamburlaine, Part One and Part Two,* 201–8.

Garnier, Robert. 1595. *The Tragedie of Antonie.* Translated by Mary Sidney. In Bullough, *Narrative and Dramatic Sources,* 5:358–406.

Geneva Bible. [1560]; 1969, facsimile. Madison and Milwaukee, Wisc.: University of Wisconsin Press.

Girard, René. 1977. *Violence and the Sacred.* Translated by Patrick Gregory. Baltimore: Johns Hopkins University Press.

———. 1987. *Things Hidden Since the Foundation of the World.* Translated by Stephen Bann and Michael Metteer. Stanford, Calif.: Stanford University Press.

Goddard, Harold. 1951. *The Meaning of Shakespeare.* 2 vols. Chicago: University of Chicago Press.

Gottschalk, Paul. 1972. *The Meanings of "Hamlet": Modes of Literary Interpretation since Bradley.* Albuquerque: University of New Mexico Press.

Greenblatt, Stephen. 1980. *Renaissance Self-Fashioning: More to Shakespeare.* Chicago: University of Chicago Press.

———. 1988. *Shakespearean Negotiations: The Circulation of Social Energy in Renaissance England.* Berkeley: Unversity of California Press.

Greenfeld, Liah. 1985. "Reflections on Two Charismas." *British Journal of Sociology* 36: 117–32.

Guerlac, Suzanne. 1990. "'Recognition' by a Woman!: A Reading of Bataille's *L'Erotisme.*" *Yale French Studies* 78: 90–105.

———. 1996. "Bataille in Theory: Afterimages (Lascaux)." *Diacritics* 26 (2): 6–17.

Guillory, John. 1988. "The Father's House: *Samson Agonistes* in Its Historical Moment." In Nyquist and Ferguson, *Re-membering Milton,* 148–76.

Gundry, Robert H. 1976. *"Soma" in Biblical Theology, with Emphasis on Pauline Anthropology.* Cambridge: Cambridge University Press.

Habermas, Jürgen. 1984. "The French Path to Postmodernity: Bataille between Eroticism and General Economics." *New German Critique* 33: 79–102.

Hale, David George. 1971. *The Body Politic: A Political Metaphor in Renaissance English Literature.* The Hague: Mouton.

Haley, Peter. 1980. "Rudolf Sohm on Charisma," *Journal of Religion* 60: 185–97.

Halpern, Baruch. 1981. *The Constitution of the Monarchy in Israel*. Atlanta: Scholar's Press.

Hardin, Richard F. 1992. *Civil Idolatry: Desacralizing and Monarchy in Spenser, Shakespeare, and Milton*. Newark: University of Delaware Press.

Helgerson, Richard. 1992. *Forms of Nationhood: The Elizabethan Writing of England*. Chicago: University of Chicago Press.

Hill, Christopher. 1993. *The English Bible and the Seventeenth-Century Revolution*. London: Penguin Books.

Holinshed, Raphael. 1807. *Chronicles of England, Scotland, and Ireland*. 6 vols. London.

Holloway, John. 1961. *The Story of the Night: Studies in Shakespeare's Major Tragedies*. Lincoln: University of Nebraska Press.

Hope, A. D. 1986. "*Tamburlaine:* The Argument of Arms." 1970. Reprinted in Bloom, ed., *Christopher Marlowe*, 45–54.

Horace. 1978. *Satires, Epistles, and Ars Poetica*. Translated by H. Ruston Fairclough. 1926. Reprint, Loeb Classical Library. Cambridge, Mass.: Harvard University Press; London: William Heinemann.

Huizinga, Johan. 1959. *Men and Ideas: History, the Middle Ages, the Renaissance*. New York: Meridian Books.

Hummel, Ralph P. 1975. "Psychology of Charismatic Followers." *Psychological Reports* 37: 759–70.

Interpreter's Bible. 1953. 12 vol. New York: Abingdon Press.

Iser, Wolfgang. 1993. *Staging Politics: The Lasting Impact of Shakespeare's Histories*. Translated by David Henry Wilson. New York: Columbia University Press.

Ishida, Tomoo. 1973. "The Leaders of the Tribal Leagues 'Israel' in the Pre-Monarchic Period." *Revue biblique* 80: 514–30.

Jaeger, C. Stephen. 1994. *The Envy of Angels: Cathedral Schools and Social Ideals in Medieval Europe, 950–1200*. Philadelphia: University of Pennsylvania Press.

———. 1997. "Charismatic Body—Charismatic Text." *Exemplaria* 9: 117–37.

Jankowski, Theodora A. 1989. "'As I Am Egypt's Queen': Cleopatra, Elizabeth I, and the Female Body Politic." *Assays* 5: 91–110.

Jay, Martin. 1973. *The Dialectical Imagination: A History of the Frankfurt School and the Institute of Social Research, 1923–1950*. Boston and Toronto: Little, Brown and Co.

Jump, John, ed. 1968. "*Hamlet*": *A Casebook*. London: Macmillan.

Kalberg, Stephen. 1994. *Max Weber's Comparative-Historical Sociology*. Chicago: University of Chicago Press.

Kantorowicz, Ernst. 1931. *Frederick the Second, 1194–1250*. Translated by E. O. Lorimer. London: Constable.

———. 1957. *The King's Two Bodies: A Study in Medieval Political Theology*. Princeton: Princeton University Press.

Kastan, David Scott, ed. 1995. *Critical Essays on Shakespeare's "Hamlet."* New York: G. K. Hall and Co.

Kaufmann, Walter. 1968. *Tragedy and Philosophy*. Princeton: Princeton University Press.

Kerrigan, William. 1994. *Hamlet's Perfection*. Baltimore: Johns Hopkins University Press.

Knight, G. Wilson. 1930. *The Wheel of Fire: Interpretations of Shakespearean Tragedy*. Oxford: Oxford University Press.

Kohut, Heinz. 1971. *The Analysis of the Self*. New York: International Universities Press.

Kuriyama, Constance Brown. 1980. *Hammer or Anvil: Psychological Patterns in Christopher Marlowe's Plays*. New Brunswick, N.J.: Rutgers University Press.

Levin, Harry. 1952. *The Overreacher: A Study of Christopher Marlowe*. Cambridge, Mass.: Harvard University Press.

Lightfoot, John. 1822. *The Whole Works of the Rev. John Lightfoot, D.D.* 12 vols. Edited by John Rogers Pitman. 1647. Reprint, London.

Low, Anthony. 1974. *The Blaze of Noon: A Reading of "Samson Agonistes."* New York: Columbia University Press.

Macfarlane, Alan. 1979. *The Origins of English Individualism: The Family, Property and Social Transition*. New York: Cambridge University Press.

Mack, Maynard. 1993. *Everbody's Shakespeare: Reflections Chiefly on the Tragedies*. Lincoln: University of Nebraska Press.

Malamat, Abraham. 1971. "The Period of the Judges." In Mazar, ed., *The World History of the Jewish People*, 3:129–63.

———. 1976. "Charismatic Leadership in the Book of Judges." In Cross, et al., *Magnalia Dei*, 152–68. Reprinted in Charles E. Carter and Carol L. Meyers, eds., 1996. *Community, Identity, and Ideology: Social Science Approaches to the Hebrew Bible*. Winona Lake, Ind.: Eisenbrauns, 293–310.

Marin, Louis. 1988. *Portrait of the King*. Translated by Martha M. Houle. Minneapolis: University of Minnesota Press.

Marlowe, Christopher. 1969. *Christopher Marlowe: The Complete Plays*. Edited by J. B. Steane. New York: Penguin Books.

———. 1981. *Tamburlaine the Great*. Edited by J. S. Cunningham. Manchester: Manchester University Press.

———. 1994. *Edward the Second*. Edited by Charles R. Forker. Manchester: Manchester University Press.

May, Thomas. 1965. *The Tragoedy of Cleopatra, Queene of Aegypt*. Acted 1626; first edition 1639. A Critical Edition by Denzell Stewart Smith. Ph.D. Diss., University of Minnesota.

Mazar, Benjamin, ed. 1971. *The World History of the Jewish People*. Vol. 3. New Brunswick, N.J.: Rutgers University Press.

McAlindon, T. 1991. *Shakespeare's Tragic Cosmos*. Cambridge: Cambridge University Press.

McIntosh, Donald. 1970. "Weber and Freud: On the Nature and Sources of Authority." *Americal Sociological Review* 35: 901–11.

McKenzie, D. A. 1967. "The Judge of Israel." *Vetus Testamentum* 17: 118–21.

Merrix, Robert P., and Carole Levin. 1990. "*Richard II* and *Edward II*: The Structure of Deposition." *Shakespeare Yearbook* 1: 1–13.

Milton, John. 1957. *The Complete Poetry and Major Prose*. Edited by Merritt Y. Hughes. Indianapolis: Odyssey Press.

Montano, Rocco. 1985. *Shakespeare's Concept of Tragedy: The Bard as Anti-Elizabethan*. Chicago: Gateway Editions.

Neely, Carol Thomas. 1985. *Broken Nuptials in Shakespeare's Plays*. New Haven: Yale University Press.

Nevo, Ruth. 1972. *Tragic Form in Shakespeare*. Princeton: Princeton University Press.

New Bible Dictionary. 1974. Organizing editor, J. D. Douglas. Grand Rapids, Mich.: Wm. B. Eerdmans Publishing Co.

Newman, Ruth G. 1983. "Thoughts on Superstars of Charisma: Pipers in Our Midst." *American Journal of Orthopsychiatry* 53: 201–8.

Nietzsche, Friedrich. 1967. *The Birth of Tragedy*. 1872. Translated by Walter Kaufmann. Reprint, New York: Vintage Books.

North, Thomas. 1880. *Shakespeare's Plutarch*. Edited by Walter W. Skeat. London: Macmillan.

Novum Testamentum, Graece et Latine. 1984. Stuttgart: Deutsche Bibelgesellschaft.

Nyquist, Mary, and Margaret W. Ferguson, eds. 1988. *Re-membering Milton: Essays on the Texts and Traditions*. London: Methuen.

Palmer, John. 1948. *Political Characters of Shakespeare*. London: Macmillan.

Peters, Edward. 1970. *The Shadow King: 'Rex Inutilis' in Medieval Law and Literature, 751–1327*. New Haven and London: Yale University Press.

Pickard-Cambridge, A. W. 1927. *Dithyramb, Tragedy, Comedy*. Oxford: Oxford University Press.

Proser, Matthew N. 1995. *The Gift of Fire: Aggression and the Plays of Christopher Marlowe*. New York: Peter Lang.

Prosser, Eleanor. 1967. *Hamlet and Revenge*. Stanford, Calif.: Stanford University Press.

Radzinowicz, Mary Ann. 1978. *Toward "Samson Agonistes": The Growth of Milton's Mind*. Princeton: Princeton University Press.

Ribner, Irving, ed. 1974. *Tamburlaine, Part One and Part Two: Text and Major Criticism*. Indianapolis: Odyssey Press.

Robinson, J. A. T. 1952. *The Body: A Study in Pauline Theology*. London: SCM Press.

Rogers, John. 1996. "The Secret of *Samson Agonistes*." *Milton Studies* 33: 111–32.

Rozett, Martha Tuck. 1984. *The Doctrine of Election and the Emergence of Elizabethan Tragedy*. Princeton: Princeton University Press.

Schweitzer, Arthur. 1984. *The Age of Charisma*. Chicago: Nelson Hall.

Sedley, Charles. [1677]; facsimile. *Antony and Cleopatra, a Tragedy*. London.

Shakespeare, William. 1954. *Antony and Cleopatra*. Edited by M. R. Ridley. Arden Edition. Cambridge, Mass.: Harvard University Press.

———. 1958. *Othello*. Edited by M. R. Ridley. Arden Edition. New York: Vintage Books.

———. 1965. *New Variorum Shakespeare: "Othello."* Edited by H. H. Furness. 1886. Reprint, New York: American Scholar Publications.

———. 1976. *Coriolanus*. Edited by Philip Brockbank. Arden Edition. London: Methuen.

———. 1982. *Hamlet*. Edited by Harold Jenkins. Arden Edition. London: Methuen.

———. 1984. *Richard II.* Edited by Peter Ure. Arden Edition. 1956. Reprint, London: Methuen.

———. 1990. *A New Variorum Edition of "Antony and Cleopatra."* Edited by Marvin Spevack. New York: Modern Language Association.

Shepard, Alan. 1993. "Endless Sacks: Soldiers' Desire in *Tamburlaine.*" *Renaissance Quarterly* 46: 734–53.

Shils, Edward. 1982. *The Constitution of Society.* Chicago: University of Chicago Press.

Shuger, Debora Kuller. 1994. *The Renaissance Bible: Scholarship, Sacrifice, and Subjectivity.* Berkeley: University of California Press.

Slater, Philip E. 1968. *The Glory of Hera: Greek Mythology and the Greek Family.* Boston: Beacon Press.

Smith, Thomas Spence. 1992. *Strong Interaction.* Chicago: University of Chicago Press.

Snell, Bruno. 1953. *The Discovery of Mind: The Greek Origins of European Thought.* Translated by T. G. Rosenmeyer. New York: Harper and Bros.

Snyder, Susan. 1972. "Othello and the Conventions of Romantic Comedy." *Renaissance Drama*, n.s. 5: 123–41.

Sohm, Rudolf. 1892. *Kirchenrecht.* Leipzig: Duncker and Humboldt.

Stallybrass, Peter. 1986. "Patriarchal Territories: The Body Enclosed." In Ferguson, et al., eds., *Rewriting the Renaissance,* 123–42.

Steadman, John M. 1987. *Milton and the Paradoxes of Renaissance Heroism.* Baton Rouge: Louisiana State University Press.

Stone, Lawrence. 1965. *The Crisis of the Aristocracy.* Oxford: Clarendon Press.

Summers, Joseph H. 1984. *Dreams of Love and Power: On Shakespeare's Plays.* Oxford: Clarendon Press.

Tanakh—The Holy Scriptures. 1988. Philadelphia: Jewish Publication Society.

Thomas, Vivian. 1989. *Shakespeare's Roman Worlds.* London: Routledge.

Tippens, Darryl. 1986. "The Kenotic Experience of *Samson Agonistes.*" *Milton Studies* 22: 173–94.

Tocqueville, Alexis de. 1967. *Democracy in America.* Translated by Henry Reeve. New York: Schocken Books.

Tucker, Robert C. 1968. "The Theory of Charismatic Leadership." *Daedalus* 97: 731–56.

Turner, Victor. 1974. *Dramas, Fields, and Metaphors: Symbolic Action in Human Society.* Ithaca, N.Y.: Cornell University Press.

Veith, Gene Edward, Jr. 1980. "'Wait upon the Lord': David, *Hamlet,* and the Problem of Revenge." In Frontain and Wojcik, eds., *The David Myth,* 71–83.

Vermes, Geza. 1973. *Jesus the Jew.* Philadelphia: Fortress Press.

Vernant, Jean-Pierre. 1988. *Myth and Society in Ancient Greece.* Translated by Janet Lloyd. New York: Zone Books.

Vickers, Brian. 1973. *Towards Greek Tragedy: Drama, Myth, Society.* London: Longman.

Wagner, Anthony. 1975. *Pedigree and Progress: Essays in the Genealogical Interpretation of History.* London: Phillimore.

Waith, Eugene. 1962. *The Herculean Hero in Marlowe, Chapman, Shakespeare and Dryden*. New York: Columbia University Press.

———. 1971. *Ideas of Greatness: Heroic Drama in England*. London: Routledge and Kegan Paul.

Walzer, Michael. 1968. *The Revolution of the Saints: A Study of the Origins of Radical Politics*. New York: Atheneum.

Weber, Max. 1946. *From Max Weber: Essays in Sociology*. Edited by H. H. Gerth and C. Wright Mills, translated by H. H. Gerth, C. Wright Mills, et al. New York: Oxford University Press.

———. 1949. *The Methodology of the Social Sciences*. Edited and translated by Edward A. Shils and Henry A. Finch. New York: Free Press of Glencoe.

———. 1952. *Ancient Judaism*. Translated by Hans H. Gerth and Don Martindale. 1921. Reprint, New York: Free Press.

———. 1956. *Wirtschaft und Gesellschaft: Grundriss Der Verstehenden Soziologie*. 2 vols. Edited by Johannes Winckelmann. Tübingen: J. C. B. Mohr (Paul Siebeck).

———. 1958. *The Protestant Ethic and the Spirit of Capitalism*. Translated by Talcott Parsons. 1904–5. Reprint, New York: Charles Scribner's Sons.

———. 1978. *Economy and Society*. 2 vols. Edited by Guenther Roth and Claus Wittich, with various translators. Berkeley: University of California Press.

Weisman, Ze'ev. 1977. "Charismatic Leaders in the Era of the Judges." *Zeitschrift für die alttestamentliche Wissenschaft* 89: 399–411.

Williams, Bernard. 1993. *Shame and Necessity*. Berkeley: University of California Press.

Willner, Ann Ruth. 1984. *The Spellbinders: Charismatic Political Leadership*. New Haven, Conn.: Yale University Press.

———. 1968. *Charismatic Political Leadership: A Theory*. Princeton: Center of International Studies, Princeton University.

———, and Dorothy Willner. 1965. "The Rise and Role of Charismatic Leaders." *Annals of the American Academy of Political and Social Science* 358: 77–88.

Winkler, John J. 1990. *The Constraints of Desire: The Anthropology of Sex and Gender in Ancient Greece*. New York: Routledge.

———, and Froma I. Zeitlin, eds. 1989. *Nothing to Do with Dionysos? The Social Meanings of Athenian Drama*. Princeton: Princeton University Press.

Woodstock, a Moral History. [ca. 1595], 1929. Transcription by Wilhelmina Frijlinck. London: Malone Society.

——— [ca. 1595], 1946. Edited by A. P. Rossiter. London: Chatto and Windus.

Zeitlin, Irving M. 1984. *Ancient Judaism: Biblical Criticism from Max Weber to the Present*. Cambridge, Mass.: Polity Press.

Ziesler, J. A. 1990. *Pauline Christianity*. Oxford: Oxford University Press.

Zimmerman, Susan, ed. 1992. *Erotic Politics: Desire on the Renaissance Stage*. New York: Routledge.

INDEX

Library of Congress Cataloging-in-Publication Data

Falco, Raphael, 1952–
Charismatic authority in early modern
English tragedy / Raphael Falco.
p. cm.
Includes bibliographical references (p.   ) and index.
ISBN 0-8018-6280-9 (alk. paper)
1. English drama—Early modern and Elizabethan, 1500–1600—History
and criticism.   2. English drama (Tragedy)—History and criticism.
3. English drama—17th century—History and criticism.   4. Charisma
(Personality trait) in literature.   5. Leadership in literature.
6. Authority in literature.   I. Title.
PR658.T7F29   2000
822'.051209353—dc21   99-38767
CIP